HISTORY
OF
THE LEICESTERSHIRE REGIMENT

MAJOR-GENERAL SIR EDWARD M. WOODWARD, K.C.M.G., C.B.
Colonel of the Regiment.

HINDOOSTAN

LEICESTERSHIRE

1688

XVII

HISTORY OF THE
1st & 2nd BATTALIONS
THE LEICESTERSHIRE REGIMENT
In the Great War

By

COLONEL H. C. WYLLY, C.B.

Printed and Published for the Regimental Committee by
GALE & POLDEN, LTD.
WELLINGTON WORKS, ALDERSHOT
ALSO AT LONDON AND PORTSMOUTH

CONTENTS

PAGE

INTRODUCTORY 1

1ST BATTALION

CHAPTER I—1914
THE BATTLE OF THE AISNE—THE FIRST BATTLE OF YPRES ... ...

CHAPTER II—1915
BATTLE OF HOOGE 16

CHAPTER III—1916
THE BATTLE OF THE SOMME 27

CHAPTER IV—1917
THE BATTLE OF CAMBRAI 43

CHAPTER V—1918
JANUARY TO MARCH
THE GERMAN OFFENSIVE—THE BATTLE OF THE SOMME 59

CHAPTER VI—1918
APRIL TO NOVEMBER
THE END OF THE GREAT WAR 74

CHAPTER VII—1918–1927
DEMOBILIZATION AND THE YEARS OF PEACE 91

2ND BATTALION

CHAPTER I—1914
BATTLE OF LA BASSÉE—BATTLE OF FESTUBERT 105

CHAPTER II—1915
THE BATTLE OF NEUVE CHAPELLE 118

CHAPTER III—1915
THE BATTLE OF FESTUBERT—THE BATTLE OF LOOS 131

CHAPTER IV—1916
THE ACTIONS AT SHAIKH SAAD, WADI AND HANNA, THE DUJAILA REDOUBT, FALLAHIYA AND SANNAIYAT 146

CHAPTER V—1916, 1917
TIGRIS, 1916—KUT-AL-AMARA, 1917—BAGHDAD 164

CHAPTER VI—1918
EGYPT AND PALESTINE 186

CHAPTER VII—1919–1927
THE YEARS OF PEACE 198

INDEX 209

LIST OF PLATES

MAJOR-GENERAL SIR EDWARD M. WOODWARD, K.C.M.G., C.B., COLONEL
OF THE REGIMENT ... ... *Frontispiece*

FACING PAGE

MAJOR-GENERAL SIR H. L. CROKER, K.C.B., C.M.G., COMMANDING 1ST BATTALION,
1914 8

MAJOR-GENERAL C. G. BLACKADER, C.B., D.S.O., COMMANDING 2ND BATTALION,
1914 8

BATTALION HEADQUARTERS, 1ST BATTALION, SEPTEMBER, 1914 20

OFFICERS OF " C " COMPANY, 1ST BATTALION, SEPTEMBER, 1914 20

OFFICERS OF THE 2ND BATTALION THE LEICESTERSHIRE REGIMENT, JANUARY,
1915 118

PRIVATE W. BUCKINGHAM, V.C. 126

LIST OF MAPS

FACING PAGE

BATTLE OF CAMBRAI, 20TH NOVEMBER, 1917 58

BATTLE OF THE 21ST MARCH, 1918 72

6TH DIVISION—BATTLE OF THE HUNDRED DAYS AND MARCH TO THE RHINE, 1918 90

BATTLE OF NEUVE CHAPELLE 130

PALESTINE—ADVANCE INTO SAMARIA 196

MESOPOTAMIA ... ... *In Pocket*

The maps of the 6th Division (Battle of the Hundred Days and March to the Rhine, 1918) and Neuve Chapelle are from the Histories of The Sherwood Foresters and 39th Royal Gharwál Rifles respectively, and have been reproduced by the courtesy of the Regimental History Committees

THE LEICESTERSHIRE REGIMENT

INTRODUCTORY

THE History of The Leicestershire Regiment, written by Lieutenant-Colonel E. A. H. Webb, brought the record down to March 31st, 1912, at which date the 1st Battalion was quartered at Aldershot, under orders for Fermoy, while the 2nd Battalion, which had landed in India on October 11th, 1906, was in March, 1912, stationed at Madras and Bellary in the Madras Presidency, and had received orders to be in readiness to move to the hill-station of Ranikhet in the United Provinces.

As the war record of the Regular battalions of the Regiment will deal with each separately, it is considered best to treat each battalion individually in bridging the interval between the conclusion of Colonel Webb's History and the opening of the Great European War in August, 1914.

1ST BATTALION.

On May 15th, 1912, His Majesty the King arrived at the Royal Pavilion, Aldershot, to spend a week among his troops, and a Guard of 1 subaltern, 2 sergeants, 2 corporals, 1 bugler and 18 privates from the Battalion was furnished during one day of the visit, while on the 17th the Band of the Battalion was commanded to play during the evening. Second-Lieutenant W. H. G. Dods was the officer in command of the Guard.

On July 28th of this year The Leicestershire Regiment experienced a great loss in the death of Major-General A. H. Utterson, C.B., who had been Colonel of the Regiment since September 23rd, 1905. He was gazetted to the 17th Foot on August 25th, 1854, served with it in the Crimea and in the Second Afghan War, commanded the 1st Battalion from 1882 to 1887, was promoted Major-General in 1891, and in that rank commanded for three years the 3rd Infantry Brigade at Aldershot, retiring from the Service in January, 1895. His funeral took place on August 1st at Weston-super-Mare, the Battalion being represented at the ceremony by Major C. G. Blackader, D.S.O., 1 colour-sergeant, 1 corporal and 1 private, while 6 colour-sergeants acted as pall bearers.

Major-General Utterson was succeeded as Colonel of The Leicestershire Regiment by Colonel and Hon. Major-General W. D. Tompson, C.B., whose appointment was announced in the *London Gazette* of September 13th, 1912. Major-General Tompson, like his predecessor, was also an old officer of the Regiment, to which he had been gazetted as far back as 1852. He served with

1

the 17th in the Crimean War, in which he was dangerously wounded, and commanded the 1st Battalion in the Afghan War of 1879-80, being mentioned in despatches and being awarded the C.B.

The time had now arrived for the move of the Battalion from Aldershot to Fermoy, and for its transfer from the 6th Infantry Brigade to the 16th Infantry Brigade of the 6th Division; on September 23rd the Brigadier, Brigadier-General C. B. Davies, C.B., made his farewell inspection, expressing his regret at losing from his brigade a battalion like the 1st Leicestershire, which had maintained, while under his command, so high a standard of excellence, equally at work and sport; and on the 27th the 1st Battalion left Aldershot for Ireland at a strength of 717 all ranks, the following officers accompanying it :—

Lieutenant-Colonel H. L. Croker; Majors B. C. Dent and B. C. Dwyer; Captains T. N. Puckle, F. Le M. Gruchy, S. O. Everitt, C. S. Davies, E. F. S. Henderson and W. C. Dixon (adjutant); Lieutenants E. S. W. Tidswell, W. F. Panton, R. S. Dyer Bennet, G. C. I. Hervey, C. C. Rolph, H. S. Pinder, H. B. Brown and J. T. Waller; Second-Lieutenants J. W. E. Mosse, A. Weyman, W. H. G. Dods and J. C. Herring-Cooper; Lieutenant and Quarter-master J. H. Greasley, with Sergeant-Major A. Measures and Bandmaster C. S. Witt.

The 6th Division, which the 1st Battalion now joined, and which was commanded by Major-General W. P. Pulteney, C.B., D.S.O., was a very scattered one, its three brigades being quartered, the 16th at Fermoy, the 17th at Cork and the 18th at Sheffield, and at these places the brigades themselves, and for the most part the units composing them, remained until the outbreak of war. Nothing of any really outstanding importance occurred, so far as the 1st Battalion The Leicestershire Regiment was concerned, during the ten months that elapsed between the beginning of October, 1913, and the early days of August, 1914, except the new organization of infantry battalions which came into force on October 1st, 1913, and under which the number of companies in each battalion was reduced from eight to four, each company being divided into four platoons, numbered consecutively from 1 to 16 throughout the battalion; while the existing colour-sergeants of these eight original companies were appointed company sergeant-majors and quartermaster-sergeants in the four reorganized companies, according to seniority.

In the 1st Battalion—

"A," or Captain C. T. M. Hare's Company, was formed from "A" and "B" Companies.

"B," or Major B. C. Dent's Company, was formed from "E" and "F" Companies.

"C," or Major B. C. Dwyer's Company, was formed from "C" and "G" Companies.

"D," or Captain F. Le M. Gruchy's Company, was formed from "D" and "H" Companies.

It was consequently under this organization that all infantry battalions, serving in the United Kingdom, India and the Dominions, took the field when the long-expected war finally broke out.

2ND BATTALION.

While quartered in Madras and Bellary—with occasional detachments for company training to Pallaverram—the 2nd Battalion The Leicestershire Regiment was in the Southern Brigade (Brigadier-General F. G. Bond, C.B.) of the 9th Division (Major-General Sir J. B. Woon, K.C.B.) of the Southern Army, commanded by Lieutenant-General Sir J. E. Nixon, K.C.B.

On September 10th, 1912, Lieutenant-Colonel L. C. Sherer completed his period of service in command of the Battalion, and was succeeded by Lieutenant-Colonel C. G. Blackader, D.S.O., who was at the time serving with the 1st Battalion, and who arrived in Madras on December 6th and took over command.

It was not until early in the new year that active preparations were set in hand for the move of the Battalion to the Bengal Presidency, when on February 4th, 1913, " B," " F," " G " and " H " Companies and the Drums rejoined Headquarters at Madras from Bellary, the whole Battalion embarking the same day in the R.I.M.S. *Northbrook* and sailing for Calcutta; this was reached on the 8th, and the 2nd Battalion proceeded thence by rail to Bareilly, where it arrived on the 11th and joined the Bareilly Brigade under the command of Major-General F. Macbean, C.V.O., C.B., of the 7th Meerut Division, the commander of which was Major-General C. A. Anderson, C.B.

At Bareilly the Battalion made but a short stay, for on March 13th and 14th it left again for its final destination—Headquarters, " A," " B," " C," " D " Companies, Band, the Signallers and the Maxim Gun Detachment leaving by rail on the 13th, arriving the next day at Kathgodam, at the foot of the hills, and marching thence to Ranikhet, which was reached on the 18th, the Battalion occupying Alma Barracks. The Left Wing followed on March 14th, under similar arrangements, and joined Headquarters on the 20th. Here the Battalion remained during the hot weather of 1913, training of all kinds being carried out by wings at Majhkali, while in June the Battalion was rearmed with the M.L.E. Mark III short rifle.

In September and October the Battalion—less " C " Company, which remained on at Ranikhet under Major Paul, D.S.O., to form a winter section— moved down to Bareilly, returning again to Ranikhet at the end of the cold weather and arriving there on March 23rd, 1914. The 2nd Battalion was not, however, to occupy its summer station at the same strength as during the preceding hot weather, for, under I.A. Order No. 704 of 1913, it had been detailed to furnish a detachment of two companies for duty at Delhi Fort; " C " and " D " Companies were detailed for this duty, and both were settled down in their new quarters by March 28th.

While stationed at Ranikhet, Lieutenant and Quartermaster A. Wood, who had been promoted Quartermaster of the 2nd Battalion from Regimental

Sergeant-Major of the 1st on October 25th, 1911, was taken ill and invalided home, dying very shortly afterwards.

There appears to be only one other event of any importance to chronicle before proceeding with the recital of the very grave and epoch-making occurrences of the late summer and autumn of 1914, and that is the appointment as Adjutant of Captain F. Latham, in the place of Captain B. F. Clarke, who had completed his tenure of that office.

1st BATTALION

CHAPTER I.

1914.

The Battle of the Aisne—The First Battle of Ypres.

THERE is no need here to repeat all that in an earlier history of the Regiment has been said as to the steps which had been taken, since the close of the war in South Africa, to make our Army in every possible way better prepared for the great continental war which the majority of thinking soldiers had envisaged. Military training had in every way been brought up to date, mobilization on a tolerably large scale had been repeatedly practised, and it is no more than the truth to say that " in every respect the Expeditionary Force of 1914 was incomparably the best trained, best organized and best equipped British Army that ever went forth to war. Except in the matter of co-operation between aeroplanes and artillery and the use of machine guns, its training would stand comparison in all respects with that of the Germans. Where it fell short of our enemies was first and foremost in numbers; so that, though not ' contemptible,' it was almost negligible in comparison with continental armies even of the smaller States."[*]

In the early part of the year 1914 the attention of the British people had been absorbed by the events which were taking place, and the even greater events which seemed to threaten the even tenour of the life of the nation, in Northern Ireland; but as the summer drew on it became increasingly certain that our domestic peace was unlikely to be seriously disturbed, and few can have had any forebodings that the end of the year would see us, in common with all the civilized nations of the world, involved in a continental war.

The story of the events which led up to and ushered in the World War has been told in all languages and from every possible point of view, and since presumably we are all well acquainted with the main facts, there seems little need and less room for their recapitulation in a purely regimental history; but it may be well to recall and place on record in these pages certain happenings, in order that we may realize their true relation to the opening military events of the coming struggle. On June 28th the heir to the Austro-Hungarian throne was, with his consort, assassinated at Serajevo, the capital of Bosnia; on July 23rd the Vienna Cabinet presented an ultimatum to the Serbian Government; two days later Austria declared war; on July 29th Russia ordered partial, and, on the 31st, full mobilization of her forces; on August 1st, Germany

---

[*] " Official History of the War," Vol. I, pp. 10 and 11.

declared war against Russia, and on the 3rd against France—having already on the 2nd of this month presented something of the nature of an ultimatum to the Belgian Government, setting forth that the Germans possessed incontestable information of the intention of the French High Command to march on the Meuse by way of Givet and Namur, and demanding of the Brussels Cabinet unresisted passage for the German armies across Belgian territory. On August 2nd, German troops crossed the Polish and French frontiers, and, on the 4th, German armies set foot in Belgium; on the same day Great Britain declared war on Germany.*

On August 5th and 6th meetings of the Cabinet were held in London, and these were attended by the chief of His Majesty's Ministers, by Lord Kitchener, who assumed the office of Secretary of State for War on the second of these dates, by Field-Marshal Sir John French, the Commander-in-Chief designate of the Expeditionary Force, and by leading soldiers and sailors; and it was decided that *for the present at least* only four infantry divisions and a cavalry division should embark for France, embarkation commencing on the 9th; and that the British forces on arrival in France should be concentrated in the region about Le Cateau and Avesnes. This last decision was not come to without considerable discussion, Lord Kitchener expressing the opinion, which the subsequent course of events seemed fully to justify, that the place of concentration had been set too far forward, but the arrangement had been come to in consultation with the leading French military authorities and it was consequently adhered to.

On September 17th, Lord Kitchener asked of the Indian military authorities that thirty-nine out of the forty-two British infantry battalions serving in India should be sent home, their places being taken by battalions of the Territorial Force.

The decision was also come to that the British Expeditionary Force should be organized in three Army Corps, of which the nucleus of one had been maintained at Aldershot, but for the two others now forming the staffs had to be improvised. The Army Corps, and Cavalry Division, Commanders were :—

The I. Army Corps, Lieutenant-General Sir Douglas Haig.

The II. Army Corps, Lieutenant-General Sir James Grierson, who, on his death a very few days after arrival in France, was succeeded by General Sir Horace Smith-Dorrien.

The III. Army Corps, Lieutenant-General W. P. Pulteney.

The Cavalry Division, Major-General E. Allenby.

Orders for mobilization were issued on August 4th, but there appears to be some difference of opinion as to the hour at which the order reached the units composing the 6th Division, in which the 1st Battalion The Leicestershire Regiment was serving, the Divisional History stating that " the order for mobilization was received at 10 p.m. on August 4th, 1914," while the war diary

* As Director of Mobilization at the War Office, 1913-14, Major-General Sir E. M. Woodward, K.C.M.G., C.B., the present Colonel of the Regiment, was largely responsible for the preparation and working of the scheme under which the British Army mobilized

of the Battalion gives the time of the receipt of the order as " 5.50 p.m." on that date.*

The Order of Battle of the Division on August 4th was as under :—

Cavalry.—One squadron, 19th Hussars.

R.E.—12th and 38th Field Companies, R.E.; 6th Divisional Signal Company.

R.A.—2nd, 24th and 38th Brigades, R.F.A.; 12th Howitzer Brigade, R.F.A.; 24th Heavy Battery, R.G.A (60-pounders).

Infantry.—16th Infantry Brigade (Brigadier-General E. C. Ingouville-Williams, C.B., D.S.O.): 1st Battalion The Buffs, 1st Battalion The Leicestershire Regiment, 1st Battalion King's Shropshire Light Infantry, and 2nd Battalion York and Lancaster Regiment.

17th Infantry Brigade (Brigadier-General W. R. B. Doran, C.B., D.S.O.): 1st Battalion Royal Fusiliers, 1st Battalion North Staffordshire Regiment, 2nd Battalion Leinster Regiment, and 3rd Battalion Rifle Brigade.

18th Infantry Brigade (Brigadier-General W. N. Congreve, V.C., C.B., M.V.O.): 1st Battalion West Yorkshire Regiment, 1st Battalion East Yorkshire Regiment, 2nd Battalion The Sherwood Foresters, and 2nd Battalion Durham Light Infantry.

The Division was now commanded by Major-General J. L. Keir, C.B.

Considering that the 1st Battalion The Leicestershire Regiment required no fewer than 579 non-commissioned officers and men to bring it up to war strength, the rapidity with which mobilization was completed is a fine tribute to the smartness with which the reservists rejoined on the declaration of war, and also to the business-like way in which the reservists were equipped at the Depot and passed on to the Battalion at Fermoy; on the afternoon of August 7th 296 reservists joined Headquarters, followed early the following morning by 230 more; on these days also detachments came in which had been away at Bantry and Berehaven, and on the 10th the arrival of 35 more reservists—2 non-commissioned officers and 33 other ranks—brought the Battalion nearly up to full strength.

While the two brigades of the 6th Division, which were quartered in Ireland, had been thus engaged in completing their mobilization, the 18th Brigade and two brigades of the 4th Division had been sent to the East Coast of the United Kingdom to guard against any possible invasion; but by August 14th it had been decided that the 6th Division should be concentrated in camps in the neighbourhood of Cambridge and Newmarket, and on this date the 1st Battalion The Leicestershire Regiment moved by wings to Queenstown, spent the night of the 14th/15th there, and embarked in three parties—in the *Heroic, Londonderry* and *Kilkenny*—on the night of the 15th and early the following morning. On arrival of these parties at Holyhead, the Battalion entrained by wings for Cambridge, where, in a camp on Coldham Common, the whole Battalion was concentrated by the 19th, when training was resumed, the three brigades now all occupying the same area.

* The Order to Mobilize was issued from the War Office at 4.40 p.m., August 4th, 1914.

B 2

In this neighbourhood nearly three weeks went anxiously by, enlivened only by the news of the early events of the war which came to hand, and varied by a move on the 27th to Grantchester, and the arrival of small parties of reservists to fill the places of men who had been found to be unfit for field service.

Then at last, on September 7th, the long-expected orders for embarkation were received, and on the afternoon of that day the 1st Battalion The Leicestershire Regiment marched to Royston, and entrained for Southampton at 11 p.m.; the port was reached at seven o'clock on the morning of the 8th, and the Battalion at once went on board the *Braemar Castle,* which steamed away the same day.* The following are the names of the officers who embarked with the Battalion for the Great War: Lieutenant-Colonel H. L. Croker, in command; Majors H. Stoney Smith and B. C. Dent; Captains F. Le M. Gruchy, J. Bacchus, R. F. Hawes, L. S. D. Tollemache, A. T. Le M. Utterson, W. C. Wilson, and M. G. B. Copeman; Lieutenants C. C. Rolph, H. B. Brown, J. T. Waller, T. Prain, J. W. E. Mosse, A. Weyman, J. G. Herring-Cooper, H. L. Bayfield, W. H. G. Dods and C. Smeathman; Second-Lieutenants H. N. H. Grimble and G. N. Wykes, Captain and Adjutant E. S. W. Tidswell; Captain and Quartermaster J. H. Greasley; Lieutenant E. C. Lang, R.A.M.C., Medical Officer; and Regimental Sergeant-Major A. Measures.

The *Braemar Castle* entered the port of St. Nazaire at eight o'clock on the morning of September 10th, but disembarkation did not take place until 10 p.m., when the Battalion marched to the Rest Camp at Grand Marais; the first person to greet the Battalion on its arrival in France was its old Commanding Officer, Lieutenant-Colonel Copley Sherer.

The divisions of the Expeditionary Force which had earlier left England had all disembarked either at Boulogne or Havre, and the reason for the change of base thus adopted by the units of the 6th Division is explained as follows in the Official History of the War : † " The rapid advance of the Germans to the west had made the bases at Boulogne and Havre unsafe, and had actually dispossessed the British of their advanced base at Amiens. The advisability of a change of base was foreseen by the Q.M.G., Major-General Sir William Robertson, as early as the 24th August, and from that date all further movement of men and stores to Havre and Boulogne was stopped. By the 27th Boulogne had been cleared of stores and closed as a port of disembarkation; and on the 29th St. Nazaire on the Loire was selected as the new base. . . . . By the 30th August the Inspector-General of Communications, Major-General Robb, had telegraphed his requirements in tonnage to Southampton; and on the 1st September the transports for the troops were ordered to Havre. . . . In four days 20,000 officers and men, 7,000 horses and 60,000 tons of stores had been shipped from Havre to St. Nazaire, a very considerable feat of organisation."

---

* The embarkation of the Battalion was supervised by two officers of the Regiment—Major W. Bryce and Captain M. Hare, then employed on the embarkation staff.

† Vol. I, p. 263.

MAJOR-GENERAL C. G. BLACKADER, C.B., D.S.O.
Commanding 2nd Battalion, 1914.

MAJOR-GENERAL SIR H. L. CROKER, K.C.B., C.M.G.
Commanding 1st Battalion, 1914.

It is obvious that these very necessary measures had retarded considerably the arrival at the front of the reinforcements required to replace the wastage in the I. and II. Corps, and also the shipment of the 6th Division to the theatre of war.

All soldiers proceeding to the front had been heartened and speeded on their way by a gracious message from His Majesty the King to his Army; it was as follows :—

" *You are leaving home to fight for the safety and honour of My Empire.*

" *Belgium, whose country we are pledged to defend, has been attacked, and France is about to be invaded by the same powerful foe.*

" *I have implicit confidence in you, My soldiers. Duty is your watchword, and I know your duty will be nobly done.*

" *I shall follow your every movement with deepest interest and mark with eager satisfaction your daily progress; indeed, your welfare will never be absent from My thoughts.*

" *I pray God to bless you and guard you and bring you back victorious.*"

To every soldier of the British Expeditionary Force, Field-Marshal Lord Kitchener addressed the following letter :—

" *You are ordered abroad as a soldier of the King to help our French comrades against the invasion of a common enemy. You have to perform a task which will need your courage, your energy, your patience. Remember that the honour of the British Army depends on your individual conduct.*

" *It will be your duty not only to set an example of discipline and perfect steadiness under fire, but also to maintain the most friendly relations with those whom you are helping in this struggle. The operations in which you are engaged will, for the most part, take place in a friendly country, and you can do your own country no better service than in showing yourself in France and Belgium in the character of a true British soldier.*

" *Be invariably courteous, considerate and kind. Never do anything likely to injure or destroy property, and always look upon looting as a disgraceful act. You are sure to meet with a welcome and to be trusted; your conduct must justify that welcome and that trust.*

" *Your duty cannot be done unless your health is sound, so keep constantly on your guard against any excesses. In this new experience you may find temptations both in wine and women. You must entirely resist both temptations, and while treating all women with perfect courtesy, you should avoid any intimacy.*

" *Do your duty bravely.*

" *Fear God.*

" *Honour the King.*"

The units composing the 6th Division made no long stay in the vicinity of St. Nazaire, for a long railway journey was before them, and the 1st Battalion The Leicestershire Regiment boarded the train at eleven on the morning of September 11th and detrained again at 1.30 a.m. on the night of the 12th/13th at Mortcerf, to the east of Paris, where the Division was concentrated in billets in the area Coulommiers—Mortcerf—Marles—Chaume.

" The period 13th to 19th September," we read in the Divisional History,* " was spent in the march to the Aisne, where the Division arrived at a time when a certain amount of anxiety was felt by the Higher Command. The Fifth French Army on the right, the British Army in the centre, and the Sixth French Army under General Maunoury on the left, had pushed the Germans back across the Marne, and on the 14th September the British troops had crossed the Aisne on the front Soissons—Bourg—the I. Corps at Bourg, the II. Corps at Vailly and Missy and the III. at Venizel. The French right attack from the direction of Rheims and the British attack by the I. Corps had progressed much faster than the left, and had reached the heights on the line Craonne—Troyon, astride the famous Chemin des Dames. These were now the object of fierce attacks by the Germans, and the 6th Division, which had been allotted originally to the III. Corps, was put into general reserve instead, only the artillery joining the III. Corps."

Leaving Mortcerf at 6.30 on the morning of the 13th and marching by Crecy, Jouarre (where the drums were left in charge of the Curé), Saacy, Château Thierry, Rocourt, Buzancy, Ambrief and Mont Notre Dame, the Battalion reached Courcelles on the afternoon of September 20th, and here it was learnt that the battalions composing the I. Corps were greatly weakened after the long and harassing retreat from Mons and all the recent hard fighting in the battles of the Marne and the Aisne, and that the 16th and 18th Brigades of the 6th Division were at once to relieve—the 18th Brigade, the 2nd Infantry Brigade on the British right, and the 16th, the 7th and 9th Brigades to the north-east of Vailly The 18th Brigade moved first and was heavily engaged on the 20th to the north and east of Troyon, incurring considerable loss, while the 16th Brigade marched from the neighbourhood of Courcelles on the 21st. The 1st Battalion The Leicestershire Regiment crossed the Aisne late in the evening and relieved the Worcestershire Regiment and the Royal Irish Rifles at eleven o'clock in trenches on the line La Fosse Marguel. Here the first casualties incurred by the Battalion in the war were suffered, and during the twenty days that the 1st Battalion remained in this part of the line 1 lance-corporal and 4 privates were killed, 1 officer—Captain R. F. Hawes—died of wounds, and 2 officers— Major B. C. Dent and Captain and Adjutant E. S. W. Tidswell—and 16 other ranks were wounded; while Lieutenants Bayfield and Waller received the congratulations of the General Officer Commanding I. Corps on the patrol work carried out by them during this period.

By this time the German pressure on the Aisne had begun to slacken, and it was becoming increasingly evident that an attempt would shortly be made by the enemy to reach and hold the Channel ports. " Towards the close of September Sir John French had suggested to General Joffre the transfer of the British Army to its former place on the left of the line. Other British troops were about to be landed in the north of France, and it was obviously desirable that all the forces of the nation should act in one body. The lines of communication also of the British Expeditionary Force would be greatly shortened by its

---

* " A Short History of the 6th Division," by Major-General T. O. Marden, C.B., C.M.G., p. 3.

being nearer the coast. The British . . . . were interested above all nations in barring the way to the Channel ports, from which the Germans could threaten the transport of troops from England to France and block the vital avenues of water-borne traffic converging on London. That the Germans had not seized Ostend and Boulogne during their first triumphant advance, when they might easily have done so, had been due to lack of troops; and that omission they were now making every effort to make good. . . . .

" Against this movement there was the obvious objection that it must be carried out gradually, so that for a time the British Expeditionary Force would be divided; and that the British, in their journey northward, must move right across the line of the French communications and would necessarily prevent the dispatch of French troops to the north for several, it was even said for ten, days. General Joffre, however, agreed to Sir John French's proposal : and on the night of the 1st/2nd October was begun the withdrawal of the British troops from the valley of the Aisne. Their movements were carefully concealed; all marches were made by night and the men confined to their billets by day, so that no sign of their departure from the Aisne should be visible to enemy aircraft."

The II. Corps moved first, then the 2nd and 1st Cavalry Divisions; these were followed by the III. Corps, composed of the 4th and 6th Divisions, less the 16th Brigade of the latter, which remained for a time with the I. Corps, this being the last to move northwards; and it was not until the night of October 12th/13th that the 1st Battalion The Leicestershire Regiment was relieved in its trenches by the 106th French Infantry, and then proceeded by rail from Fismes to Cassel, and thence by road to Croix Blanche, in the neighbourhood of which the 16th Brigade finally rejoined its Division on October 17th. The night of the 17th/18th was spent in a defensive position at Croix Blanche, and that of the 19th/20th was passed in billets at Bois Grenier; so that the 16th Brigade was not concerned in the fighting in which the other brigades of the Division had been engaged from October 13th to the 19th, during which period the 6th Division had advanced from Hazebrouck to the western portion of the ridge between Armentières and Lille at a cost of some 750 casualties.

On the morning of October 20th the Germans attacked very heavily along their whole front, and the 1st Leicestershire Regiment, leaving Bois Grenier at 10 a.m., took up a position on the line Rue du Bois—La Houssoie; but about 4.30 in the afternoon fresh orders were received to move to the " E " of Boulogne on map and entrench a line thence to Porte Egale. Thenceforward the German pressure on the five-mile front caused the receipt of many and varying orders for the Battalion to proceed to strengthen points where other units of other brigades were putting up a gallant fight against great odds, and, as often as not, with one or both flanks in the air; and at 8 p.m. on the 21st the Battalion was sent to relieve the West Yorkshire Regiment, of the 18th Brigade, in the line—Chemical Factory—Rue du Bois, holding on here under repeated attacks and continuous enfilade gun fire, until the 26th, when the Battalion was withdrawn to billets at Bois Grenier.

The events of October 25th and 26th are described as follows by one who was there :—

October 25th.—" At 6 p.m., 25th, reports were received from O.C. Leicestershire Regiment that hostile shelling had compelled his battalion to evacuate this trench line from just south of the Rue du Bois to Le Quesne, that his men were lying in the open along the railway line and that the enemy's infantry were massing in the area Le Quesne—Distillery and that he considered their attack imminent. The G.O.C. 16th I.B. and one company of the Buffs proceeded to the railway station, La Houssoie, headquarters 1st Leicestershire Regiment, with the object of initiating a counter-attack. From reports on arrival such action was, however, considered impracticable, the enemy was in considerable strength, the night was very dark, and the ground very much broken. The enemy was undoubtedly in occupation of the large Distillery buildings and a group of houses east of the railway crossing south of the station.

" It was decided that The Leicestershire Regiment should continue to hold their ground immediately south of Rue du Bois, and bend back their line to the railway line about 250 yards off the Rue du Bois cross-roads, and continue the line along a deep ditch bordering the west of the railway to the railway crossing south of the station. At this point the defensive line was to cross the east of the railway along the bank of a shallow cutting about 18 inches deep through which the railway runs to a culvert about 500 yards south.

" Although direct touch on the line occupied was established with the K.S.L.I. (on the right) during the night, it was realized that the 1st Leicestershire Regiment had indifferent cover and were badly placed if the enemy made a determined attack during the following day."

October 26th.—"At dawn the enemy attempted to penetrate between the inner flanks of the Battalion and the K.S.L.I., and the situation up to 11 a.m. was critical.

" The Leicesters' line was intact from Rue du Bois to the barrier at the level crossing south of the station. Close hand-to-hand fighting took place throughout the day at the barrier, the Germans, being in considerable strength, making repeated assaults on the barrier, covered by rifle fire from the house at a few yards' range.

" The enemy throughout the day never took advantage of the initial success gained by them shortly after dawn. This inability to do so was in a measure undoubtedly due to the excellent work performed by the machine gun section of the K.S.L.I. and the stubborn resistance offered by the company of The Leicestershire Regiment occupying the road barrier at the level crossing and on the railway north of this point. Another reason undoubtedly was that the German commanders could not have known the situation on this front, and the German troops who had penetrated the gap appeared lost and in many cases wandered about aimlessly until shot down."

During these days the enemy shelling was very heavy, while our guns could make little or no response, for, as we learn from the Divisional History, " during the whole period, 20th to 30th October, the guns were woefully short of ammunition, and consequently a greater strain was thrown on the infantry." The German attacks continued until October 31st, when trench warfare set in, the 6th Division having by then been driven back from the top of the ridge to the low ground on the line Rue du Bois—La Boutillerie, at a cost of nearly 4,000 casualties. Those in the 1st Battalion Leicestershire were by no means negligible, and amounted to: killed or died of wounds—Captain F. Le M. Gruchy, Lieutenants T. Prain, W. H. G. Dods and C. Smeathman and 47 other ranks; wounded—Lieutenant-Colonel H. L. Croker, Captains J. Bacchus, A. T. Le M. Utterson, Lieutenants J. T. Waller and H. L. Bayfield and 134 non-commissioned officers and men; while 106 other ranks were missing—a total of 287 casualties.

The last day of the month found Headquarters and " C " and " D " Companies at Grise Pot, near Bois Grenier, the other two companies being at Touquet, in reserve; the 16th Infantry Brigade had been drawn back to the line Touquet—Flamengrie Farm—Rue du Bois, where positions had already been prepared in view of a withdrawal from the forward line becoming necessary.

" Active fighting now died away on this front," so we read in the Divisional History, " but its place was taken by constant shelling and the heavy sniping which claimed so many victims at this time. The weather during November and December was truly appalling. All trenches were knee-deep in mud and water. Parapets would not stand and were so flimsy that many men were shot through them." In November there was one fortnight of continuous frost followed by a thaw, during which the banked-up earth of the parapets simply crumbled away; there were no materials for revetment, while trench stores were practically unknown and even sandbags were obtained only with much difficulty and in wholly insufficient numbers; the trench periscope was only now, belatedly, beginning to make its appearance, and the British hand-grenade—of the jampot pattern—had but lately been evolved.

These two months were passed monotonously—but by no means unexcitedly —in holding trenches and " resting " in reserve billets. The periods of duty in the trenches varied from five to twelve days in length and the portion of the front line occupied was not always the same—at one time the 1st Battalion The Leicester-shire Regiment took up a line about Porte Egale Farm, another tour was spent on the line Rue de Petillon—Rouges Bancs, again at Touquet—Flamengrie Farm, and finally at Rue du Bois—Grande Flamanderie; while billets were almost equally varied, at one time being at Rue Duquesne, at another at Bac St. Maur, at another at Fleurbaix, while the Battalion was again billeted at Grise Pot towards the end of the year.

The behaviour of the enemy during these months was very changeable; at times the Battalion War Diary records nothing but " Quiet all day," while at others we read of heavy bombardments. Casualties occurred almost daily, for there was no immunity from shell fire even in the billets well in rear of the front line, and during November and December the loss in killed and wounded experienced by the Battalion amounted to the following: Captain P. E. Viney died of wounds received on December 14th in the trenches, and 24 non-commissioned officers and men were killed, while Captain C. C. Rolph and 25 other ranks were wounded; the severity of the weather also may be gauged from the fact that several men were admitted to hospital suffering from frost-bite. Fortunately these losses and others earlier incurred were in some measure made good by the arrival of reinforcements from the base or from England; on November 1st, Captain C. A. Bamford, 3rd Battalion, and 59 other ranks joined; on the 3rd, Second-Lieutenant C. H. O. D. Burrell, 3rd Battalion, reported his arrival; on the 14th, Lieutenant M. Brown joined with 86 non-commissioned officers and men; and finally on December 18th a small party, 30 strong, arrived at Battalion headquarters. But these reinforcements, welcome as they undoubtedly were, can hardly have gone far to replace the wastage of the fighting in which the 6th Division had taken part during the months of October and November alone, for by the end of the latter month this amounted in the 6th Division to 183 officers and 5,136 other ranks killed and wounded.*

In the last month of this year His Majesty the King paid one of his greatly appreciated visits to his armies at the front, and on December 2nd the 1st Battalion The Leicestershire Regiment marched to Bac St. Maur and was inspected by the King with other units of the 6th Division.

Of the last days of the first year of the war we can perhaps hardly do better than quote from the account of one who was there and who served throughout with the 1st Battalion from the beginning to the Armistice.†

" A few days before Christmas," he writes, " the 1st Battalion took over the front-line trenches in the Armentières—Bois Grenier sector. The trenches were in a terrible state owing to the continuous downpour of rain and the scarcity of sandbags, shovels or trench pumps to combat the deluge. Daybreak showed that part of the trenches occupied by ' C ' Company was a ditch running through two fields and the water at this part was knee-deep, numerous things were floating about and the Company had to work continuously with tins baling out the water. After a few days of this wretchedness a sharp frost set in and froze the ground like flint, excepting the trench bottom, which remained very muddy and uncomfortable, so that fires for cooking, or a decent rest, were impossible, the cold was intense and the Battalion experienced its first cases of frost-bite. The enemy trenches appeared to be in good condition, for throughout the cold days the smoke curled up from their numerous trench fires.

" To the rear of the Battalion trenches was a small wood, and paths through it led to the main road in rear. Through this wood the Battalion ration and ammunition parties used to file off to the limbers on the road in rear, and many exciting times and numerous casualties were experienced on these trips, for at this time the enemy employed huge searchlights at night which swept the trenches and the ground in rear, every object caught in the beam showing up as clear as day. Often, as the parties entered the wood the beam of light would be thrown upon them, whistles would be blown by the enemy sentries as they detected the ration parties floundering about to dodge the dazzling light, and a volley of rifle and machine-gun fire, with a few shells to add to the discomfort,

---

* " The Official History of the War," Vol. II, p. 466.
† Sergeant E. B. Hayball, D.C.M., " C " Company.

would be directed on to the wood. Sometimes it would be nearly daybreak before the parties could return to the trenches.

"Christmas Eve found the Battalion trenches covered with snow, and a brilliant moon lit up No Man's Land and the enemy trenches. After dusk the sniping from the German trenches ceased and the enemy commenced to sing; their Christmas carol grew louder as their numerous troops in the reserve trenches joined in, and eventually ended with loud shouts and cheering. 'A' Company of our Battalion then began a good old English carol, the regiments on right and left joining in also, and this was received by the enemy with cheers and shouts of, 'Good! Good!'

"On Christmas Day snow fell heavily, and, as the enemy did not snipe when the men exposed their heads, several of 'B' Company got out of their trench and stood upright in full view of the enemy; they were surprised to see the Germans do likewise, waving their hands and shouting in broken English. Orders were given by the Commanding Officer for sentries to be posted on the alert in case the enemy attempted any treachery, and the remainder of the Battalion, quick to take advantage of the opportunity, set to work repairing the trench parapet and collecting wood for fires. At dusk the sentries manned the parapet as usual, but the enemy remained quiet, all except his artillery, who continued to shell the back areas. That night the ration parties were again subjected to the glare of the searchlight on reaching the wood, and, expecting a volley of bullets, the men threw themselves flat, but the enemy infantry did not fire, and after arriving safely back with the rations, etc., the troops gave the Germans a rousing cheer!

"Next day rain fell, thaw set in, the trenches collapsed during the day, the enemy recommenced to snipe and shell, Christmas was over and they were back to business. The trenches by this time were in a shocking state in places, owing to the sides falling in, being here and there almost as wide as a country lane, with scarce any cover from the enemy snipers. After being under these conditions for twenty-two days the Battalion was relieved and took over billets in rear for a few days' rest."

At this season the Commander-in-Chief caused the following message of goodwill to be published to his Army in France and Flanders :—

"*In offering to the Army in France my earnest and most heartfelt good wishes for Christmas and the New Year, I am anxious once more to express the admiration I feel for the valour and endurance they have displayed throughout the campaign, and to assure them that to have commanded such magnificent troops in the field will be the proudest remembrance of my life.*"

CHAPTER II.

1915.

BATTLE OF HOOGE.

THE opening months of the year 1915 were, for the units composing the 6th Division, tolerably uneventful ones, in so far that the Division took no part in any major operations, remaining in that portion of the front of which it had been in occupation at the end of the previous year. " But if there was no heavy fighting, the trench casualties from sniping and enemy shell fire were quite considerable. We had practically no artillery ammunition with which to worry the enemy, as the following extract from the Divisional War Diary shows :—

" 24th April, 1915.—In view of the fighting in progress in the north (Second Battle of Ypres) the Corps Commander allots an extra ten rounds of shrapnel per gun for 18-pounders, with a view to making a demonstration by fire to hold the enemy in front of us."

On January 1st, 1915, the following officers were present with the 1st Battalion The Leicestershire Regiment : Lieutenant-Colonel H. L. Croker; Majors H. Stoney Smith and A. H. Buchanan-Dunlop; Captains C. T. M. Hare, F. I. Ford (3rd Battalion), C. A. Bamford (3rd Battalion), L. S. D. Tollemache, W. C. Wilson, M. B. G. Copeman and H. B. Brown; Lieutenants J. W. E. Mosse (Transport Officer), A. Weyman (Machine Gun Officer), J. G. Herring-Cooper, G. N. Wykes, C. W. Herbison, S. Waring, L. Dowding, J. E. Garbutt, F. J. Diggins and M. Brown; Second-Lieutenants C. H. O. D. Burrell (3rd Battalion), Captain and Adjutant E. S. W. Tidswell, Captain and Quartermaster J. H. Greasley and Lieutenant E. C. Lang, R.A.M.C.; the total strength of the Battalion was 24 officers and 955 non-commissioned officers and men.

During the months January to April the Battalion moved regularly from billets in Armentières to the trench-line about the Rue du Bois, and its numbers fluctuated as officers and men became casualties and others came out in drafts to take their places. In January there appears to have been little or no wastage, and consequently no reinforcements seem to have been sent out, but in February 6 men were killed and 3 officers—Major Stoney Smith, Captain Wilson and Lieutenant Brown—and 30 other ranks were wounded, while the loss was more than made good by the arrival at various dates of Major B. C. Dent, Second-Lieutenants C. E. Morrison and H. Pickbourne and 73 non-commissioned officers and men. In March, 6 men were killed and 11 were wounded, while the reinforcements were Second-Lieutenant J. Wright and 30 men. On the 20th Colonel Croker left the Battalion to take command of the 81st Brigade : he was succeeded in command of the 1st Battalion by Major Stoney Smith. In April

16

the losses were 2 killed and 30 wounded, the latter exclusive of Captain Copeman and Second-Lieutenant Dowding, who were injured by the premature explosion of a hand grenade; but at the end of the month a large draft, 92 strong, joined Headquarters. Finally, in May, at the end of which month the Division quitted the Armentières sector, Second-Lieutenant Morgan was killed and 2 officers and 24 other ranks were wounded.

During these months the troops of the Canadian Expeditionary Force had begun to arrive on the Western Front, and several platoons of these were attached for instruction and for various periods to the Battalion; further, Territorial battalions were now beginning to come out in ever-increasing numbers, and each brigade of the 6th Division was allotted one of these as a fifth battalion, the 5th Battalion The Loyal North Lancashire Regiment being posted to the 16th Infantry Brigade on February 15th.

Rumours of an approaching move had been for some little time now in circulation, and late in May the 6th Division was informed that, on relief by the 27th Division, it was to move north to the Ypres Salient and join the newly-formed VI. Corps, to the command of which Major-General Sir John Keir had just been appointed. This promotion occasioned a vacancy among the Divisional Commanders, and Major-General Congreve moved up from the command of the 18th Infantry Brigade to that of the 6th Division.

Marching from Armentières on May 30th by way of Bailleul and Poperinghe, the 1st Battalion The Leicestershire Regiment relieved the 1st Hampshire Regiment on June 2nd on the line Wieltje—Ypres Road—West Roosebeke Road, where heavy casualties almost at once commenced to be incurred. "" By the night of the 31st May-1st June the Division,'' so we read in the Divisional History, "" took over its new front in the Ypres Salient, commencing its long tour in that unsavoury region, and trench casualties almost doubled immediately. It continued in the Salient up to the end of July, 1916, with three periods of rest, each of about a month's duration; the first spent in the neighbourhood of Houtkerque and Poperinghe in November and December, 1915; the second in the Houtkerque—Wormhoudt area, with one brigade at a time back at Calais from mid-March to mid-April, 1916; and the third again in the Houtkerque—Wormhoudt area from mid-June to mid-July, 1916. . . . . The line was just hardening after the Second Battle of Ypres when the Division moved up to the Salient, and no active operations took place on the actual front taken over by the Division ''; but once at least in June—on the 16th— the Battalion was called out and remained in reserve during an attack made by the 3rd Division—on the right of the 6th—upon Bellewaarde Farm, north-west of Hooge.

During June the casualties amounted to Lieutenant E. Harrison* and 20 men killed, Captain J. T. Waller and 73 men wounded, while to make up—somewhat inadequately—for these losses, Captain J. T. Waller, Second-Lieutenants F. Passmore and C. A. Hine had joined. In this month, too, Lieutenant A. Weyman took the place, as adjutant, of Captain E. S. W. Tidswell, who was appointed Brigade Major to the 81st Brigade.

* A remarkably efficient young officer, known as " Baby Harrison "—he was only seventeen.

During June and July the enemy frequently bombarded the trenches and the back areas with gas shells, but happily an improved gas mask had recently been issued and the men did not suffer so much as they might otherwise have done; in July, Second-Lieutenant F. Passmore was wounded.

"On the 30th July the 14th Division was attacked at Hooge and driven back to Sanctuary and Zouave Woods. Their counter-attacks, gallantly delivered, but under the circumstances giving very little prospect of success, failed, and for a time the situation was critical. The 16th Infantry Brigade was moved up to the area about Goldfish Château* (half a mile north-west of Ypres) as a precautionary measure, and was for a time in danger of being thrown in to make a hasty counter-attack. Fortunately this proved unnecessary, and on the 31st July the Corps Commander decided to relieve the whole Division, and to allot to it the task of restoring the line at Hooge in a carefully-prepared attack."†

In the meantime the 1st Leicestershire Regiment had been withdrawn from the neighbourhood of Zillebeke Lake, where it had met the 5th Battalion of the Regiment, to the ramparts of Ypres, near the Menin Gate; here it was called upon to supply working parties of 400-600 men nightly, and here the Battalion bombers were in considerable request, these last, when lent to the 8th Battalion King's Royal Rifles, having a very rough time of it on the night of August 2nd-3rd, all their bombs being destroyed by shell fire, while 6 men were killed, and Lieutenant C. J. Burn, Second-Lieutenant P. R. Milner and 21 men were wounded between the 2nd and 8th of the month.

On the 6th the Division took over its front of attack and the preparatory bombardment began; this had been very carefully thought out and arranged, and was generally acknowledged to have been one of the most effective which had up to this been put down by the British artillery. The attack began at 3.15 a.m. on August 9th, the 18th Brigade on the right, the 16th on the left—the two covering a front of some thousand yards—and the 17th Brigade in reserve, and was completely successful, all objectives being quickly gained. The 1st Battalion The Leicestershire Regiment did not play as important a part in the action as some other units of their Brigade, for they remained in reserve in the ramparts at Ypres, only moving forward at ten o'clock that night to relieve the Buffs in the trenches and having no more than 4 men wounded during the operations.

The same day Lieutenant F. J. Thorpe joined and was wounded within twenty-four hours of his arrival, Lieutenant S. Waring being also wounded the same day.

The Battalion was back again in the ramparts by dark on the 13th, and next day the enemy shelled the position at a range of sixteen miles with 17-inch howitzers, firing "an enormous shell which made a noise like a railway train as it came, and sent earth and bricks 300 feet high at least, and the dust was fearful after each explosion. One shell came regularly every ten minutes, three landing

---

* The Battalion War Diary says : "Moved off hurriedly 9 p.m. 31st to W. edge of Zillebeke Lake as general reserve to 14th Division."

† "History of the 6th Division," p. 14.

within 50 yards of Battalion Headquarters and making a crater 60 feet across and about 30 feet deep. A few men buried by debris, but no one killed—9 wounded."

Three further extracts may here be given from the Battalion War Diary of this month, as showing the activity which prevailed and the spirit with which all ranks were carrying out their instructions to harass the enemy in every way possible.

"Night of 22nd-23rd August a patrol of 'D' Company, under Corporal Bullimore, came upon a German covering party in front of a digging party. They bombed the covering party with great success and then retired without loss. On the way back, one man—No. 9720 Private Bradbury—died of wounds as the result of the premature explosion of one of his bombs. He was carried in by Corporal Bullimore, who displayed conspicuous ability and bravery during the fracas.

"24th, 3 a.m. Two Alsatians crept over and surrendered to 'D' Company. They brought no arms with them. Their reason for coming over to us was that the Germans distrusted all Alsatians, and there was a rumour that all Alsatians were to be sent to the Russian front. A great deal of most useful information was got out of them. They also confirmed our bomb exploit of the night before, and said that one man had been killed and an officer wounded by our bombers.

"25th. Private Cherry did good work patrolling, and reconnoitred German saphead; was challenged and fired upon, but got back safely."

On this day Second-Lieutenant T. Forbes reported his arrival.

On September 4th the announcement was made of the award of the Distinguished Conduct Medal to No. 8186 Lance-Corporal T. Paling, of the Battalion, for gallantry in action at Hooge, and few men can have earned it better. He was detailed to take a party, carrying a supply of bombs, up to the York and Lancaster Regiment in the firing line, and, having successfully performed this duty, he was marching his party back, when it was caught in a heavy burst of shell fire at the railway cutting on the Menin—Ypres road. Five of the party were wounded, and Lance-Corporal Paling bound up their wounds in the open, under heavy shell fire, and then carried them to a dug-out and thence to a dressing station in the neighbourhood. He then took charge of some German prisoners who were being marched to the rear, and whose escort had been killed by artillery fire, and shepherded them safely into Ypres.

September 9th found the Battalion occupying the front line about Wieltje, the 1st Shropshire Light Infantry being on the right and the 3rd Rifle Brigade on the left, and the three battalions were subjected next day to a most intense bombardment by guns of all calibres, shrapnel and high explosive, while a trench mortar sent over a 50 lb. shell which did enormous damage to the parapets; three German aeroplanes also flew low over the British trenches spotting for the enemy gunners. The bombardment commenced about 6.35 a.m. and was distributed impartially along the whole of the 16th Brigade front; it was most incessant, and it was estimated that in action against this front there were two batteries of 8-inch guns, two batteries of 4·5-inch guns, not fewer than three batteries firing shrapnel, and four trench mortars. The shells from these did especial damage, " part of ' A ' Company's trenches being absolutely blown in, and great craters and gaps made communication with the right of this company impossible except by a big detour. The damage to trenches by shell fire was also very great, and the communication trenches in rear of ' A ' and ' C ' Companies were absolutely flattened. ' B ' and ' D ' Companies also had damage done to them, their barbed wire being blown to bits. The casualties were extremely few, considering the intensity and length of the bombardment. ' A ' Company casualties were Second-Lieutenant W. H. Reynolds killed—some men had been buried and he dug them out and saved them, but was killed instantaneously almost immediately after—3 men killed and 7 wounded. ' B ' Company had 3 men wounded, 2 very slightly; ' C ' Company 3 killed; ' D ' Company 5 wounded. Many men were badly bruised and buried, but they were rescued and not sent to hospital."

All must have been thankful when the relief came on the 15th and the companies moved back to the canal bank, though here there was but little rest, working parties of 340 strong being called for nightly for carrying up trench supplies and for digging, laying wire and assisting in the construction of a light railway.

On the last day of September the enemy artillery turned their attention to all the rearward communications, and the Battalion transport had a lucky escape, a shell bursting over a wagon and frightening the horses, who threw the driver and bolted. The man did not, however, lose his head, for he secured a loose horse, galloped after the wagon, and headed the runaways into a field, where he recaptured his wagon and brought it and his horses safely back to the dump.

During the greater part of October, when the Battalion was either occupying trenches in the Potijze sector or else obtaining such rest and shelter in rear as was afforded by the canal bank, things seem to some extent to have quieted down and casualties were comparatively few, though the sick rate slightly increased, due to the appearance of the disease known as " trench feet "; then, on the 21st, Lieutenant W. C. Williams was very slightly wounded, and on the following day the Battalion suffered a very heavy loss—one deeply regretted by all ranks of the 1st Leicestershire Regiment—in the death of Lieutenant-Colonel H. Stoney Smith, who was killed by a sniper about 11.30 a.m. while going round the trenches, dying within thirty minutes of being hit. His body was taken to Vlamertinghe the same evening, and he was buried next day in the Military Cemetery at Poperinghe, his funeral being attended by Major-General Congreve, but unfortunately only three officers of his Battalion and one man per company could be spared from trench duty to attend. The 2nd Battalion Durham Light Infantry very kindly sent their buglers. Of Colonel Stoney Smith one who knew him well has recorded that at the front " he was an example to all in fearlessness and courage. Few men have lived such a life of devotion to the Service and to the Regiment, and few men have done more to encourage that unconquerable regimental spirit, to which His Majesty the King ascribed the victory of the British Army at the First Battle

BATTALION HEADQUARTERS, 1ST BATTALION, SEPTEMBER, 1914.

LT.-COL. H. L. CROKER. CAPT. E. C. LANG, R.A.M.C. CAPT. E. S. W. TIDSWELL. MAJOR H. STONEY SMITH.
(ADJT.)

OFFICERS OF "C" COMPANY. 1ST BATTALION, SEPTEMBER, 1914.

CAPT. J. BACCHUS. LIEUT. H. BARRINGTON BROWN 2/LT. H. L. BAYFIELD. LT. T. PRAIN.

of Ypres. Faithfulness to the Regiment was the most noticeable feature in Colonel Stoney Smith's career."

Major A. H. Buchanan-Dunlop assumed command of the Battalion in place of Lieutenant-Colonel Stoney Smith.

About the 24th of this month intimation was received that the 1st Battalion The Leicestershire Regiment was to be transferred from the 16th to the 71st Infantry Brigade, which, commanded by Brigadier-General M. Shewen, was to take the place in the 6th Division of the 17th Brigade, transferred to the 24th Division. This change necessitated a redistribution of battalions among the brigades of the 6th Division, and the 71st Brigade was now to be composed of the 9th (Service) Battalion The Norfolk Regiment, the 9th (Service) Battalion The Suffolk Regiment, the 1st Battalion The Leicestershire Regiment, and the 2nd Battalion The Sherwood Foresters. So far, however, as the Leicestershire Regiment was concerned, the transfer did not actually take place until November 17th.

On the Battalion leaving the 16th Brigade, the Brigadier published the following very flattering farewell order :—

"*The Brigadier-General, 16th Infantry Brigade, wishes to express to the Officers, Non-Commissioned Officers and Men of the 1st Battalion Leicestershire Regiment his great regret at the departure of the Battalion from the Brigade, and his great appreciation of the magnificent work it has done, both in action and in the yet more trying work of trench duty during the time it has been under his command.*

"*The Brigadier-General will watch the future career of the Battalion with much interest, and feels sure that the high standard of gallantry in action, steadfast endurance of hardship, and soldierlike behaviour at all times, which it has attained, will be fully maintained.*"

On October 29th the Battalion, while in occupation of the Potijze trenches, had another experience of a heavy bombardment by the German artillery; to quote from the War Diary : "Intense bombardment of Battalion Headquarters, from 6 to 6.40 a.m., 7.45 to 8.30 a.m., 9.45 to 11 a.m. and 9 to 10 p.m. Every dug-out but one was broken in, and the whole of Battalion Headquarters had to remain in this all day. Shells varied from shrapnel and H.E. shrapnel up to 11-inch shells. One direct hit on the top of the Headquarters dug-out about 8 a.m., made by an 8-inch shell, made an enormous crater but did not penetrate. The dug-out is a tunnel through a mound, about 80 feet long, each side strutted with wood, and great beams on the roof. Another high explosive shell burst in our ammunition and bomb reserve, but luckily did not explode the bombs which were near the Headquarter dug-out; this shell nearly brought down the end of the Headquarter dug-out. The telephone dug-out was smashed at about 6.20 a.m., the shell bringing down part of the roof, none of the four telephonists hurt but two telephones smashed. Casualties nil !"

During October, 3 officers—Second-Lieutenant C. A. McConchie, L. J. Clarence and H. S. Roberts—and 75 non-commissioned officers and men joined the Battalion.

C

In the first week in November, when in billets in Poperinghe, the Battalion had a new experience, the billets being heavily bombarded one morning by armour-piercing shells from a German naval gun many miles distant in the Houthulst Forest, north-north-east of Ypres; and then, as already stated, on the 17th the transfer of the Battalion from the 16th to the 71st Infantry Brigade was effected, and, having been relieved on the canal bank by the 1st Battalion The Buffs, the 1st Leicestershire Regiment went forward to the re-entrant between the Wieltje and Forward Cottage Salients, where the line was taken over from the 9th Battalion Norfolks and the companies were distributed as follows :—

" B " and half " D " Company in the front line;

" C " and half " D " Company in X line and St. Jean defences;

" A " Company in the canal bank;

Machine Guns in Poperinghe;

and the condition of the trenches appears to have left much to be desired, for they are described as " fearfully wet and quite impassable in places; communication trenches between X line and front line impassable."

On November 14th, Major-General C. Ross, D.S.O., had assumed command of the 6th Division on the appointment of Major-General W. N. Congreve, V.C., to command the XIII. Corps, and on the 25th the Battalion marched to Poperinghe, where the whole of the 71st Brigade was concentrated and marched in column of route past General Sir H. Plumer, the Commander of the Second Army, and Major-General Ross, the new General Officer Commanding 6th Division. Both Sir H. Plumer and Brigadier-General Shewen had many complimentary things to say about the marching and general turn-out of the Battalion.

The draft that joined the Battalion during November was a very small one, consisting of *nine* men only, every one of whom had been at least once wounded during the war while serving with the 1st Battalion; four officers also arrived from the 3rd Battalion of the Regiment—Second-Lieutenants A. H. Pinder, H. A. Dolby, W. North and F. G. H. Grimsley.

Before the month of December came to an end the Battalion was to have a very trying experience of a severe attack by poison gas, and the manner of it was in this wise. On the 18th, in the afternoon, the companies entrained at Poperinghe, left the train at the Asylum, a quarter of a mile to the west of Ypres, and marched thence to the trenches at Wieltje, there taking over the line from the 2nd Battalion Sherwood Foresters and having the 2nd Durham Light Infantry on the right and the 9th Norfolks on the left, with a gap between themselves and the right battalion, for the patrolling of which gap the 18th Brigade was responsible. " A " and " B " Companies were on the right and left of the Battalion firing line respectively, " C " and half " D " were in support, the remainder of " D " being in rear in the canal bank.

The night passed quietly enough, but at 5.10 on the morning of the 19th the enemy sent up red lights all along their front, and the sentries of " A " —the right—Company saw two German soldiers come out of their trenches and advance to within a hundred yards of our trenches and bend down, apparently turning on a tap, and before the sentries could open fire the gas was upon them.

It came out of cylinders, and could be heard, like the escape of steam, at a distance of at least 200 yards in rear of the front line. It was later discovered that the gas was chlorine and phosgene, and, being extremely volatile, it travelled with the fresh easterly breeze at high speed and was received at Battalion headquarters—1,000 yards behind the front line—before the telephone message could get through that gas was being used. It was especially deadly in character, and though the Battalion had had constant practice in the use and application of gas helmets, such men as could not speedily get at their helmets were overcome by its effects in about five minutes, remaining in a comatose state for no more than two or three hours before death overtook them.

One curious feature of the gas was its "delayed action"; at noon on the 19th the casualties reported were no more than 3 died and 8 suffering from its effects; but by 6 p.m. over 100 men in the front line were suffering very severely from the delayed action of the gas, and many who attempted to reach the dressing station at St. Jean fell on the way thither and were picked up insensible. The stretcher bearers worked all through the night of the 19th-20th carrying men down to the road on anything available, and collecting them on the company carts.

About 6.20 a.m. on the 19th small parties of the enemy were seen moving about in front of their lines, but no serious attack was then made; a few minutes later, however, all the roads in rear of the trenches, all the houses and villages as far to the rear as Poperinghe, as also the main roads in its vicinity, and Poperinghe itself were also heavily shelled, as were Ypres and Vlamertinghe with shells of all calibres, including some 17-inch. The British batteries were all shelled with lachrymatory-gas shells.

On the evening of this day the following message was received by the Brigade from the General Officer Commanding 6th Division: "*G.O.C. wishes to inform Brigadier much pleased with the behaviour of the troops under trying conditions. In view of the severity and duration of the gas the remarkably few cases of gassing which occurred shows that training had been thorough and discipline admirable when decisive moment arrived.*"

It seems clear that many more gas cases developed after receipt of the above message.

The bombardment was continued with varying intensity for forty-eight hours, and all the roads round about became veritable death-traps. Telephone communication between Battalion Headquarters and the companies was almost at once destroyed by shell fire, and orderlies had to be employed; these did their very dangerous work splendidly, "carrying on" under the heaviest fire, and the casualties among them were remarkably few and every message was delivered. The village of St. Jean, in a cellar of which Battalion Headquarters was located, and also the dressing station, were shelled with unceasing fury, and movement was very difficult, if not indeed wholly impossible. "A" Company suffered most heavily, as the gas was let off only 100 yards from their trenches. During the actual gas attack the enemy kept up a sustained rifle and machine-gun fire on the Battalion trenches, and this was as far as possible replied to.

C 2

The bombardment was maintained throughout the 20th with varying intensity, but the Battalion transport managed to get rations up to the forward companies, running the gravest risks in doing so, as all the roads were under continuous shell fire; and this day there were nearly 40 casualties, including 3 officers—Second-Lieutenant S. C. Lawrence being badly wounded, while Captain R. H. Gillespie and Lieutenant D. V. Webb were badly gassed—but neither would go to hospital.

The enemy artillery kept up the shelling all through the night of the 20th-21st and until about 7 a.m. on the latter date, when happily the wind changed and the shelling ceased, the remainder of the day being tolerably quiet.

The Divisional gunners estimated that during the bombardment the Germans had fired some 400,000 shells into the 6th Division area alone, and from December 18th to the 21st the Battalion had 9 men killed, 7 died of the effects of gas, 19 men were wounded, 88 were suffering from the effects of gas, while 5 men were missing; and during the whole month 21 non-commissioned officers and men were killed or died from gas, while 115 were wounded, suffering from gas or missing. Fortunately substantial reinforcements arrived at Battalion Headquarters during December, amounting to 2 officers—Second-Lieutenants J. G. Kennedy and F. B. Robertson, both from the Cadet School at St. Omer—and 165 other ranks.

The above "official" account of the experiences of the Battalion during these terrible December days may be supplemented by extracts from what was at the time written by one who was then serving with the 1st Battalion : " the stretcher bearers," he writes, " worked strenuously with the wounded, and tried to evacuate them from the trenches, but the road was so fiercely shelled that it was found impossible to attempt to carry them out; many slightly gassed or wounded who left the trenches were afterwards found dead on the road, having been caught in the terrible barrage the enemy put down.

" After subjecting the Battalion to an hour of gas and bombardment " (this was in the early morning of December 18th), " the enemy lifted the range of his guns and concentrated on the already battered support trenches, occupied by ' C ' Company, who already had a large number of killed, wounded and gassed. The increased roar of rifle fire from the Battalion fire-trenches indicated that the enemy infantry had attempted to leave their trenches to assault. The Sherwood Foresters were turned back and attempted to reinforce the Battalion, but after enduring many casualties in the attempt to reach the front line were placed in some old trenches near St. Jean and had a rough time indeed.* Communication between companies and Battalion Headquarters had been entirely cut off, and during this trying period great gallantry was shown by Private Folwell, of ' C ' Company, who carried and delivered safely messages to all Company Commanders, each time traversing the shell-swept road on which many dead and wounded lay. On one of these dangerous errands, a piece of shrapnel penetrated his gas helmet, but, securing the rent with string, he got through safely."

* The War History of the 1st and 2nd Battalions Sherwood Foresters makes no mention of this.

Later the writer describes how " C " Company was sent forward to reinforce the front line, but " to attempt to reach the front by way of the road would have been disastrous, so intense was the barrage, so ' C ' Company was sent up by platoons in extended order across the intervening two hundred yards of ground, and, after an exciting few minutes and the loss of a number of men, the company managed to reach the remainder of the Battalion in the trenches and took up position. With daybreak could be seen the damage done by the enemy guns during the night—parapets were blown in, so that parties of men were isolated by day, for to move across the gaps would have invited instant death at the hands of the busy snipers. Throughout this, as in all other actions, the Battalion stretcher-bearers showed great gallantry, working day and night to ease the sufferings of the wounded."

The 1st Battalion The Leicestershire Regiment spent their second Christmas Day of the war in billets; not forgotten, we may be very sure, by their many friends at home, and remembered, as always on every Christmas Day of those four years of war, by His Majesty the King, who caused the following gracious message to be promulgated among all ranks of his Army in the field :—

" *Another Christmas finds all the resources of the Empire still engaged in war, and I desire to convey on My own behalf, and on behalf of the Queen, a heartfelt Christmas greeting and Our good wishes for the New Year, to all who, on sea and land, are upholding the honour of the British name. In the officers and men of My Navy, on whom the security of the Empire depends, I repose, in common with all My subjects, a trust that is absolute. On the officers and men of My Armies, whether now in France, in the East, or in other fields, I rely with an equal faith, confident that their devotion, their valour and their self-sacrifice will, under God's guidance, lead to victory and an honourable peace. There are many of their comrades now, alas, in hospital, and to these brave fellows also, I desire, with the Queen, to express Our deep gratitude and Our earnest prayers for their recovery.*

" *Officers and men of the Navy and Army, another year is drawing to a close, as it began, in toil, bloodshed and suffering; but I rejoice to know that the goal to which you are striving draws nearer into sight.*

" *May God bless you and all your undertakings.*

(Sd.) "GEORGE R.I."

Just a week before Christmas a change had taken place in the command of the British Expeditionary Force, which on December 19th Field-Marshal Sir John French resigned into the able hands of General Sir Douglas Haig, the leader of the First Army, Sir John French proceeding to England to assume charge of the Home Defences and to supervise the training of the new armies still coming into existence.

On leaving France the Field-Marshal issued the following farewell order :—

" *In relinquishing the command of the British Army in France, I wish to express to the officers, non-commissioned officers and men with whom I have been so closely associated during the last sixteen months, my heartfelt sorrow in parting with them before the campaign, in which we have been so long engaged together, has been brought to a victorious conclusion. I have, however, the firmest conviction that such a glorious ending to their splendid and heroic efforts is not far distant, and I shall watch their progress towards this final goal with intense interest, but in the most confident hope.*

" The success so far attained has been due to the indomitable spirit, dogged tenacity which knows no defeat, and the heroic courage so abundantly displayed by the rank and file of the splendid Army which it will ever remain the pride and glory of my life to have commanded during over sixteen months of incessant fighting.

" Regulars and Territorials, Old Army and New, have ever shown these magnificent qualities in equal degree. From my heart I thank them all.

" At this sad moment of parting my heart goes out to those who have received life-long injury from wounds, and I think with sorrow of that great and glorious host of my beloved comrades who have made the greatest sacrifice of all by laying down their lives for their country.

" In saying good-bye to the British Army in France, I ask them once again to accept this expression of my deepest gratitude and heartfelt devotion towards them, and my earnest good wishes for the glorious future which I feel to be assured."

At the end of the year 1915, the following were the officers serving with the 1st Battalion The Leicestershire Regiment :—

Lieutenant-Colonel A. H. Buchanan-Dunlop in command.

Captain A. Weyman, Adjutant.

Captain J. W. E. Mosse, Transport Officer.

Lieutenant H. Pickbourne, Bombing and Intelligence Officer.

Second-Lieutenant C. H. O. D. Burrell, Machine Gun Officer.

Captain and Quartermaster J. H. Greasley.

Captain W. J. Adie, R.A.M.C., Medical Officer.

" A " Company: Captain R. H. Gillespie, Second-Lieutenants A. H. Pinder and H. A. Dolby.

" B " Company: Captain M. K. Wardle, Lieutenant C. E. Morrison, Second-Lieutenants P. R. Milner and F. B. Robertson.

" C " Company : Temporary Captain C. W. Herbison, Second-Lieutenants G. A. Brounsworth, W. M. Bailey and J. G. Kennedy.

" D " Company : Lieutenant D. V. Webb and Second-Lieutenant F. G. H. Grimsley.

CHAPTER III.

1916.

The Battle of the Somme.

DURING the greater part of the first three months of the year 1916, the battalions composing the 71st Infantry Brigade remained on in occupation of the same portion of the Ypres Salient, holding the trenches in the Wieltje section when up in the line and retiring to billets in Poperinghe—usually divided, so far as the 1st Battalion The Leicestershire Regiment was concerned—between the Asylum, the Elverdinghe Road and the Rue des Furnes.

The daily report when in the trenches in January usually describes the situation as " very quiet indeed," which may perhaps be regarded purely as relative terms as compared with other and more exciting portions of our far-flung line. There was a good deal of patrolling of the enemy trenches, " B " Company being especially active, and one night, when Second-Lieutenant F. B. Robertson was sent out to try to discover the strength of the German wire and the positions of their listening posts, he returned with the useful information that the enemy wire was very strong and in excellent repair, consisting of one row of concertina wire heavily barbed, the meshes being no more than half an inch apart, then ordinary wire entanglements about 12 yards thick, with iron uprights, all very strong; listening posts, too, had by this enterprising young officer been located in the old Canadian trench running north-west and south-east about 200 yards in front of the German line.

Activities such as these could not of course be carried out without a certain amount of loss, while the enemy shelling and sniping continued to cause casualties; and at the end of January these numbered for the month 2 killed and 7 wounded, among the latter being two officers, Lieutenants D. V. Webb and H. Pickbourne. There was a good deal of sickness, as was only to be expected, so that the substantial reinforcements which arrived during January were very welcome; these amounted to 9 officers and 180 non-commissioned officers and men. The officers were Captain R. S. Dyer Bennet, who vacated his appointment as Adjutant of the 4th Battalion and rejoined the 1st; Lieutenants G. H. Salmon and G. W. Grossmith, Second-Lieutenants S. S. English, J. H. Hill, W. J. Gardner, R. N. Davis, C. L. Seton-Browne and S. F. Mackay.

Early in February there was a re-arrangement of divisions, whereby the 6th Division now became part of the XIV. Corps and was taken out of the VI., to which for some time it had belonged under Major-General Sir John Keir, its old Divisional Commander; the XIV. Corps now contained the Guards, the 6th and the 20th Divisions, and was commanded by Lieutenant-General the

Earl of Cavan. At the time when this change took place " the troops of the XIV. Corps were holding the left of the British front—the northern portion of the Ypres Salient from the Bellewaarde stream, north-west of Hooge on the right, to the junction with the French Army just south of the village of Boesinghe on the left. The 6th Division was on the right of the line and the 20th Division on the left, the boundary between the two divisions running just north of Wieltje Farm."*

The XIV. Corps was in the Second Army commanded by General Sir Herbert Plumer.

March was not so " quiet " a month as January, in the Battalion Diary, is stated to have been, and on the night of the 8th, when the 1st Leicestershire relieved the 2nd Sherwood Foresters in the St. Jean (Wieltje) sector, the relief is described as " the most unpleasant we have had for months, furious shelling of roads and a great deal of transport caught—none of our own, luckily. How the Battalion got in without heavy casualties it is hard to conceive, as all roads were shelled most impartially and everybody had narrow shaves."

During the next two or three days the German guns were incessantly in action, shells of all calibres being distributed along the front, while Poperinghe, Hooge and Hill 60 were heavily bombarded, and the enemy aircraft were also very active, dropping bombs on the rest billets and rearward communications. On the night of February 13th-14th " the Germans put a field gun on our Battalion Headquarters, and we had a whizz-bang every thirteen minutes between 10 p.m. and 3 a.m. Each shell was within twenty yards of our Headquarter dug-out; one bomber killed outside the dug-out."

Towards the end of the month snow fell and the cold was intense, but though there was a good deal of sickness—nearly 90 men being admitted to hospital, the casualties from enemy action were comparatively few, 3 men being killed and 25 wounded, among these latter being Captain M. K. Wardle, who was wounded for the second time since arrival in France.

March may be considered a bad month for trench casualties, inasmuch as on the 19th the 71st Brigade was taken out of the line for a prolonged rest to a locality actually beyond the hearing of the guns, but it did not leave before it had incurred nearly 70 more casualties. On the 18th, then, the 1st Battalion The Leicestershire Regiment was relieved by the 2nd Grenadier Guards and 3rd Coldstream Guards, and left Poperinghe next day by motor bus for Wormhoudt, which was again left on the 26th and the Battalion marched by way of Herzeele, Houtkerque, Watou and St. Jan-Ter-Bierzen to a camp near the last-named place, whence fatigue parties of 4 officers and 200 other ranks were daily supplied for work on a new railway between the Poperinghe—Crombeke and Poperinghe—Proven roads.

Here on the last day of the month the 1st Battalion saw something of the 11th (Service) Battalion of the Regiment, which was passing through to join the 6th Division as Pioneer Battalion.

This month 4 officers—Captain G. C. Dickinson, Lieutenant G. A. Quale, Second-Lieutenants S. C. Lawrence and H. Humberston—and 212 other ranks

* " The Guards Division in the Great War," Vol. I, p. 116.

joined or rejoined the Battalion—67 of these were rejoining on discharge from hospital; but the Battalion was called upon to give up its experienced Machine Gun Section—Second-Lieutenant F. G. H. Grimsley, 2 sergeants and 27 other ranks—to join the 6th Division Machine Gun Company. "They took," so the Diary records more in sorrow than in anger, "our four Maxim guns and full kit and two 4-horsed limbers. The 71st Infantry Brigade Machine Gun Company arrived, but had had little training and none previously at the front."

During the first week in April the whole of the 71st Infantry Brigade was concentrated in one large camp some little distance outside Calais on the Dunkerque road, and here for some ten days training of all kinds was assiduously carried on in weather which was fine but cold. On April 15th the first of several movements took place, the Brigade marching first to the Zutkerque area, then, on the 16th, the 1st Leicestershire and 9th Norfolks to Bollezeele and the two remaining battalions to Merkeghem; and on the following day by way of Zeggers Cappel and Esquebec to the Wormhoudt area, the Brigade being inspected on the march by General Sir H. Plumer, who expressed himself as being "very pleased."

On the 18th the march was resumed via Herzeele, Houtkerque, Watou and Poperinghe to Camp "E," two and a half miles from Poperinghe, whence late on the following night the Battalion was hurriedly sent off to the neighbourhood of Brielen, in support of the 16th Infantry Brigade, in whose trenches the Germans, after a very intense bombardment, had managed to gain a footing. Here the Battalion was disposed as follows: Headquarters, "A" and "B" Companies about the Château Trois Tours, 100 rifles of "C" Company in some trenches known as L.2, and the remainder of the Battalion in the Brielen defences. On the night of the 21st the Germans were turned out of the portion of the trenches they had captured, and the Battalion provided that night and the next day fatigue parties to carry up R.E. material and ammunition and to evacuate the wounded from the ground over which the recent fighting had taken place.

Here on the 23rd the 1st Battalion The Leicestershire Regiment relieved the 1st Battalion The Buffs, their old comrades of the 16th Brigade, in what was known as the Forward Cottage line in trenches described as "easily the worst we have been in since Hooge, 1915, and portions, having come in for enemy bombardment on the 19th-20th, are merely a succession of isolated posts and do not exist as trenches. Also the three days' rain has made every place full of water." Both sides here were very busily engaged in repairing and strengthening their trenches, each doing its very best, by heavy artillery bombardment, to hinder the efforts of the opponent, while patrols frequently met in No Man's Land and bombed each other with vigour. Here again Second-Lieutenant F. B. Robertson was especially conspicuous.

The casualties in April were few—3 killed and 16 wounded, while the drafts contained 1 officer—Second-Lieutenant S. L. Crowe—and 29 other ranks.

May was passed in very much the same way, but early in the month the Battalion experienced a severe loss in the death of a valuable young officer—Lieutenant G. A. Brounsworth, who had gone out with a party carrying some torpedoes intended to be placed at a spot where an enemy patrol usually passed through a wire entanglement on its nightly rounds. Unfortunately, by some mishap, the cause of which was never satisfactorily explained, one of the torpedoes exploded unexpectedly while the party was withdrawing, and caused several casualties, Lieutenant Brounsworth being terribly wounded, and dying on the 27th in No. 10 Casualty Clearing Station at Poperinghe.

On the 30th an accident of a somewhat similar character was averted through the bravery of No. 8052 Lance-Corporal J. England, "D" Company. While four bombers under his command were cleaning bombs in a fire-bay in one of the trenches, the lever of a Mills grenade flew up, striking the fingers of the man who was cleaning the grenade and causing him to drop it in the bay. The man shouted a warning and ran out of the trench, but Lance-Corporal England, seeing what had happened, rushed to the spot, picked up the grenade and hurled it over the parapet, where it exploded almost before reaching the ground. But for the lance-corporal's calm courage four men would almost certainly have been blown up, together with some fifty bombs.

This month 3 officers and 95 other ranks joined the Battalion, the officers being Lieutenant Lee, 9th Suffolks, who was attached temporarily as Transport Officer, and Second-Lieutenants F. E. Shelton and J. C. Webb; while at the end of the month there was a change in the command of the 71st Brigade, Brigadier-General M. Shewen vacating on relief by Brigadier-General FitzJ. M. Edwards, D.S.O., from the command of the Meerut Cavalry Brigade.

June, happily, was a tolerably quiet month, in view of the great events in which the 1st Battalion The Leicestershire Regiment was shortly to play its part, and the losses by enemy action numbered no more than 18 killed, wounded and missing, while nearly 60 non-commissioned officers and men joined from home or rejoined on discharge from hospital; the Rev. B. W. Keymer was attached to the Battalion as Chaplain; Captain H. B. German, R.A.M.C., took over duty as Medical Officer from Captain Adie, who was posted to No. 7 General Hospital; Captain J. Langdon Thomas, 1st Battalion 4th Gloucesters, joined as Transport Officer, and Second-Lieutenants J. H. John, B. Kidd, F. B. Stevenson, G. H. Gristwood and J. Burnett reported their arrival. Company Sergeant-Major A. Cummins was, on June 6th, promoted Second-Lieutenant.

Early in the month the Battalion, in common with the 2nd Battalion of the Regiment, received one of those complimentary letters from the armies of our allies, which seemed so hopeful of the success of joint endeavours to end the war, but which later the defection of Russia caused to seem something of a mockery.

"*From the Grand Quartier Général, Russie, to The Leicestershire Regiment.*

"*The 17th Archangelogordski Infantry of His Highness the Grand Duke Vladimir Alexanderovitch congratulate their comrades in arms on the birthday of His British Majesty King George V, and they wish the valiant Leicestershire Regiment success and glory.*"

To this the following reply was returned :—

" *To the O.C. 17th Archangelogordski Regiment.*

"*All ranks of the 1st Battalion Leicestershire Regiment join in thanking their gallant brothers in arms of the 17th Archangelogordski Infantry of His Highness the Grand Duke Vladimir Alexanderovitch for their kindly and felicitously expressed congratulations on the occasion of His Majesty King George V's birthday. May we meet after a glorious victory which will give lasting peace to the world.*"

The first half of July was spent in billets in Volkeringhove and Wormhoudt and in a training camp, where the Division was exercised over dummy trenches for an attack intended to be carried out on the Pilckem Ridge in conjunction with the Guards. This attack was, however, abandoned when the 6th Division moved to the Somme, as will now be described, but it formed the basis of the very successful attack delivered by the Guards and Welsh divisions in July, 1917. The time away from the immediate front was not, however, wholly given over to training for war, for on one afternoon Brigade sports were held, when the Battalion won the Brigade Championship prize for the highest points obtained.

For the last few days of the month the Battalion returned to the front-line trenches, and here an unfortunate accident occurred, a bomb exploding in the hands of Private Nicholls, killing him, Sergeant Faulkner and Private Potter, and wounding more or less severely six other men, all of " A " Company.

On August 1st the 1st Battalion The Leicestershire Regiment was relieved in the trenches by the 1st Battalion King's Own Scottish Borderers, and proceeded to Camp N, near Proven, and on this date the following were the officers serving with the Battalion :—

Lieutenant-Colonel R. H. Gillespie; Major R. S. Dyer Bennet; Lieutenant J. A. Hill, Adjutant; Lieutenant A. H. Pinder, Signalling Officer; Second-Lieutenant C. H. O. D. Burrell, Lewis Gun Officer; Second-Lieutenant F. B. Robertson, Bombing and Intelligence Officer; Captain J. H. Greasley, Quartermaster; Captain H. B. German, R.A.M.C., Medical Officer; the Rev. B. W. Keymer, Chaplain; and Captain J. Langdon-Thomas, Transport Officer.

"A" Company: Captain J. W. E. Mosse, Lieutenant G. Grossmith; Second-Lieutenants J. C. Webb, S. L. Crowe, F. B. Stevenson and A. Cummins.

"B" Company: Captain H. Pickbourne, Second-Lieutenants R. N. Davis, P. R. Milner, C. L. Seton-Browne, H. B. Kidd, H. A. Graves and W. Blacklock.

"C" Company: Lieutenant G. H. Salmon, Lieutenant C. E. Morrison, Second-Lieutenants J. H. John, G. W. Tanner, J. G. Kennedy, H. W. Brooker and A. G. Douglas.

"D" Company: Captain C. W. Herbison, Second-Lieutenants F. E. Shelton, G. H. Gristwood, J. Burnett and R. Pickersgill.

The following officers of the Battalion were absent on command: Lieutenant D. V. Webb, Second-Lieutenants W. Gardner and S. F. Mackay.

Entraining at Proven at 7.14 p.m. on August 2nd, the Battalion arrived at Candas early the next morning, an accident occurring during the journey which might very easily have had serious results. As the train was passing near Frevant its rear portion, containing the major part of the Battalion and nearly all the horses, broke away while ascending a rather steep incline, when the detached portion at once began to run backwards down the descent. Possible loss of life was prevented by the coolness and presence of mind of a pointsman, who, seeing what had occurred, and realizing that another train was about due on the same line, switched the detached portion of the train on to a dead-end, where it ran into buffers and was brought up, three carriages, however, being derailed and partly overturned. The casualties were 7 men and 5 horses slightly injured.

From Candas the Brigade moved by march route via Beauval and Leal-villers to a camp in Mailly-Maillet Wood, where Sunday, August 6th, was spent, and on the 14th the 1st Battalion Leicestershire relieved the 2nd Battalion Grenadier Guards in the right sector of the Brigade line in front of Beaumont Hamel.

Here, early the next morning, Lieutenant Douglas was killed by shrapnel.

About this time His Majesty the King had just concluded one of his very welcome and greatly-appreciated visits to his Army on the Western Front, and in the following Special Order of the Day, dated August 15th, he gave expression to the pleasure it had given him to come among his troops, and the pride he felt in their valour, endurance and remarkable cheerfulness.

" *Officers, Non-Commissioned Officers and Men.*

" *It has been a great pleasure and satisfaction to Me to be with My Armies during the past week. I have been able to judge for Myself of their splendid condition for war and of the spirit of cheerful confidence which animates all ranks, united in loyal co-operation to their chiefs and to one another.*

" *Since My last visit to the front there has been almost uninterrupted fighting on parts of our line. The offensive recently begun has been resolutely maintained by day and by night. I have had opportunities of visiting some of the scenes of the later desperate struggles, and of appreciating to a slight extent the demands made upon your courage and physical endurance in order to assail and capture positions prepared during the past two years and stoutly defended to the last.*

" *I have realized, not only the splendid work which has been done in immediate touch with the enemy—in the air, under ground, as well as on the ground—but also the vast organizations behind the fighting line, honourable alike to the genius of the initiators and to the heart and hand of the workers. Everywhere there is proof that all, men and women, are playing their part, and I rejoice to think their noble efforts are being heartily seconded by all classes at home.*

" *The happy relations maintained by My Armies and those of our French Allies are equally noticeable between My troops and the inhabitants of the districts in which they are quartered, and from whom they have received a cordial welcome ever since their first arrival in France.*

"*Do not think that I and your fellow-countrymen forget the heavy sacrifices which the Armies have made and the bravery and endurance they have displayed during the past two years of bitter conflict. These sacrifices have not been in vain; the arms of the Allies will never be laid down until our cause has triumphed.*

"*I return home more than ever proud of you.*

"*May God guide you to victory.*

(Sd.) " GEORGE, R.I."

Already as early in this year as February 16th the Allied Commanders had agreed upon the desirability of seriously taking the offensive against the enemy during the forthcoming summer. The choice of front to be attacked was governed by the knowledge that neither of the allied armies was in itself sufficiently strong to undertake an attack unaided upon a large enough scale to promise useful results. None the less, all possible preparations had early been made, but for some considerable time no decision was come to as to the actual date on which such an attack should open. For more reasons than one, General Sir Douglas Haig wished to postpone operations as long as possible; his armies were certainly growing in numbers, for he had now seventy divisions in the field, numbering in all some 600,000 sabres and bayonets;* but many of the new organizations were still far from being trained up to the standard of the older ones, and the longer the opening of the offensive could be deferred, the more efficient would these new units become. On the other hand, the enemy was pressing the French more and more strenuously in the Verdun battle, which had now been long in progress, while the Austrians had gained substantial successes against the Italians in the Trentino. Against this it may be said that, early in June, the Russian offensive had drawn certain German formations away from the western to the eastern front, but the strain in and about the French portion of the allied line was becoming over-heavy, and the allied generals then resolved that a combined offensive must be launched and that its commencement must not be delayed later than the end of June.

The necessary preparations were on a very vast scale; huge stocks of ammunition and military stores of all kinds had to be brought up and garnered in convenient places near the front; roads, railways and tram-lines had to be made or improved, shelters and magazines provided and mining operations undertaken, while 120 miles of water-pipes had to be laid down so as to ensure an adequate water supply for the troops as they moved forward.

" The enemy's position to be attacked was of a very formidable character, situated on a high, undulating tract of ground, which rises to more than 500 feet above sea-level, and forms the watershed between the Somme on the one side and the rivers of south-west Belgium on the other. On the southern face of this watershed, the general trend of which is from east-south-east to west-north-west, the ground falls in a series of long irregular spurs and deep

* *Vide* his despatch of December 23rd, 1916.

depressions to the valley of the Somme. Well down the forward slopes of this face the enemy's first system of defence, starting from the Somme near Curlu, ran at first north for 3,000 yards, then west for 7,000 yards to near Fricourt, where it turned nearly due north, forming a great salient in the enemy's line. Some 10,000 yards further north of Fricourt the trenches crossed the River Ancre, a tributary of the Somme, and, still running north, passed over the summit of the watershed about Hébuterne and Gommecourt, and then down its northern spur to Arras. On the 20,000 yards front between the Somme and the Ancre the enemy had a strong second system of defence, sited generally on or near the southern crest of the highest part of the watershed, at an average distance of from 3,000 to 5,000 yards behind his first system of defence."*

The operations known as the First Battle of the Somme are usually considered in three phases; the first began on July 1st and ended about the 17th; the second then commenced and went on until the end of the first week in September; and the third and final phase began on September 9th, continuing until November 18th, and it was in this concluding part of the great battle that the 1st Battalion The Leicestershire Regiment was engaged.

On August 27th the Battalion left its camp in Mailly Wood, and, marching by Louvincourt, Beauval, Flesselles, Cardonette and Mericourt l'Abbé, arrived at the assembly area in the vicinity of Meaulte on September 11th, here occupying some old German trenches, and officers and men being busily employed during the next day carrying up bombs and rifle ammunition to a dump in Trônes Wood.

The 6th Division, still forming part of the XIV. Corps, was now in the Fourth Army commanded by General Sir H. Rawlinson, and the distribution of this army, from south to north, was as follows :—

XIV. Corps : 56th Division, 6th Division, Guards Division.

XV. Corps : 14th Division, 41st Division, New Zealand Division.

III. Corps : 47th Division, 50th Division, 15th Division.

The XIV. Corps was thus the right of the British attack, and had its right resting on the north bank of the Somme.

In the operations which had been in progress during July and August the Fourth Army had forced the enemy back for some distance, but casualties had been heavy and fresh troops were badly needed. "On the 9th September a successful attack had given us Ginchy and Leuze Wood, but the Germans were holding very strongly the high ground which lies in the form of a horse-shoe between the above-named points, and which dominates the country for some distance to the south. The trenches followed the shape of the spur roughly at the back end of the horse-shoe, and covered access was given to them by a sunken road leading back to the deep valley which runs north from Combles. At the top of the spur, just south of the railway and communicating with the sunken road, was a four-sided trench in the form of a parallelogram of some 300 yards by 150 yards, called by us the Quadrilateral. It was this strong point and the adjoining trenches which had held up the advance of the Fourth Army on the 9th September, and it was the first task of the 6th Division to obliterate the

* Despatch of December 23rd, 1916.

horse-shoe and straighten the line preparatory to a general attack on the 15th September."*

On the 13th, the 16th and 71st Infantry Brigades made a joint attack upon the enemy, with the view of strengthening the line by capturing the Quadrilateral, but not very much ground was gained, while the casualties were heavy; in this attack only the 2nd Sherwood Foresters and 9th Suffolks of the 71st Brigade were engaged.

Preparations were now made to include the Quadrilateral in a general attack on September 15th, instead of making it a subsidiary operation as had originally been intended, and the objective was now the line Gueudecourt—Flers—Les Bœufs—Morval, the Guards and the 6th Division being detailed to capture the two last-named places.

This was the first occasion on which tanks were employed, but, of the three allotted to the 6th Division, two broke down before starting, while the third, moving off in advance of the infantry, had its periscope shot away, its peepholes blinded, was riddled by armour-piercing bullets and had to return whence it came, having achieved no useful result whatever.

At 6.20 p.m. on the 14th, Operation Orders were issued to all concerned, and these may be summarized as follows :—

" The Fourth Army will attack the enemy's defences between the Combles Ravine and Martinpuich on the 15th with the object of seizing Morval, Les Bœufs, Gueudecourt and Flers and breaking through the enemy's system of defence. The French are undertaking an offensive simultaneously to the south and the Reserve Army on the north.

" The capture of Morval and Les Bœufs will be undertaken by the Guards and 6th Divisions, the main object of the 56th Division on the right of the 16th Infantry Brigade will be the clearing of Bouleaux Wood and the formation of a protective flank covering all the lines of advance from Combles.

" The attack of the 6th Division will be carried out with the 16th Brigade on the right, the 71st on the left and the 18th Brigade in reserve.

[The objectives were indicated by certain trenches lettered on the map.]

" The 1st Leicesters and 9th Norfolks will form up to-night under cover of darkness in attack formation, facing north-east along the general line of the sunken road which runs due south from Ginchy, Norfolks on the right, Leicesters on the left; each battalion on a front of about 250 yards, with 2 companies in the front line and 2 in support; each company on a one-platoon front. The left of the Leicesters will be close up to Ginchy and the right of the Norfolks on the sunken road near the point where the railway crosses it." The Norfolks were to direct. Zero hour was fixed at 6.20 a.m. on September 15th.

The 1st Battalion The Leicestershire Regiment moved into its attack position during the night, and was finally settled down ready for the attack by 4.30 a.m. on the 15th.

To facilitate reorganization should the casualties in the coming action prove to be heavy, the following were left behind; Major R. S. Dyer Bennet,

* " Short History of the 6th Division," pp. 20, 21.

Lieutenants D. V. Webb, M.C., and S. T. Hartshorne, Second-Lieutenants A Cummins, R. N. Davis and P. R. Milner, with Regimental Sergeant-Major Measures, Orderly-Room Sergeant H. Judd, all the company quartermaster-sergeants, 15 per cent. of the non-commissioned officers and 10 per cent. of the privates; this left Lieutenant-Colonel R. H. Gillespie in command, with the companies officered as follows:—

"A" Company: Captain J. W. E. Mosse, Second-Lieutenants J. C. Webb, S. J. Crowe and F. B. Stevenson.

"B" Company: Captain H. Pickbourne, Second-Lieutenants H. B. Kidd, H. A. Graves and W. Blacklock.

"C" Company: Captain G. H. Salmon, Lieutenant J. H. John, Second-Lieutenants J. G. Kennedy and H. W. Brooker.

"D" Company: Captain C. W. Herbison, Second-Lieutenants G. H. Gristwood, J. Burnett and R. Pickersgill.

The Commanding Officer decided to attack with "D" (Captain Herbison) and "B" Company (Captain Pickbourne) on the left and right of the front line respectively, and "A" (Captain Mosse) and "C" (Captain Salmon) on the left and right of the second line. Two Lewis guns were detailed to accompany each company, which also contained two bombing squads each of ten bombers, and every man of the four companies carried two Mills bombs.

The strength of the Battalion on going into action was 23 officers—inclusive of the Chaplain and Medical Officer—and 643 non-commissioned officers and men.

At zero hour the leading companies moved off at a steady pace, advancing in four lines at 30 paces interval, the supporting companies following in the same formation 300 yards in rear, and the enemy at once opened a heavy machine-gun fire.

The mist and smoke were very thick and permitted of no observation by the supporting companies or by Battalion Headquarters, moving in rear of the last wave of the support, and nobody knew exactly what was happening to the leading companies, which had failed to advance quite in the desired direction, with the result that a small gap opened near the centre of the line; this was, however, at once filled up by the supporting companies.

Fortunately, the enemy barrage came down too late to do much harm, but throughout the advance the Battalion suffered heavily from machine-gun fire, and did not succeed in gaining its objective, being held up under this fire by very strong and wholly undamaged enemy wire in front of a trench leading from the north-west corner of the Quadrilateral, the existence of which does not appear to have been previously known.

"A" Company now entrenched itself on a small ridge, and at once set about locating the positions of the remaining companies, when it was discovered that "B" and "C" had lost very heavily and had entrenched themselves in a position where they were wholly unsupported, while "D," which had also suffered many casualties, was either advancing with the Guards or holding shell holes between the new line and the German wire. Grave difficulties were experienced in keeping in touch with Brigade Headquarters owing to the impossibility of using visual signalling, while the heavy barrage kept up throughout the day made it almost impossible for any runners to get through. Private Parry, " A " Company, however, did very excellent work, running the gauntlet no fewer than three times during the day, while after his fourth journey he was detained by Brigade Headquarters, who refused to allow him to venture again.

During the 15th the trenches occupied were improved as much as possible, so that by night all their occupants had tolerably good cover; and at dark the supporting companies were moved up to the new line, which was extended to the right and left. The night was quiet except for some very continuous sniping in front of " C " Company.

During the attack the Battalion appears to have been opposed to the 9th Bavarian Infantry Regiment.

The 16th opened quietly, the only sign of enemy activity being the appearance about 8 a.m. of nine enemy aeroplanes which circled over the British line. Then at nine o'clock the Guards on the left of the Battalion advanced, and when, towards evening, their right was counter-attacked, one of the Battalion Lewis guns, commanded by Corporal Tyers, rendered material assistance.

In the course of the afternoon of the 16th intimation was received that the Battalion would be relieved about 9.30 that evening by the 1st West Yorkshire Regiment, but this relief did not materialize, and patrols sent out established the fact that the " relief " was occupying a position some 200 yards in rear of that held by the 1st Leicestershire, and had received no orders as to relieving them !

Lieutenant-Colonel Gillespie now decided that he had better evacuate his position, as the West Yorkshire battalion was well placed for occupying it, if necessary, and he was, in fact, in the act of doing so when a message was received from the Brigade directing him to withdraw without relief, as the heavy artillery was about to bombard the Quadrilateral. The Battalion then left its trenches and fell back to bivouacs in Maltz Horn Farm, arriving here about 5.30 on the morning of September 17th.

Again had the 1st Battalion The Leicestershire Regiment experienced very grievous losses, no fewer than 14 officers and 410 non-commissioned officers and men having been killed and wounded during these two days' fighting, while this total was to be slightly increased before the month came to an end.

Such little rest as was obtainable at Maltz Horn Farm was not of a very prolonged character, for before midday on the 18th the Battalion was moved back to the front, being placed at the disposal of the General Officer Commanding 16th Infantry Brigade; but it was withdrawn again the same night and marched back to Maltz Horn Farm. Here, however, no accommodation was available, and the Battalion was finally sent to billets at Ville sur Ancre, which was reached on the afternoon of the 19th. From here sudden orders took the Battalion back once more to the front on the afternoon of the 26th, being again placed at the disposal of the General Officer Commanding 16th Infantry Brigade, who at first held the Battalion in reserve, and twenty-four hours later sent it up to trenches east of Morval. Here, having relieved the 16th Warwicks

D

and the 1st Cheshires, the companies settled down to the usual " improvement " of trenches, for those appear to have left even more than usual to be desired— no battalion in the course of the whole war ever admits having taken over trenches in a really satisfactory state ! But here " A " and " B " Companies occupied Thunder Trench with a gap of 500 yards between the two companies, while it is seriously stated that " A " Company on the right " shared a trench with the Germans " ! " A " Company seems to have done its very best to persuade their fellow-occupants that their companionship was not desired, for we read in the War Diary—" Huns harassed all day by rifle grenades and bombs " ! These very broad hints seem to have been effectual !

On the 28th the Battalion was again relieved, and marched back to billets in the neighbourhood of Guillemont.

During these days—the last half of September—the losses in the 1st Battalion The Leicestershire Regiment amounted to 14 officers and 442 non-commissioned officers and men killed, wounded and missing ; the officers were : killed, Lieutenant A. H. Pinder, Second-Lieutenants J. C. Webb and J. G. Kennedy ; died of wounds, Captain C. W. Herbison, Second-Lieutenants G. H. Gristwood, J. Burnett and J. G. Gardner ; wounded, Captains H. Pickbourne, G. H. Salmon and H. B. German, R.A.M.C., Lieutenant J. H. John, Second-Lieutenants F. B. Stevenson, H. A. Graves, W. Blacklock and R. Pickersgill ; of the other ranks, 119 were killed, 259 were wounded, while 34 were missing.

As a result of these losses the Battalion entered upon the month of October with an officer-corps numbering twelve only, including the Medical Officer.

On September 16th the following message had been sent by Major-General C. Ross, the Commander of the 6th Division, to the Brigadier and battalions of the 71st Brigade :—

" The Major-General wishes the G.O.C. 71st Infantry Brigade to convey to his Battalions and Machine Gun Company his great appreciation of the splendid fashion in which they carried out the task given to them. The general situation demanded an attack on a strongly entrenched, an unreconnoitred, and, as it proved, a well-wired enemy, without much preparation. This, the most difficult task which can be given to soldiers, was carried out with unflinching gallantry and devotion."

Then, on the day following, the Commander-in-Chief of the British Army in France wrote as follows to General Sir H. Rawlinson, commanding the Fourth Army :—

" The great successes won by the Fourth Army on the 15th are most satisfactory, and have brought us another long step forward towards final victory. The further advance yesterday after such severe fighting was also a very fine performance, highly creditable to the troops and to Corps, Divisional and Brigade Staffs. Our new engine of war, the Heavy Section Machine Gun Corps, acquitted itself splendidly on its first trial, and has proved itself a very valuable addition to the Army. My warmest congratulations to you and the Fourth Army on a very fine achievement."

His Majesty the King also sent his congratulations on the successes of this month :—

"*I congratulate you and My brave troops on the brilliant success just achieved. I have never doubted that complete victory will eventually crown our efforts, and the splendid result of the fighting yesterday confirms this view.*"

Those successes, moreover, were not gained over inferior or dispirited troops; the enemy everywhere fought well and " the German defence was worthy of the highest praise."*

" On 7th October the XIV. Corps (20th and 56th Divisions) attacked with only partial success, and the 6th Division was brought in again on the night of the 8th-9th October for a general attack on the 12th October. The enemy had dug a series of trenches named by us Rainbow, Cloudy, Misty, Zenith, etc., a portion of which had been captured by us, making a somewhat pronounced salient. All three brigades were in the line, with one battalion in front trenches, the 71st Brigade (Brigadier-General F. Feetham)† being in the salient, with the 16th Infantry Brigade on the right and the 18th Infantry Brigade on the left. The objective of the attack of the 12th October was the line of trenches running north from Le Transloy."‡

With these operations, however, the 1st Battalion The Leicestershire Regiment had but little to do; when they commenced on October 8th, only one battalion of the 71st Brigade was sent up to the front, the Leicestershire and Norfolks remaining behind in reserve in the camp they were then occupying. Later the 1st Leicestershire Regiment was moved nearer the front, but took no part in any serious attack, being chiefly employed in carrying up stores and providing stretcher and other parties for the troops more closely in contact with the enemy.

By October 21st the Battalion was back in billets at Corbie, where intimation was received that the 6th Division, less artillery, was to be prepared to entrain on any date after the 26th for transfer to the First Army. The move, however, as far as the Battalion was concerned, commenced on the 24th, when it entrained at Corbie, detrained next day and marched to Sorel; entraining again at Pont Rémy on the 29th, it arrived the same afternoon at Fouquereuil and marched from there to billets at Fouquières les Béthune, the 6th Division being now in Corps Reserve of the I. Corps, commanded by Lieutenant-General A. E. A. Holland, C.B., D.S.O., M.V.O., of the First Army under General Horne.

The 6th Division had taken part in three general attacks on the Somme, and had suffered casualties amounting to 277 officers and 6,640 other ranks.

The results of the Somme battles were thus summed up by the British Commander : " Verdun had been relieved; the main German forces had been held on the Western Front; the enemy's strength had been very considerably worn down. Any of these three results is in itself sufficient to justify the Somme battle. The attainment of all three of them affords ample compensation for the splendid efforts of our troops and for the sacrifices made by ourselves and our

---

* " The Guards Division in the Great War," Vol. I, p. 160.
† Took over command on October 6th.
‡ " Short History of the 6th Division," p. 25.

Allies. . . . . The total number of prisoners taken by us in the Somme battle between the 1st July and the 18th November is just over 38,000, including over 800 officers.   During the same period we captured 29 heavy guns, 96 field guns and field howitzers, 136 trench mortars and 514 machine guns.''

There is a tendency among certain of our post-war writers to contend that our successes in the summer and autumn fighting of this year cannot be considered as worth the sacrifices which they entailed; but it seems very clear that the leaders of the German Army were not in agreement with these gloomy views.   Writing of the German situation as he found it in the middle of November, 1916, General Ludendorff has written : '' Our position was uncommonly difficult and a way out was hard to find.   We could not contemplate an offensive ourselves, having to keep our reserves available for defence. . . . . If the war lasted our defeat seemed inevitable.''

The 6th Division was now in the La Bassée sector, which included Givenchy Ridge and the Cuinchy Brickstacks, and the list of officers present with the Battalion on November 1st shows how relatively few these had become in number, and how many of the old names were missing :—

Major R. S. Dyer Bennet, in command; Captain J. W. E. Mosse, second-in-command; Second-Lieutenant C. H. O. D. Burrell, Acting Adjutant; Second-Lieutenant P. R. Milner, Brigade Bombing Officer; Second-Lieutenant W. A. Charlesworth, Brigade Lewis Gun Officer; Second-Lieutenant H. W. J. Brooker, Signalling Officer; Captain H. B. German, R.A.M.C., Medical Officer; and Captain the Rev. B. D. Wilkins, Chaplain.

> '' A '' Company : Lieutenant S. T. Hartshorne, Second-Lieutenants H. D. Muggeridge, D. F. M. Hackett and W. B. Bonas.
>
> '' B '' Company : Lieutenant J. E. Garbutt, Second-Lieutenants H. B. Kidd and W. A. Savage.
>
> '' C '' Company : Lieutenants D. V. Webb, M.C., and F. E. Shelton, Second-Lieutenants A. L. Gray and C. E. Lancaster.
>
> '' D '' Company : Second-Lieutenants G. W. Tanner, M.C., C. H. Hassall and W. H. Thomas.

For the greater part of November the Battalion remained in reserve engaged in training of all kinds, especially in that for the many '' specialists '' now required to be maintained by battalions; but on the 25th it went up to the front again, moving by Bèthune, La Bassée Canal and Pont Fixe, and relieved the 1st Battalion The Devonshire Regiment in the front and support line trenches from the canal bank towards the south—a frontage of approximately 1,200 yards.   This tour was a comparatively brief one, lasting four days only, when the Battalion went back to billets in Harley Street, leaving, however, five platoons up in the line.   '' The outstanding feature of this tour,'' writes the Battalion diarist, '' has been trench-mortaring, at which our men excelled. Retaliation in each case was effective, the number of our mortar shells being greatly in excess of the Boche's.   Seven men had to be admitted to hospital suffering from trench feet, although before entering the trenches the feet of the whole Battalion were rubbed with whale oil, and socks were changed every day by a fresh pair being sent up from the laundry for each man.''

The casualties during this month were low—only 4 killed or died of wounds and 5 wounded.

Of the events of December there is but little to chronicle, beyond that on the 15th Lance-Corporal B. Curtis, of the Battalion, brought in a wounded German non-commissioned officer belonging to an enemy patrol, who had been left behind by his party when dispersed by a burst of Lewis-gun fire; he proved to belong to the 393rd Infantry Regiment.

Christmas Day, 1916, was spent by the 1st Battalion The Leicestershire Regiment out of the line, in huts at La Bourse : " Church Parade with Drums, marched to Y.M.C.A. Hut for the service, big dinner arranged in company messes—a great success. Soccer match, 1st Leicestershire v. 9th Suffolks, score 2—2, a very exciting match. All the officers dined together, a very successful dinner."

During the final tour at the close of the year the Battalion Diary tells us that " the trenches have been in an awful condition, in places knee-deep in mud and even higher. The Boche ' special ' on this front is ' rum-jars,' but considering the amount of stuff sent over, the casualties were wonderfully light "; these, indeed, totalled only 1 killed and 18 wounded, but the sick numbered 52.

Again at this, the third Christmas of the war, His Majesty the King sent his usual kindly message to his troops; in the one addressed more particularly to those at the front, he said :—

" *I send you, My sailors and soldiers, hearty good wishes for Christmas and the New Year. My grateful thoughts are ever with you for victories gained, for hardships endured, and for your unfailing cheerfulness. Another Christmas has come round and we are still at war, but the Empire, confident in you, remains determined to win.*

" *May God bless and protect you.*"

Another message was addressed more especially to the sick and wounded, and was as follows :—

" *At this Christmastide the Queen and I are thinking more than ever of the sick and wounded among My sailors and soldiers. From Our hearts we wish them strength to bear their sufferings, speedy restoration to health, a peaceful Christmas, and many happier years to come.*"

On December 7th of this year, Major-General Tompson, C.B., who had been Colonel of the Leicestershire Regiment since September, 1912, died at Windsor, and he was succeeded by Major-General Sir E. M. Woodward, K.C.M.G., C.B. General Woodward joined the Regiment in 1882, was promoted Captain ten years later, Major in 1902, Lieutenant-Colonel in 1907, and Colonel in 1911. He served at Malta as D.A.A.G. from 1893-6, was Brigade Major at the Curragh in 1899, and Staff Captain, Intelligence Division, 1900-1903. He served in Ireland as D.A.A.G. from 1899-1900; D.A.Q.M.G., Army Headquarters, 1904-5; D.A.A.G., War Office, 1906-1911, and was Director of Mobilization from 1913-14. He served in Uganda from 1897-98, was mentioned in despatches and was awarded a Brevet Majority, a medal and two clasps; in East Africa, 1903-4, despatches, medal and clasp; and in the Great War he served with the Mediterranean Expeditionary Force from 1915-16, and was three times mentioned in despatches, awarded the C.B., the British and Victory Medals, and was promoted Major-General. From 1916-17 he was Director of Organization, and was created K.C.M.G. in 1917.

From the day that General Woodward was gazetted Colonel of the Regiment the interests of his old corps have never been out of his mind. In very many ways he helped all battalions during the war, and urged the claims of deserving officers and men; while, after the war, both battalions have found in their Colonel a man they could lean on and get help from in numberless ways.

CHAPTER IV.

1917.

THE BATTLE OF CAMBRAI.

IN the Field-Marshal's despatch of May 31st, 1917, he wrote as follows :—

" Our operations prior to the 18th November, 1916, had forced the enemy into a very pronounced salient in the area between the Ancre and the Scarpe valleys, and had obtained for us greatly improved opportunities for observation over this salient. A comparatively short further advance would give us complete possession of the few points south of the Ancre to which the enemy still clung, and would enable us to gain entire command of the spur above Beaumont Hamel."

In the middle of November, 1916, the Allied Commanders-in-Chief, General Joffre and Field-Marshal Haig, had made their plans for the ensuing year, and under these the pressure upon the Germans was to be kept up throughout the winter, the troops holding themselves ready for an offensive early in the New Year; the British Armies, it was arranged, should attack about February 1st between Bapaume and Vimy Ridge, while the French were to strike between the Oise and the Somme. By December 16th, 1916, however, a change had come about in the command of the French Armies, General Nivelle having taken the place of General Joffre, and the scheme was then remodelled, the arrangement now being that, as a main operation, the French were to endeavour to break through on the Aisne by the employment of an overpowering number of divisions. To obtain this great preponderance of force, it was necessary that as many French divisions as possible should be replaced by a corresponding number of British units, and Sir Douglas Haig was asked to extend his line south of the Somme as far as a point opposite the town of Roye. This request was loyally complied with, and the required extension of our line was completed by February 26th, 1917. " This alteration entailed the maintenance by British forces of an exceptionally active front of 110 miles, including the whole of the Somme battle-front, and, combined with the continued activity maintained throughout the winter, interfered to no small extent with my arrangements for reliefs. The training of the troops had consequently to be restricted to such limited opportunities as circumstances from time to time permitted."*

During the closing weeks of the Somme struggle the Germans had already begun to prepare defensive lines behind their front for their armies to fall back upon and hold; these they called after different legendary heroes—the Woden, Siegfried, Brunhilda lines, etc.—but by the Allies these were collectively known

* Despatch of May 31st, 1917.

43

as the Hindenburg Line, after the soldier who had now been summoned from the Russian to the Western Front; the northern flank of the Hindenburg Line rested on Vimy Ridge, and the southern on the St. Gobain Forest and on the Chemin des Dames.

The general disposition of the British forces, after the extension to the south above mentioned, was as follows : General Plumer's Second Army was about the Ypres Salient; south of him, in the Armentières sector, was the First Army, under General Horne; while General Allenby's Third Army carried on the line to the south of Arras. From the point upon which the British line had hinged during the previous year's operations, General Gough's Fifth Army took over the front, joining on to the Fourth Army, commanded by General Rawlinson, near the old French position.

With the opening of the New Year came a period of very severe frost, with heavy snowstorms, but when the worst of this weather was past and offensive operations could be resumed, the enemy was driven, during the first half of January, from as much of the Beaumont Hamel spur as he was then still holding; while during the early days of February the success of some hard fighting brought the British line forward north of the Ancre to a point level with the centre of Grandcourt, thus obliging the Germans to vacate the last remaining portion of their second line system in these parts. " Further British offensives towards the middle of February led to the evacuation of Miraumont and Serre; and between the 25th February and the 2nd March a series of attacks was carried out against a strong secondary line of defence, which, from a point in the Le Transloy—Loupart line due west of the village of Beaulencourt, crossed in front of Ligny—Tilloy and La Barque to the southern defence of Loupart Wood."

The month of January, 1917, was spent by the 1st Leicestershire Regiment by turns in the front line and at rest in Mazingarbe, furnishing working parties for the trenches; during this month a draft of 122 non-commissioned officers and men arrived under Lieutenant Stevens; and on the 30th-31st, a patrol sent out by the Battalion from the North Crater to investigate the enemy sap, encountered a small party of the enemy, who were evidently lying in wait to ambush the men of the patrol but were seriously discomfited. The patrol was composed of Second-Lieutenant Savage, Sergeant Wragg and five men, and on the enemy opening rapid fire the officer was hit in the foot and was placed in a shell hole, while Sergeant Wragg, having reorganized the party, proceeded to bomb the aggressors. One man was seen to run away and Sergeant Wragg shot a second with his revolver. On advancing to the spot whence fire had been opened by the enemy, nobody was seen, and Sergeant Wragg then brought in his patrol, being highly commended for his conduct by Brigadier-General Feetham.

During February there was considerable activity on both sides and many raids were carried out from the trenches occupied by the 71st Infantry Brigade, but 1 officer, Second-Lieutenant W. A. Charlesworth, and 8 other ranks were killed, while Lieutenant P. C. Watson and 25 non-commissioned officers and men were wounded in the course of the month. On the 17th the 6th Division was relieved by the 21st, the 10th Yorkshire Regiment of the 62nd Brigade taking the place in the front line of the 1st Leicestershire, which then marched by companies to Sailly Labourse, and on the following day to Bèthune, where the non-commissioned officers and men were accommodated in Montmorency Barracks, while the officers were billeted in private houses.

Towards the end of February, however, notice was received that between March 1st and 6th, the 6th Division would relieve the 37th Division in the Loos, 14 Bis and Hulluch sectors and also part of the 62nd Brigade of the 21st Division in the Quarries sector, and the move took place on the last day of February and March 1st, when the Division, with all three of its brigades in line, occupied a front 11,000 yards in length extending to the north from the Double Crassier at Loos; this month was, however, tolerably quiet.

On April 10th orders were issued for the Battalion to carry out a one-company raid on the enemy trenches on the night of the 17th-18th, with the object of securing identifications, killing Germans, obtaining enemy documents and destroying all dug-outs and emplacements. " C " Company was detailed for the raid, and the following officers took part : Captain C. H. V. Cox was O.C. raid; Lieutenant D. V. Webb, M.C., was O.C. assaulting party; Lieutenant A. L. Stevens was O.C. first wave; Second-Lieutenant A. Wherry was O.C. second wave; and Second-Lieutenant C. H. Watson was in charge of the torpedo and wire-cutting party. The password for the operations was the wholly appropriate one of " Tiger."

The raiding party left its trenches at 2 a.m. on the 18th and the raiders were back again in billets at Philosophe by 6 a.m., having in the meantime thoroughly wrecked and blown in several dug-outs containing Germans, destroyed by bombing an enemy machine gun and brought in one unwounded prisoner. Several Germans were found dead in the front line, having evidently been killed by the British barrage. The losses among the raiding party totalled 27, 1 man being killed, while Second-Lieutenant A. Wherry and 21 other ranks were wounded, and Lieutenant A. L. Stevens and 3 men were missing.

The Battalion was now—on the 22nd—withdrawn into billets at Maroc, but on the march thither a shell exploded under the horse of the Transport Officer, Second-Lieutenant W. H. Muggeridge, who was bringing up rations, killing the horse and wounding the rider.

About this time a battalion reorganization was directed to be carried out in the 71st Brigade, each company to be henceforth composed for fighting purposes of three platoons, each of a minimum strength of 28, plus platoon and company headquarters, the remainder of the fourth platoon being left in rear in the event of the battalion going into action.

" During ten days," we now read in the History of the 6th Division, " the Division had been engaged in continuous fighting on the front of one brigade, whilst holding with the other two a front of approximately 7,000 yards. Four battalions from other brigades, in addition to its own four, had passed through the hands of the 16th Infantry Brigade, which was conducting the fighting. Battalions relieved from the fighting front one night were put straight into the line elsewhere on the following night, and battalions which had already done a long continuous tour in the trenches were relieved one night, put into the fighting front on the following night, and twenty-four hours later had to deliver an attack.   The enemy, concerned about the fate of Hill 70, concentrated a very formidable artillery fire on the narrow front involved, and the bombardments and barrages on the front of attack were of exceptional severity.   The extent to which the Division was stretched on the rest of its front is exemplified by two incidents.   On one occasion an enemy raid penetrated our front and support lines without being detected or meeting anyone, and came upon our reserve line by chance at the only place on the front of the brigade concerned where there was one company in that line.   At another part of the front it was found, when normal conditions were restored, that in an abandoned part of our front line between two posts, the enemy had actually made himself so much at home that he had established a small dump of rations and bombs.

" For the manner in which the Division had followed up and pressed the enemy withdrawal it received the thanks of the Commander in Chief."

The greater part of the month of May was passed in the usual manner, the Battalion being either up in the front line about Loos or in rear in billets in Les Brebis or in Philosophe, when in the line incurring casualties, among which were Lieutenant H. A. Dolby killed by an enemy sniper, and Second-Lieutenant L. C. Morton severely wounded by aerial darts;* while of other ranks 4 men were killed and 20 wounded.   On the 22nd, " B " Company, under command of Captain G. N. Wykes, with Lieutenants P. R. Milner, H. A. Graves and G. Delmer and 132 non-commissioned officers and men, raided the German front and support line trenches, bombing several dug-outs and inflicting many casualties on the enemy, at a loss to the raiding party of 6 wounded.

In this month Captain H. B. German, R.A.M.C., was relieved by Captain N. P. Boulton, of the same corps.

From January to May of this year the 1st Battalion The Leicestershire Regiment, in common with other units of the Brigade and Division, had been engaged in tolerably continuous fighting, losing experienced officers and men who could only with difficulty be replaced, but it had not so far taken any part in the more important actions which, during the same period, had been fought on the Western Front, and of which some general mention must now be made.

The German retreat to the Hindenburg Line had commenced on March 14th and came to an end on April 5th, being followed by an event of the very greatest significance, when, on April 6th, the United States House of Representatives, by a majority of 373 votes to 50, passed a resolution declaring the existence of a state of war with Germany, authorizing President Wilson " to employ the entire naval and military forces of the United States and the resources of the Government to carry on war against the Imperial German Government; and, to bring the conflict to a successful termination, all the resources of the country are hereby pledged by the Congress of the United States."

On April 9th the Battle of Arras opened with the hard fighting on Vimy Ridge and on the River Scarpe, was continued with the Second Battle of the

* Died later of his wounds.

Aisne and endured until May 4th; while the Battle of Bullecourt, which commenced on May 3rd, did not end until the 17th. Finally, the results of the battles of the spring of this year were summed up as follows by the British Commander-in-Chief in his despatch of December 31st of this year: "On the British front alone, in less than one month's hard fighting, we had captured over 19,500 prisoners, including 400 officers, and had also taken 257 guns, including 98 heavy guns, with 464 machine guns, 227 trench mortars, and immense quantities of other war material. Our line had been advanced to a greatest depth exceeding five miles on a total front of over twenty miles, representing a gain of some sixty square miles of territory. A great improvement had been effected in the general situation of our troops on the front attacked, and the capture of Vimy Ridge had removed a constant menace to the security of our line."

On June 4th—the Battalion being then engaged in training at Verquin—it was notified that the 46th Division, which at this date was holding the front opposite Lens, would shortly be engaged in offensive operations, and that the 6th Division should do everything in its power to attract the enemy's attention to its front and convey the impression that an attack was about to be launched therefrom—cutting the enemy's wire with torpedoes, raiding his trenches by small parties, and opening a heavy bombardment upon his front line and back areas. June was consequently a month of constant small activities and equally of some ceremonial, for on the 27th His Royal Highness the Duke of Connaught visited this front, when a Guard of Honour of the Battalion paraded at Advanced Army Headquarters; the Guard was composed of Captain J. W. E. Mosse, M.C., Second-Lieutenants R. N. Davis and J. O. Vessey, two warrant officers, four sergeants and 100 rank and file. On the next day the following was issued from the Division to the General Officer Commanding 71st Brigade:—

"*The G.O.C. has directed me to communicate the following with reference to yesterday's Guard of Honour:—*

"*H.R.H. the Duke of Connaught was much impressed by the appearance, turn-out and physique of the Guard of Honour of the 1st Leicestershire Regiment, and especially by the way in which the men handled their arms.*

"*The Guard of Honour reflected credit on the Battalion, the Brigade and on the Division.*"

During the early part of July Their Majesties the King and Queen had been engaged in a visit to the Western Front, and on the 11th His Majesty the King inspected representatives of the First Army. He had taken special steps to have it given out that he hoped to see as many of his troops as possible, and, accordingly, the road along which he was to pass was lined by all soldiers from the different units of the Army who were not on duty. Unfortunately, the 1st Leicestershire at the time was holding the front in the St. Elie sector, and consequently does not appear to have been represented on this historic occasion; but the following Special Order of the Day, issued by command of the King on July 14th, applied equally to all ranks of the Battalion as to those of the regiments and battalions, more fortunate, which on this occasion had come immediately under the Royal eye.

" *Officers, Non-Commissioned Officers and Men.*

" *On the conclusion of My fourth visit to the British Armies in the field, I leave you with feelings of admiration and gratitude for past achievements, and of confidence in future efforts.*

" *On all sides I have witnessed the scenes of your triumphs.*

" *The battlefields of the Somme, the Ancre, Arras, Vimy and Messines have shown Me what grand results can be attained by the courage and devotion of all arms and services under efficient commanders and staffs.*

" *Nor do I forget the valuable work done by the various departments behind the fighting line, including those who direct and man the highly developed system of railways and other means of communication.*

" *Your comrades, too—the men and women of the industrial army at home— have claims on your remembrance for their untiring service in helping you to meet the enemy on terms which are not merely equal, but daily improving.*

" *It was a great pleasure to the Queen to accompany Me and to become personally acquainted with the excellent arrangements for the care of the sick and wounded, whose welfare is ever close to Her heart.*

" *For the past three years the armies of the Empire and workers in the home-lands behind them have risen superior to every difficulty and every trial.*

" *The splendid successes already gained, in concert with our gallant Allies, have advanced us well on the way towards the completion of the task we undertook.*

" *There are doubtless fierce struggles still to come and heavy strains on our endurance to be borne. But be the road before us long or short, the spirit and pluck which have brought you so far will never fail, and, under God's guidance, the final and complete victory of our just cause is assured.*

(Sd.) " GEORGE, R.I."

On July 14th intimation was received that *part* of the 6th Division would very shortly be relieved by a portion of the 1st Canadian Division, but as this notice contained the further announcement that this relief would not affect the area for which the 71st Infantry Brigade was responsible, no particular excitement was aroused among the battalions thereof; but on the 25th a complete relief by the Canadians actually took place, with a view to an attack by the latter on Hill 70, and the 6th Division withdrew into the Monchy—Breton area, the headquarters of the Division being at Ourton, and the Battalion proceeding by motor lorries to Magnicourt-en-Compte.

" Thus was the 6th Division relieved after a continuous tour on the Loos front of just under five months—a period of particularly bitter and severe trench warfare. Trench mortaring was continuous on both sides on the greater part of the front held, and shelling heavy. The artillery suffered no less severely than the infantry, owing to the very restricted choice of positions and the advantages of the observation enjoyed by the enemy. Raids and counter-raids were numerous. An analysis of the diary shows that during the six months from the end of January to the beginning of July the Division carried out 30 raids, of which 13 were successful in obtaining their objectives and securing prisoners (total for the 13 raids, 50), 11 secured their objectives, but failed to yield any prisoners, and only 6 definitely failed. During the same period the enemy attempted 21 raids, of which only 4 succeeded in taking prisoners, 5 entered our trenches without securing any prisoners, and 12 were entire failures. Three of the enemy's attempted raids yielded no prisoners, and 4 yielded identifications. The low average of prisoners taken by us in successful raids is attributable to two causes—first, the extraordinary precautions taken by the enemy in the latter part of the period to avoid losing prisoners by evacuating his trenches on the slightest alarm or remaining in his dug-outs, and, secondly, the fierceness engendered in our troops by the severity of the bombardment, and particularly the trench mortaring to which they were normally subjected.''*

During the six months from January to June of this year the Battalion had taken part in no great battle, but the casualties incurred during that period had been by no means negligible, amounting as they did to 36 killed, 198 wounded and 4 missing.

The battalions composing the Division had been but a very few days in the rest area when two of its battalions—the 1st Leicestershire and the 9th Norfolk— were temporarily lent to the 57th Division of the XI. Corps, to assist in a relief at the time of the gas shelling of Armentières; the transport of the Battalion left Magnicourt by road at midnight on July 30th, and at seven the next morning 29 officers and 717 other ranks were "embussed," reached Bac St. Maur at midday and marched thence to billets in Fleurbaix, one platoon per company moving into the reserve line behind La Boutillerie. The Battalion was away a very few days only, being back again at Magnicourt by the afternoon of August 5th.

The Division remained during the greater part of August in the Monchy— Breton area, its units going through a tolerably strenuous training, pursuing a course of rifle practice, and taking part in athletic competitions of all kinds; the weather was not especially kind, for a good deal of rain fell, but the change and rest were much needed, and all ranks were very much the better when the month came to an end and the 6th Division, in its turn, relieved the Canadians.

During August the commands both of the 6th Division and of the 71st Infantry Brigade changed hands, Major-General C. Ross being relieved by Major-General T. O. Marden, C.M.G., on the 19th, while, on the 20th, Brigadier-General P. W. Brown, D.S.O., took the place in the 71st Brigade of Brigadier-General Feetham, promoted to the command of the 39th Division, at the head of which he was killed in March, 1918. Early in July, Captain A. Weyman, M.C., of The Leicestershire Regiment, was appointed Brigade Major of the 71st Infantry Brigade.

On August 24th the Division commenced relieving the 3rd Canadian Division on the Hill 70 front, the 16th and 18th Brigades moving first and taking over a new line between Loos and St. Elie; two days later the 71st Brigade followed, the Battalion marching on the 26th from Magnicourt by way of Frevillers—Hermin—Mesnil-les-Ruitz and Barlin to a camp in Houchin, the 71st Brigade being at the outset in divisional reserve; " the month spent

* "Short History of the 6th Division," pp. 31-32.

in this sector," so we read in the Divisional History, " was one of hard work for all ranks, consolidating the newly won position, but was without important incident." Then, on September 24th, the Division moved into the Cité St. Emilie sector, just north of Lens, and commenced preparations for an attack north of that town, to be carried out in conjunction with a projected attack by the Canadian Corps on Sallaumines Hill; but this project was later abandoned.

At the end of September the Battalion was in South Maroc, and early in October at Nœux les Mines, where, on the 7th, it provided a Guard of Honour for the French Cabinet Minister, Monsieur Loucheur, who distributed decorations to certain French civilians; the Guard was composed of Lieutenant J. C. Wratislaw, Second-Lieutenant C. F. Atter and 50 non-commissioned officers and men.

There was now a period of many moves before the Battalion; on October 18th a warning order was received from headquarters, 71st Brigade, advising the prospective relief of the 6th by the 11th Division, the Brigade relief to take place on the nights of the 20th-21st and 21st-22nd and the battalions to withdraw to General Headquarters Reserve in the St. Hilaire area. In consequence of the above the Battalion was on the 20th relieved by the 5th Dorsetshire Regiment, and marched by Mazingarbe to Houchin; here the Battalion entrained for Nœux les Mines, and reached Lillers on the afternoon of the 22nd and Ligny-les-Aires the same evening, the entraining strength being 29 officers and 620 other ranks. On the 29th, Ligny-les-Aires was again left, and the Battalion—now at a strength of 32 officers and 847 non-commissioned officers and men—marched via Monchy-Breton to Manin, in the Liencourt area, here joining the III. Corps of the Third Army for the Battle of Cambrai.

The following officers were serving with the 1st Battalion The Leicestershire Regiment on November 1st, 1917: Lieutenant-Colonel H. B. Brown, D.S.O.; Major J. W. E. Mosse, M.C.; Captain H. W. J. Brooker, Signalling Officer; Lieutenant R. N. Davis, Acting Adjutant; Lieutenant G. W. Tanner M.C., Lewis Gun Officer; Second-Lieutenant P. A. Crouch, Bombing Officer; Second-Lieutenant D. F. M. Hackett, Transport Officer; Hon. Major and Quarter-master J. H. Greasley, M.C.; Lieutenant F. Taylor, United States Medical Service, Medical Officer; and Lieutenant-Colonel C. H. Jones, C.M.G., attached.

" A " Company: Captain S. T. Hartshorne, Lieutenant J. O. Vessey, Second-Lieutenants C. E. Lancaster, G. C. Colborne-Smith, A. B. Entwistle and E. H. Butler.

" B " Company: Captain J. H. John, Second-Lieutenants P. A. B. Wrixon, J. Wacks, A. N. Bagshaw and J. H. Connell.

" C " Company: Lieutenants W. Wilson and R. J. Huntley, Second-Lieutenants C. H. Watson, C. F. Atter and D. H. Sims.

" D " Company: Captain J. Harbottle, Lieutenant J. C. Wratislaw, Second-Lieutenants F. N. Spencer, G. Delmer, M.C., D. Etherington, T. J. Atkinson and H. V. Lancaster.

On November 6th the Third Battle of Ypres, which had been in progress during the preceding three months, came to an end with the taking of Passchendaele, and though many of the German divisions had suffered very heavy losses in this fighting, the winter was now fast approaching during which any large-scale operations must be suspended, thus giving the enemy time to recuperate and reinforce; while to meet any offensive to be undertaken by the Allies in the spring, Germany might reasonably hope to bring, in reinforcement of her armies on the main or Western Front, many divisions which it was now possible to withdraw from her eastern frontier, consequent on the defection of Russia.

Italy at this time was in somewhat desperate case on the Piave, and was sending repeated demands for a diversion by her Allies, and the British Commander-in-Chief now determined to undertake something of the nature of a surprise attack under entirely novel conditions, carried out upon the Cambrai front.

The reasons for his selection of this point of attack are given in the Field-Marshal's despatch of February 20th, 1918, and are as follows :—

" Our repeated attacks in Flanders, and those of our Allies elsewhere, had brought about large concentrations of the enemy's forces on the threatened fronts, with a consequent reduction in the garrisons of certain other sectors of his line. Of those weakened sectors the Cambrai front had been selected as most suitable for the surprise operation in contemplation. The ground there was, on the whole, favourable for the employment of tanks, which were to play an important part in the enterprise, and facilities existed for the concealment of the necessary preparations for the attack.

" If, after breaking through the German defence systems on this front, we could secure Bourlon to the north and establish a good flank position to the east in the direction of Cambrai, we should be well placed to exploit the situation locally between Bourlon and the Sensée River and to the north-west. The capture of Cambrai itself was subsidiary to this operation, the object of our advance towards that town being primarily to cover our flank and puzzle the enemy regarding our intentions. The enemy was laying out fresh lines of defence behind those which he had already completed on the Cambrai front; and it was to be expected that his troops would be redistributed as soon as our pressure in Flanders was relaxed."

The ground hereabouts was especially well suited to a surprise offensive, including the use of tanks on a really large scale; it was mainly a country of rolling downs, with here and there large woods, in or in rear of which the concentration of these engines of war could be concealed, while the surface was everywhere dry and favourable to their unhindered advance.

The German defences on this front had been considerably improved and enlarged since the opening of the Allied offensive in April, and comprised three main systems of resistance. " The first of these three trench systems, constituting part of the Hindenburg Line proper, ran in a general north-westerly direction for a distance of six miles from the Scheldt Canal at Banteux to Havrincourt. There it turned abruptly north along the line to the Canal du Nord for a distance of four miles to Mœuvres, thus forming a pronounced salient in the German front. In advance of the Hindenburg Line the enemy had constructed a series of strong forward positions, including La Vacquerie and the north-east corner of Havrincourt Wood. Behind it, and at a distance respectively varying from a little less to rather more than a mile and from three and a half to four and a half miles, lay the second and third main German systems, known as the Hindenburg Reserve Line, and the Beaurevoir, Masnières and Marquion Lines.''*

The conduct of the forthcoming operations was entrusted to General the Hon. Sir J. Byng, who had recently relieved General Allenby in command of the Third Army, which had not been seriously engaged since the Battle of Arras. The main front of attack extended for six miles, and was occupied, from left to right, by the 36th, 62nd, 51st, 6th, 20th and 12th Divisions, while on the left, in the Bullecourt area, the 3rd and 16th Divisions were to carry out a subsidiary attack. In immediate support, in the main area of attack, was the 29th Division, while the 1st, 2nd, 4th and 5th Cavalry Divisions were at hand, ready to exploit any success which might be gained.

At the commencement of the Battle of Cambrai the enemy, on this front, was in inferior strength, for he had no more than eleven divisions in line—belonging to the Second German Army, under General von der Marwitz—while actually in the threatened area he had but six, three in line and three in support, but a seventh was then on its way to join from the Russian front.

" The 6th Division was ordered to attack on the front Villers Plouich—Beaucamp, with the 71st Infantry Brigade on the left, next to the 51st Division, and the 16th Infantry Brigade on the right, next to the 20th Division. These two brigades were to advance about 3,000 yards to the first objective (Ribécourt and spur to the south-east of it) and another 1,000 yards to the second objective —the German support system. The 18th Brigade was ordered to advance through the 71st and secure the third objective about a mile further on (Premy Chapel Ridge) throwing back a defensive flank towards Flesquières for the further operations of the 51st Division on its left, and securing the flank of the 29th Division on its right. The latter division, passing through the right of the 6th Division and the left of the 20th Division, was charged with securing the crossings of the St. Quentin Canal at Marcoing and Masnières and seizing the high ground at Rumilly, thus facilitating exploitation to the south-east, preventing a concentration against the widely-stretched defensive flanks of the III. Corps, and threatening Cambrai.

" Opposite the 6th Division the Hindenburg Line commenced with an outpost line 750 yards distant on the left and 250 yards on the right. This was out of sight of our front trenches by reason of the curve of the ground. Half a mile behind this came the main system, consisting of two trenches 200 yards apart, the whole guarded by most formidable belts of wire about 150 yards in depth. The interval between outpost and main systems was sown with well-sited and concealed machine-gun positions. A mile further on, and on the opposite side of the valley for the most part, ran the support system, similar to the main system. One and a half miles further back again was the reserve system, of which only machine gun dug-outs were completed, and a small amount of wire had been erected.

* Despatch of February 20th, 1918.

" Two battalions of tanks, each of 36 tanks, were allotted to the Division. ' B ' Battalion operated with the 16th Infantry Brigade, and ' H ' Battalion with the 71st Infantry Brigade. The 18th Brigade advanced without tanks. The only points which caused anxiety, provided that the tanks functioned properly, were Couillet Wood on the right of the 16th Brigade front, in which tanks could not operate, and Ribécourt Village on the left of the 71st Infantry Brigade front."[*]

The first two weeks of November were passed in the neighbourhood of Manin, preparing and training for the battle now expected very shortly to commence; and the battalions of the 6th Division were sedulously exercised in the practice of combined attacks by infantry and tanks upon trenches, special trenches having been dug for the purpose and unusually thick belts of barbed wire having been put up; and on the 14th all officers and non-commissioned officers visited a plan of the battle-ground worked out on a piece of country near Bullecourt. On this day, too, orders were issued for the move of the Battalion on the 15th to Moislans, by way of Frevent and Peronne.

Leaving Manin on that day at 9.30 in the morning, the Battalion—strength 25 officers and 639 non-commissioned officers and men—marched to Frevent and proceeded from there to Peronne, whence the Battalion moved by road to Moislans, arriving here at 1 a.m. on the 16th and moving on late the same afternoon, by a road greatly congested with traffic of all descriptions, to Dessart Wood, east of Fins; here the following orders for the attack by the 6th Division were issued :—

" The 6th Division is to carry out an attack on a date and at a time to be notified later. The 20th Division will be on its right and the 51st Division on its left. The 29th Division will be in Corps Reserve. Secrecy is an absolute essential to success and every possible precaution regarding it must be taken.

" The 6th Division is attacking with the 16th Infantry Brigade on the right and the 71st Infantry Brigade on the left. The 11th Bn. Essex Regiment will be attached to this Brigade for this operation. These two infantry brigades will capture the 1st and 2nd Objectives, shown in blue and brown on the maps issued on 14th November to officers commanding units. The 3rd Objective (Red Line) will be taken by the 18th Infantry Brigade. . . . .

" The 71st Infantry Brigade will attack in three waves :—

" (a) First Wave, consisting of 1st Bn. Leicestershire Regiment and 9th Bn. Suffolk Regiment, will attack and capture the Hindenburg Front Line System, each battalion dropping special parties to mop up Plush Trench.

" (b) The Second Wave, consisting of 9th Bn. Norfolk Regiment and Half 2nd Sherwood Foresters, will attack and capture the Blue Line.

" (c) The Third Wave, consisting of 11th Bn. Essex Regiment and 2nd Bn. Sherwood Foresters, will attack and capture the Brown Line.

" The O.C. 1st Leicestershire Regiment will detail special parties to work down that portion of Unseen Trench and Unseen Support West of the Sector to be attacked by his left section of Tanks in order to join hands with the 152nd Infantry Brigade. . . . .

* " Short History of the 6th Division," pp. 37-38.

E

" On reaching their Objectives, Battalion Commanders will at once throw out Battle Outposts. . . .

" The 1st Battalion Leicestershire Regiment and the 9th Bn. Suffolk Regiment will be formed in rear of the first wave of Tanks. . . ."

The greater part of the 19th was spent in drawing and issuing all the extra battle stores required for the forthcoming action, and then at 6.30 p.m. the Battalion moved forward from Dessart Wood to the position of assembly east of Beaucamp, the marching-out strength being 20 officers and 555 other ranks; the following are the names of the officers: Lieutenant-Colonel H. B. Brown, D.S.O.; Captain H. W. J. Brooker, Signalling Officer; Lieutenant R. N. Davis, Acting Adjutant; Lieutenant R. J. Huntley, Lewis Gun Officer; Lieutenant F. Taylor, Medical Officer.

" A " Company: Captain S. T. Hartshorne, Second-Lieutenants F. H. Jeeps, C. E. Lancaster and A. B. Entwistle.

" B " Company: Lieutenant P. A. B. Wrixon, Second-Lieutenants A. K. Purdy, A. N. Bagshaw and J. H. Connell.

" C " Company: Captain F. E. Shelton, Second-Lieutenants C. F. Atter, D. H. Sims and M. Mills.

" D " Company: Lieutenant J. C. Wratislaw, Second-Lieutenants D. Etherington and H. V. Lancaster.

By midnight the Battalion was in position between Argyll Road and Lancaster Road on a frontage of some 600 yards, the companies being disposed in the following manner :—

" B " Company: No. 7 Platoon, right front; No. 8 Platoon, left front; each behind a section of three tanks, with orders to occupy the enemy front line at Plush Trench, and, after the other companies should have pushed on, to occupy the German second line—Unseen Trench—and support " C " Company.

" D " Company, right front company; " A " Company, left front company; their objectives being the capture and occupation of the enemy third line— Unseen Support Trench.

" B " Company (remaining two platoons) in reserve, its objective being to reinforce the two front companies and help them to retain their positions, with especial reference to the protection of their flanks. " C " Company in support.

Battalion Headquarters was in Beaucamp Support Trench.

The following account of what happened is extracted from the Battalion War Diary :—

" 20th November, 6.20 a.m.   Tanks commenced to move forward.

" Barrage opened. Infantry and tanks by this time well under weigh. Enemy barrage very slow in opening and very weak indeed—no regular barrage line established, simply promiscuous shelling.   The attack was very successful.   The tanks breached very strong belts of wire with ease, and the following infantry had no difficulty in passing through the gaps made. The enemy appeared to be taken completely by surprise and put up practically no opposition. All objectives were taken without difficulty, and at 9.30 a.m. Battalion Headquarters was established in Unseen Trench. Companies were in position as follows: *Unseen Support Trench:* ' D ' Company *plus* one platoon ' B ' Company, right; 'A' Company *plus* one platoon 'B' Company, left. *Unseen Trench:* 'B' Company *less* two platoons right; Battalion H.Q., centre; 'C' Company, left.

"The casualties sustained by the Battalion in penetrating the Hindenburg Line were: killed, Second-Lieutenant A. K. Purdy and four other ranks; wounded, Lieutenant J. C. Wratislaw, Second-Lieutenants H. V. Lancaster, D. Etherington and F. H. Jeeps and 44 non-commissioned officers and men.

"Attack continued throughout the morning, all Brigade objectives were captured after very slight opposition, and during the afternoon the cavalry were being pushed forward past the positions occupied by the Battalion. We captured 37 prisoners, 3 heavy machine guns, 3 light machine guns, one heavy trench mortar and two aerial dart machines. The prisoners captured belonged to the 387th Regiment and were not conspicuous by reason of the strength of their opposition or by their soldierly bearing.

"Remained in the captured trenches throughout the night."

Of the events of November 20th, Major-General Marden has written:—

"The Division had a most successful day, with very light casualties (about 650), capturing 28 officers and 1,227 other ranks, 23 guns, and between 40 and 50 machine guns and many trench mortars, and receiving the congratulations of the Corps Commander. Everything had gone like clockwork."

The Battalion remained in the captured position throughout the 21st and up to midday on the 22nd, when orders were received for a move, and by 3 p.m. that afternoon the three brigades of the 6th Division were thus disposed: the 16th in the front line about Noyelles and Marcoing: the 18th in support in the vicinity of Nine Wood, and the 71st in reserve 1,000 yards south-west and west of Marcoing, occupying the Hindenburg Support System from Couillet Wood to Premy Ridge in the following order from right to left—Suffolk, Leicestershire, Foresters and Norfolk Regiment.

From the 23rd to the 26th the situation on the immediate front of the 6th Division remained tolerably quiet, but on other parts of the front there was heavy and somewhat resultless fighting, mainly about Fontaine, Bourlon and Bourlon Wood; but on the 26th the 71st Brigade relieved the 16th, and by night the Battalion was disposed about Noyelles, three out of the four companies being in occupation of the high ground between the St. Quentin Canal and the Noyelles—Marcoing road.

"The 6th Division now held a rectangular strip 2,500 yards by 7,000 yards, with the head at Cantaing and Noyelles, and the rear in the Hindenburg main line. . . . . Comparing the position with the back of a man's left hand, the 6th Division occupied the third finger, the 29th Division the main finger, the 20th Division the index finger, the 12th Division the portion below the index finger down to the lower portion of the thumb when fully extended, the 55th Division occupied the thumb. Such was the situation when the enemy delivered a heavy counter-attack, on the morning of the 30th November, on the 29th, 20th and 12th Divisions of the III. Corps and the 55th Division of the VII. Corps, driving the 20th and 12th Divisions on to the main finger, except for a few posts, and occupying the thumb."*

E 2   * "Short History of the 6th Division," p. 40.

It had been noticed on the Battalion front during the 29th that the enemy aircraft seemed especially active, while the German artillery fire appeared to be increasingly heavy, but the night of the 29th-30th passed quietly, and patrols sent out returned reporting nothing of a disturbing or unusual character.

At eight on the morning of the 30th, however, the Germans opened a very heavy bombardment, distributed over a wide area, chiefly to the south and apparently preliminary to an attack. All communication to front and rear, except by runners, was soon cut off, and " B " Company was now the only one from which information of any kind was obtainable. At 9.30 the 9th Suffolks on the left reported that a smoke barrage was to be seen north-west of Noyelles; and a couple of hours later it was stated that the enemy had broken through between the 20th and 29th Divisions, and that German infantry had been seen advancing between Masnières and Marcoing, the latter town being heavily shelled.

At 12.30 p.m. a message was received—" Enemy reported massing between Fontaines and Cantaing "—thus threatening the left flank, and all necessary arrangements were now made and orders issued in the event of it becoming necessary for the 71st Brigade to fall back.

At this time the situation seemed somewhat critical; patrols sent into Marcoing established the fact that the enemy had gained possession of that place during the morning, but that it was now again in British hands; but late in the evening the enemy attacked the right and right rear of the 6th Division position very strongly, broke through the original British front and captured Gonnelieu and Gouzeaucourt, Divisional Headquarters and the transport only just succeeding in getting clear in time.

During the course of the night Battalion Headquarters joined that of the 9th Suffolk Regiment in a quarry in Nine Wood, so as to be available to co-operate with that regiment, with which the 1st Leicestershire shared the responsibility for holding the Brigade front should the enemy attack. Late in the night headquarters was visited by the Brigade Major, 71st Brigade, who confirmed the report that the Germans had made a heavy and successful attack that day upon the right, penetrating as far as Gouzeaucourt and making large captures of men, guns and material. A simultaneous effort against the left in the Bourlon Wood direction had been held up before any really material progress had been made, and hope was afforded that the Battalion might be relieved on the night of December 1st should nothing unforeseen occur.

During the 1st the enemy bombardment was heavy, especially on the left about Cantaing, and he attempted an attack, but this, being made in insufficient force, was easily driven back, and that night the Battalion was relieved and withdrawn to Flesquières Ridge in Brigade Reserve.

So far as the 71st Brigade was concerned the Battle of Cambrai had now come to an end, the battalions composing it not being again engaged; but the next few days were ones of no little anxiety, as may be seen from the following extracts from the Battalion War Diary :—

" 2nd December, 12.30 a.m. Quiet night. General situation still obscure and unsatisfactory. No definite knowledge obtainable as to position or intentions of enemy. . . . . Position on flanks very uncertain. Right flanks of 'C,' 'B' and 'D' Companies thrown back to protect Battalion from attack expected from direction of Marcoing.

"3rd December. Uneventful day on immediate front. 3.55 p.m. Brigade order received advising dispositions to be taken up by units of Brigade in the event of the enemy capturing Marcoing.

"4th December. Uneventful day on immediate front, though enemy attacks on either flank beginning to render position, especially of units holding the front line of the Brigade sector, very precarious. Brigade order received advising that withdrawal of the Brigade to new position in Hindenburg Support Line was to be effected during the night."

This withdrawal was duly carried out on the 5th, as arranged, but the situation continued to be anything but clear, and on December 6th the Diary records :—

"Enemy attack on Flesquières on our left in the afternoon, but was driven back, the attacking troops suffering heavily under our artillery and machine-gun fire. Trenches occupied by the Battalion in very incomplete condition, practically no cover at all for the men and trenches very shallow, unprotected by wire. Enemy attack expected at any time, so all energy concentrated on wiring and deepening trenches. Men beginning to show signs of wear and tear owing to prolonged tour in trenches, and *morale* not improved by constant changes of position, mostly towards the rear.

"7th December. Uneventful day, cold and frosty. Enemy aircraft very active, ours conspicuously absent. Enemy apparently digging in along the Marcoing—Premy Chapel road and uncertain as to our position and intentions. Work being done on line as far as condition of men would permit.

"8th December. Two prisoners who had lost their way captured by 'A' Company in the early hours of morning, belonged to the 227th Regiment. Quiet day. . . . . Working parties again at full pressure wiring and consolidating. Weather turned wet, making trenches and general conditions very. bad.

"9th December. A prisoner, 232nd Regiment, captured by 'A' Company in early morning, blundered into our trenches, having lost his way. . . . . Patrolling continually indulged in, but no trace of the enemy discovered. Wiring and trench digging carried on during night.

"10th December. A prisoner, 30th Regiment, a corporal who had lost his way, captured by 'A' Company in early morning. Very clear day and much *enemy* aeroplane activity. One machine brought down by Lewis-gun fire from our trenches.

"11th December. Quiet day. Little activity on either side except for occasional bursts of artillery fire by us on likely enemy assembly points."

On the 12th the Battalion was relieved by the 6th Wiltshire Regiment, having been practically continuously in contact with the enemy for some three weeks, and withdrew to a camp at Étricourt, the relief being complicated by the ignorance by the Battalion of the areas in rear, and the relieving battalion's ignorance of those in front; the 1st Leicestershire came out of the trenches at a strength of 18 officers and 482 non-commissioned officers and men, the casualties since November 20th inclusive totalling, all ranks, 15 killed, 94 wounded and 3 missing.

From Etricourt and neighbourhood the Division was now ordered to the Basseux area, south-west of Arras, and, leaving camp on the morning of the 14th, embussed at Manancourt and proceeded to Bellacourt, where Christmas and the remainder of the year were passed.

In the following letter, published on December 15th of this year, the Corps Commander expressed his appreciation of the services of the 6th Division while under his command during the Battle of Cambrai :—

"*The Corps Commander wishes to thank all ranks of the 6th Division for the endurance shown under difficult circumstances, and to congratulate the Division on its fighting qualities. The dash displayed by the troops on the 20th November, and the subsequent stubborn resistance to attack were of a high order, and equalled the reputation which the Division acquired in the first year of the war. The Corps Commander is especially gratified to testify this to a Division that he has been connected with for so many years.*"*

The success of the initial operations of the battle had drawn from His Majesty the King the following telegram, dated November 27th, addressed to the General Commanding the Third Army :—

"*I congratulate you, General Byng and the troops concerned, on the successful operations in the neighbourhood of Cambrai. The complete surprise effected under such novel conditions of warfare has been received with the utmost satisfaction throughout the Empire, while holding out great hopes for the future. It is especially gratifying that the tanks, a purely British invention, should have played so important a part in your victory.*"

In his despatch of February 20th, 1918, Field-Marshal Sir Douglas Haig thus summed up the general results of the Battle of Cambrai :—

"We had captured and retained in our possession over 12,000 yards of former German front line from La Vacquerie to a point opposite Boursies, together with between 10,000 and 11,000 yards of the Hindenburg Line and Hindenburg Reserve Line and the villages of Ribécourt, Flesquières and Havrincourt. A total of 145 German guns were taken or destroyed by us in the course of the operations, and 11,000 German prisoners were captured. On the other hand the enemy had occupied an unimportant section of our front line between Vendhuille and Gonnelieu.

"There is little doubt that our operations were of considerable indirect assistance to the Allied Forces in Italy. Large demands were made upon the available German reserves at a time when a great concentration of German divisions was still being maintained in Flanders. There is evidence that the German divisions intended for the Italian theatre were diverted to the Cambrai front, and it is probable that the further concentration of German forces against Italy was suspended for at least three weeks at a most critical period, when our Allies were making their first stand on the Piave line."

---

* The III. Corps Commander was General Sir J. L. Keir.

BATTLE OF CAMBRAI,
20TH NOVEMBER, 1917.

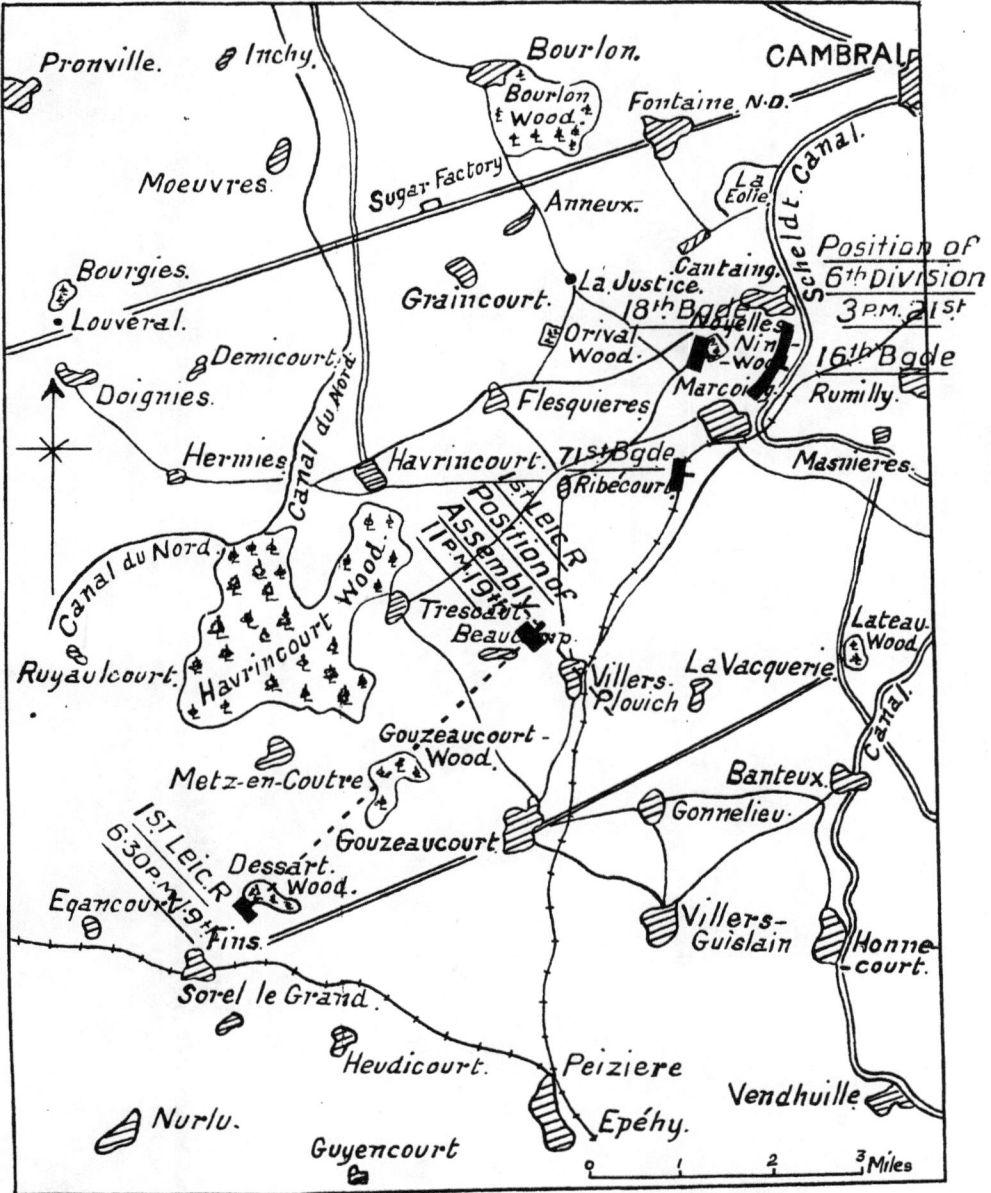

Pronville.

Inchy.

Bourlon.

CAMBRAI.

Bourlon Wood.

Fontaine N.D.

Moeuvres.

Sugar Factory

Anneux.

La Eolie

Position of 6th DIVISION 3 P.M. 21st

Bourgies.

Graincourt

La Justice.

Cantaing.

16th Bgde

Louveral.

Demicourt

Orival Wood.

18th Bgde

Noyelles

Nine Wood

Marcoing

Rumilly.

Doignies.

Flesquieres.

Canal du Nord

Masnieres.

Hermies.

Havrincourt.

71st Bgde

Ribecourt.

9th Leic.R.

Canal du Nord.

Position of Assembly 11 P.M. 19th

Havrincourt Wood.

Tresault

Beauc

Lateau Wood.

Ruyaulcourt.

Villers Plouich

La Vacquerie.

Canal.

Metz-en-Coutre.

Gouzeaucourt-Wood.

Banteux.

Gonneliev.

Dessárt Wood.

1ST Leic.R 6.30.P.M. 19th

Gouzeaucourt.

Villers-Guislain

Egancourt.

Fins.

Honne-court.

Sorel le Grand.

Heudicourt.

Peiziere

Vendhuille.

Nurlu.

Guyencourt

Epéhy.

0   1   2   3 Miles

CHAPTER V.

1918.

JANUARY TO MARCH.

THE GERMAN OFFENSIVE—THE BATTLE OF THE SOMME.

THE opening weeks of the year 1918 were passed by the units composing the 6th Division under almost peaceful conditions, giving no indication whatever of the tremendous events which were shortly to follow.

In the early part of January the Battalion was at Courcelles, but on the 17th the 6th Division moved forward and commenced to relieve the 51st Division in the front line between Hermies and Boursies, the Battalion moving on the 18th through Fremicourt and Beugny—undergoing some enemy shelling of the road by which it marched, but happily incurring no casualties—and relieving the 1/4th Gordon Highlanders in the trenches on the Mœuvres front, an unusually quiet sector, where the opposing lines were nearly everywhere some 800 yards apart and the enemy not particularly enterprising. There was a good deal of work to be done here, but much of it could be carried on during the day-time, uninterfered with by the enemy. When out of the line the Battalion was usually in Luck and Lindop Camps, in the vicinity of Fremicourt, but though the enemy aircraft was now developing an increased activity and frequently bombed the back areas, the Battalion appears to have suffered no casualties.

On February 19th and 20th the 6th Division moved slightly to the north and relieved the 25th Division in the Lagnicourt area, where, when out of the line, large parties were furnished daily for work on the defences.

On March 1st the following were the officers serving with the Battalion: Lieutenant-Colonel F. Latham, D.S.O., in command (this officer having joined and taken over on February 25th); Major D. L. Weir, D.S.O., M.C.; Captains R. N. Davis, Acting Adjutant, and H. W. J. Brooker, Signalling Officer; Lieutenant R. J. Huntley, Lewis Gun Officer; Second-Lieutenants M. Mills, Battalion Bombing Officer, and D. F. M. Hackett, Transport Officer; Captain F. Taylor, United States Medical Service, Medical Officer; Quartermaster and Hon. Major J. H. Greasley, M.C.; and Second-Lieutenant C. E. Lancaster, Assistant Adjutant.

"A" Company: Captain S. T. Hartshorne, Second-Lieutenants E. H. Butler, R. J. Croker and N. G. Fidoe.

"B" Company: Captain J. H. John, Lieutenant S. C. Lawrence, Second-Lieutenants A. N. Bagshaw, A. E. W. Paterson, A. H. Muggeridge and J. Houston.

" C " Company: Lieutenants C. H. Watson and C. F. Atter, Second-Lieutenants T. C. A. Clarke, D. H. Sims and G. A. Roberts.

" D " Company: Captain J. Harbottle, Second-Lieutenants F. N. Spencer, G. Mansfield and L. Faulks.

For some time past the military authorities had been greatly exercised in their minds in regard to the strain caused to the man-power of the nation by the increasing demand for more and yet more men to fill up the ranks; and during the early part of this year it had been considered necessary to reorganize the infantry divisions of the British Army in France, and this reorganization was completed during February, when the number of battalions in a division was reduced from thirteen to ten, and the battalions of a brigade from four to three. " Apart from the reduction in fighting strength involved by this reorganization, the fighting efficiency of units was to some extent affected. An unfamiliar grouping of units was introduced thereby, necessitating new methods of tactical handling of the troops and the discarding of old methods to which subordinate commanders had been accustomed."*

The effect of this, as regards the 6th Division, was that three Service battalions were withdrawn from their respective Brigades—the 9th Suffolks from the 71st Infantry Brigade, and the 8th Bedfords and 14th Durham Light Infantry from the 16th and 18th Brigades.

Moreover, during the past winter, in consequence of some pressure exerted upon the British Government by the French authorities, the front held by the armies under command of Sir Douglas Haig had been appreciably extended, their right reaching by the end of January, 1918, when the movement was completed, nearly as far as the village of Barisis, immediately south of the River Oise. The additional front thus taken over amounted to 28 miles, so that the British were now holding an active front of 125 miles in length with weakened forces and reorganized units.

During the past month the Allies had gained certain not unimportant successes over the enemy in other theatres of the World War, but these could not seriously affect the outcome of affairs in western Europe, where the balance of armed strength was rather against than in favour of the Allies. Russia could now no longer be taken into account, Roumania had been overwhelmed by her hostile neighbours and forced to make terms, and thus the whole strength of Germany and Austria was now ranged against Great Britain and France alone, for American troops were only just beginning to arrive in the European theatre of war in any appreciable strength. In the course of the preceding winter, German divisions, no longer required on the Eastern frontier, had been rapidly transferred by train from Russia to France and Flanders; and, in some measure to meet this menace, certain British and French divisions, which had been sent to Italy after the disaster of Caporetto, had been hurriedly recalled to the front where the real issue was to be fought out.

As early as the beginning of February there were persistent rumours that the Germans were massing troops and elaborating measures for an attack on an unusually large scale; on February 6th the Battalion War Diary records:

* Despatch of the 20th July, 1918.

" Strong rumours of expected enemy attack in the near future," and again, on the 12th, " Preparations completed in view of enemy attack at dawn "—while on at least two occasions the Division " stood to " in expectation of a German offensive.

" Some description of the ground and defensive organization of the Division will not be out of place here.

" The front held by the Division was generally on a forward slope opposite the villages of Quéant and Pronville. No Man's Land averaged three quarters of a mile in width. The whole area was downland and very suitable for the action of tanks. The position lay astride a succession of well-defined, broad spurs and narrow valleys (like the fingers of a partially opened hand), merging into the broad transverse valley which separated the British line from the two villages above mentioned. All the advantages of ground lay with the defence, and it seemed as if no attack could succeed, unless by the aid of tanks. A large portion of the front line, notably the valleys, was sown with 2-inch trench-mortar bombs with instantaneous fuses, which would detonate under the pressure of a wagon but not of a man's foot. In addition, five anti-tank 18-pounder guns were placed in positions of vantage. The wire was very broad and thick. The position would, indeed, have been almost impregnable had there been sufficient time to complete it, and had there been separate troops for counter-attack.

" The ground was a portion of that wrested from the enemy in the Cambrai offensive of November-December, 1917, but had only improvised trenches. A month's hard frost in January had militated against digging, and though there were a complete front trench and reserve trench, the support trenches hardly existed, and dug-outs were noticeable by their absence. The front was 4,500 yards in extent, the three brigades in line—18th on right, 71st in centre, 16th on left—approximately on equal frontages. The depth from front or outpost zone to reserve or battle zone was about 2,500 yards. With only three battalions in a brigade, there was no option but to assign one battalion in each brigade to the defence of the outpost zones, and keep two battalions in depth in the battle zone. With battalions at just over half-strength, and with the undulating nature of the ground, the defence resolved itself everywhere into a succession of posts with a very limited field of fire.

" A good Corps line, called the Vaux-Morchies Line, had been dug, the nearest portion a mile behind the reserve line, and this was held by the Pioneers and Royal Engineers, owing to scarcity of numbers."*

The following was at this time the composition and distribution of the Third and Fifth Armies, upon which the main enemy attack was about to fall : the Third Army was commanded by General Sir J. Byng, and contained four Army Corps, the XVII. in the Arras—Monchy sector, the VI. between that and Bulle-court, the IV. carrying on the line to opposite Cambrai, while the V. covered a gap in the Hindenburg Line through which an attack might possibly be pressed. In the IV. Corps, under General Harper, were the 6th and 51st Divisions on left and right respectively. The Fifth Army, under General

* " Short History of the 6th Division," pp. 44-45.

Gough, consisted of the VII. Corps in the southern portion of the Cambrai district, the XIX. from south of Ronssoy to Maissemy, the XVIII. in front of St. Quentin, and the III. covering the ground from Orvillers to Barisis.

In his despatch of October 21st, 1918, the Field-Marshal states that "the general principle of the defensive arrangements on the fronts of those armies, was the distribution of our troops in depth. With this object three defensive belts, sited at considerable distance from each other, had been constructed or were approaching completion in the forward area, the most advanced of which was in the nature of a lightly-held outpost screen covering our main positions. On the morning of the attack the troops detailed to man these various defences were all in position. . . . . In all at least 64 German divisions took part in the operations of the first day of the battle, a number considerably exceeding the total forces comprising the entire British Army in France. . . . To meet this assault the Third Army disposed of eight divisions in line on the front of the enemy's initial attack, with seven divisions available in reserve. The Fifth Army disposed of fourteen divisions and three cavalry divisions, of which three infantry divisions and three cavalry divisions were in reserve. The total British force on the original battle front, on the morning of March 21st, was twenty-nine infantry divisions and three cavalry divisions, of which nineteen infantry divisions were in line."

During the days and nights immediately preceding the German offensive, our troops were everywhere indefatigable in the endeavour to capture enemy prisoners in order to discover what were the intentions of the occupants of the opposing trenches; the Battalion patrols were very busy, while the inactivity of the enemy was no less remarkable. On the 15th the front line company of the Battalion managed to capture a propaganda balloon laden with ten copies of the *Gazette des Ardennes,* a paper published in French by the Germans for distribution among the inhabitants of the occupied territory.

On the following night "B" Company of the Battalion provided a raiding party of 36 men and 4 stretcher bearers, with Captain J. H. John, Lieutenant S. C. Lawrence and Second-Lieutenant A. N. Bagshaw, with two Lewis gun detachments, each of one non-commissioned officer and six men, the party being divided into four; the following is the report of what happened :—

"Raid left assembly point according to plan at 8.15 p.m. and proceeded in single file across No Man's Land, marching due north just on the far side of the middle belt of wire. Raid formed up according to orders in the following manner: No. 12184 Lance-Corporal T. W. Boote and two other ranks 20 yards in front as screen, rest of raid in three worms at 20 yards interval; on the left, party B; in the centre, O.C. assault, torpedo party, Second-Lieutenant A. N. Bagshaw with party A; on the right, parties C and D. At 8.45 p.m. raid moved forward in above order. Main party halted. O.C. assault and torpedo party crawled up to enemy's wire. Here it was found that there were two belts, 10 yards apart; in case the second should be thick it was decided to cut through the first—a single apron of concertina wire, and this was accordingly done very silently and quickly by No. 16378 Lance-Corporal J. B. Buckler and No. 17256 Private Frost of the torpedo party; the second belt was, however, found to be useless, as it was so badly cut about that we could walk through it easily. I decided that the torpedo was unnecessary, and started back to bring in A party when the barrage opened, a minute and a half before its time. I started doubling, shouting 'come on' as loud as possible, upon which Lieutenant Bagshaw, with No. 18174 Sergeant J. Bexon and the leading section of party A, dashed through the gap; here a slight confusion occurred, as the rear sections had not heard my shouts and were still waiting for the torpedo to go up. This was quickly corrected and parties carried on according to plan, O.C. assault with party B going along the enemy wire on the outside to the post named Magpie's Nest. Finding the wire weak, party B walked through it and joined party A in the Nest. Nothing could be seen of the enemy, nor any traces of identification, though a thorough search was made, in particular, a shallow dug-out with about 6 feet of cover, dug underneath Poultry, was reached by the two officers, but without result.

" As there was nothing further to be gained by remaining in the enemy's post, the order to withdraw was given by O.C. assault; this was done in an orderly manner, the rear party consisting of O.C. assault, No. 8474 Lance-Corporal W. Yardley and two other ranks, tape party, No. 16378 Lance-Corporal J. B. Buckler hauling in the tape.

" Raid re-entered trench at 10 p.m.

" One man slight concussion from one of our shells.

" The failure to secure prisoners was in my opinion due to the artillery, in that, first, the barrage started one and a half minutes before zero hour, and, secondly, it was short, not giving party A a chance to catch up with the retreating enemy without running into the barrage. Some shells were so short that they fell right amongst the raiding parties."

In the Divisional History it is stated that " on 20th March aeroplane photographs disclosed ammunition pits for seventy extra batteries opposite the divisional front. . . . . Warning had been given overnight for all troops to be in battle positions by 5 a.m., but it came too late to stop working parties, and the reserve battalions of all brigades had marched ten miles before the battle commenced."

This latter statement is borne out by the Battalion War Diary; on March 17th the 1st Leicestershire had gone back into Brigade Reserve, when the companies were thus distributed : Battalion Headquarters, " B " and " D " Companies at Camp No. 12, Favreuil, " C " Company in billets at Vaulx, and "A" Company in dug-outs in the Sunken Road; and when, at midnight on the 20th, after " a quiet day," a telephone message was received from the Brigade Major ordering the Battalion to " stand to " at 5.30 a.m. on the 21st in battle positions, three large working parties were away and could not be immediately recalled; thus, 6 officers and 216 other ranks were away on this duty from " B " and " D " Companies, one officer and 76 men from "A" Company, and the same number from " C " Company; so that when at 4.30 on the morning of the 21st the Battalion Headquarters moved forward to the assembly area, it was accompanied by no more than 5 officers and 110 non-commissioned officers and men, the detached parties not having by then returned from work. On arrival in the assembly position at 5.32, however, it was found that " C " Company had already come in during a heavy enemy bombardment which opened at five o'clock, and nobody appears to have had any doubt that this time the alarm was a genuine one.

Opinions seem to differ among commanders of larger units as to whether the fog, which this morning was very thick all along the front of the Third and Fifth Armies, did or did not assist the German attack. Major-General Marden, commanding the 6th Division, considers that it did, for he writes * that " Fog favoured the Germans in that it prevented our seeing when the attack was launched." On the other hand, General Sir H. Gough, commanding the Fifth Army states † that it did *not* assist the enemy, taking all factors into consideration; " at first," he has written, " say, for a couple of hours, fog was a great disadvantage to the defence. Had it not been present, many of our machine guns, very skilfully hidden, would have taken a terrible toll. . . . . But as soon as the foe had broken through the first line of resistance and was pushing on, he must have found that command, co-operation and communication became increasingly difficult. . . . . On the whole, then, it may be said that the fog favoured our Fifth Army."

The enemy appeared to be advancing by the Noreuil Valley on the left, the Lagnicourt Valley in the centre and the Morchies Valley on the right, thus avoiding the spurs, where a heavy fire would probably have met him, and assisting in the enveloping of the garrisons of these latter.

At 6.30 a.m. the large working party which had been furnished by " B " and " D " Companies reported in the assembly area. This party did not reach camp, on recall, until 5.15, and was much exhausted, having done a heavy night's work and having marched five miles each way, the return journey having naturally been something of the nature of a forced march.

Just before 8 a.m. information was received from the Brigade that enemy troops were concentrating in Cornhill Valley, and an hour and a half later Lieutenant-Colonel Latham visited Brigade headquarters and was ordered to move two companies to the left flank of the Brigade sector, where the line had been driven in. " C " and " D " Companies, commanded respectively by Lieutenant Watson and Captain Harbottle, accordingly moved off, " C " Company being placed at the disposal of the Officer Commanding 9th Norfolk Regiment, while " D " Company was detailed to hold certain trenches about Lagnicourt Switch. Of the situation on the IV. Corps front at this time it may be said that the northern stretch from Dernicourt to Lagnicourt, occupied by the 6th Division, was very much more heavily attacked than was the southern portion occupied by the 51st Division, and that the 71st Infantry Brigade in the Lagnicourt sector was particularly hard pressed, having been heavily attacked by the 195th German Infantry Division, including the 1st Prussian Guards, which, at one time, practically surrounded the 9th Battalion Norfolk Regiment.

At 2.10 p.m. Headquarters and " B " Company of the Battalion were ordered to move into the Vaulx—Morchies line, and took up a position between

---

* " Short History of the 6th Division," p. 46.
† Sparrow, " The Fifth Army in March, 1918," pp. 56-60.

the Lagnicourt—Maricourt Wood road and Vaulx Wood, moving under very heavy machine-gun fire about Vaulx Wood, but gained the trench without many casualties and ejected a small body of the enemy who had succeeded in forcing an entry into the Vaulx—Morchies line. The trench was held in greater strength on the left than on the right, but any attempt to equalize matters and distribute the defenders better was fraught with difficulty, owing to the trench here not being continuous, while the many gaps to be crossed were swept by machine-gun fire and marked down by German snipers; also, touch could not be obtained with the troops on the right of the Lagnicourt—Maricourt Wood road, since for some distance there was no trench line at all.

At 5.35 p.m. a company of a battalion (2nd South Lancashire) of the 25th Division, made its appearance and was added to the left of the Brigade line, " B " Company moving more to the right to make way for it; the remaining portion of the sector on the right, as far as Lagnicourt—Maricourt Wood road, being held by part of the 509th Field Company, R.E., and by " C " Company of the 11th Leicestershire Regiment (Pioneers) under Captain Spencer. Then, at 6.40, Battalion Headquarters was moved to a position between Vaulx and Beugnâtre. Up to this no news had reached Battalion Headquarters as to the whereabouts or doings of the remaining three companies, but about 8.30 in the evening a runner managed to get through from " A " Company, bringing the following information : " A " Company, less one platoon which had been practically wiped out during the morning, was in the battle position in the Vaulx—Morchies line, where was also " D " Company, while " C " Company shortly after was reported as being also there in position, to which line the 9th Norfolks and 2nd Sherwood Foresters had now withdrawn.

The distribution of the 71st Infantry Brigade, from right to left, was now as follows : 9th Battalion Norfolks, " A " and " C " Companies 1st Leicestershire, 2nd Sherwood Foresters, 459th Field Company, R.E.—*nine* men only—one machine gun, and " D " Company of the Battalion. The strength of the various units so gallantly " holding on " was approximately as under :—

" B " Company, 4 officers and 110 other ranks.
Battalion Headquarters, 4 officers and 40 other ranks.
" A " Company, 1 officer and 70 other ranks.
" B " Company, 4 officers and 110 other ranks.
" C " Company, 1 officer and 37 other ranks.
" D " Company, 3 officers and 112 other ranks.
9th Battalion Norfolks, about 120 all ranks.
2nd Foresters, about 120 all ranks.

The enemy was by this time in possession of the villages of Doignies, Boursies, Louverval and Lagnicourt, their total penetration, from Boursies in the south to Ecoust in the north, a frontage of seven miles, averaging about 300 yards.

During the course of the night, which passed fairly quietly, rations were brought up and issued, while Second-Lieutenant G. Mansfield, who had been on leave at home, rejoined " D " Company of the Battalion.

The morning of March 22nd opened with a thick fog, but as soon as it became light the enemy put down a very heavy barrage on the Vaulx—Morchies line and also on Vaulx itself, and at 8.30 the Battalion Headquarters was ordered to move to dug-outs said to be east of Maricourt Wood, and the Commanding Officer, Adjutant and a few men left, giving orders for the remainder to follow under Captain Brooker; but, no dug-outs being discoverable at the spot indicated, Battalion Headquarters was established at some cross-roads, where also was the headquarters of the 2nd South Lancashire Regiment; while the 9th Norfolks and 2nd Foresters had also withdrawn from the Vaulx—Morchies line on relief by some of the 2nd South Lancashire.

From this time onwards reports came in recording the increasing pressure of the enemy all along the line, describing the efforts which were being made to hold up the German advance, stating the losses everywhere met with and asking for reinforcements sufficient to enable "the perished linesmen" to maintain such positions as they had taken up.

Thus at 11 a.m. the 2nd South Lancashire reported that the enemy had broken through a weakly-held portion of the Vaulx—Morchies line, while a very few minutes later an officer of that corps stated that the breach had been made on a frontage held by two companies of his regiment, one of the 11th Battalion The Leicestershire Regiment and one of the 8th Battalion The Border Regiment, and a request was sent to the 9th Norfolks and 2nd Foresters to move up and cover the valley from about the Sunken Road. A defensive flank was also organized for the high ground east of Vaulx Wood by the South Lancashire, bombing parties were sent forward to recover the lost ground, and reinforcements were sought for to strengthen the left of the Brigade front. At 11.40 the Germans were noticed massing in front; the commander of "C" Company of the 11th Leicestershire reported that he had now only 37 men left and that the enemy was in Vaulx Wood; an officer and 40 men of another company of the same battalion, which had fallen back from the Vaulx—Morchies line, now arrived at Battalion Headquarters; and rather later—about 2 p.m.— "B" Company, 1st Battalion, appeared to be gaining or regaining ground by bombing up the line, helped by an officer and 60 other ranks of the 2nd South Lancashire Regiment.

The gun fire on both sides now increased in intensity, but soon after 3 p.m. German infantry could be discerned from Battalion Headquarters advancing rapidly between the Lagnicourt—Maricourt Wood road and Vaulx Wood, and it now seemed tolerably certain that the breach was effective and that the situation was becoming—if, indeed, it had not already become—very serious indeed. "B" and "C" Companies were practically destroyed in this advance, "A" Company alone succeeding in withdrawing through Morchies cemetery under a heavy 4·2 barrage.

Towards 4 p.m. a withdrawal commenced, infantry and machine gunners occupying and holding one position after another, finally taking up a line north of Beugny, where the remnants of three battalions of the 71st Brigade were now assembled about 8 p.m. and were disposed in sections of the trenches to the left rear of the 58th Brigade; these survivors of the great fight numbered, all told, approximately :—

9th Battalion Norfolk Regiment, under Lieutenant C. P. Bassingthwaite, about 80.

1st Battalion The Leicestershire Regiment, under Lieutenant-Colonel F. Latham, about 40.

2nd Sherwood Foresters, under Captain G. H. A. Giles, about 40.

This last position was held under heavy shell and machine-gun fire until 3 a.m. on the 23rd, when what was left of the 6th Division was relieved by troops of the 41st Division, the 71st Brigade by the 123rd. The relief was completed by four o'clock that morning, and all moved out of the line by way of the Bapaume—Cambrai road, the Battalion, on reaching Fremicourt, being in the first instance ordered to move to a camp near Achiet-le-Petit, but it eventually found itself, about 8 a.m., in Berkeley Camp, Bihucourt, where 4 officers and 46 other ranks were all that could at that time be collected together, the total casualties sustained during the preceding forty-eight hours having amounted to 20 officers and 459 other ranks killed, wounded and missing.

The following are the names of the officers who were in battle position with the Battalion on the morning of March 21st, 1918: Lieutenant-Colonel F. Latham, D.S.O., in command; Captain R. N. Davis, Adjutant; Captain H. W. J. Brooker, Signalling Officer; Captain F. Taylor, Medical Officer, *wounded;* and Lieutenant C. E. Lancaster, Assistant Adjutant, *killed.*

" A " Company: Captain S. T. Hartshorne, *wounded;* Second-Lieutenants N. G. Fidoe, *killed,* and W. Jones, *wounded.*

" B " Company: Captain J. H. John, *missing;* Lieutenant S. C. Lawrence, *missing;* Second-Lieutenants A. N. Bagshaw, *missing,* and O. T. Harper, *missing.*

" C " Company: Captain F. E. Shelton, *killed;* Lieutenants C. H. Watson, *wounded, and* C. F. Atter, *killed;* Second-Lieutenants A. G. Escudier, *wounded,* and G. A. Roberts, *killed.*

" D " Company: Captain J. Harbottle, *killed;* Second-Lieutenants M. Mills, *missing,* A. C. Ansell, *missing,* and G. Mansfield (rejoined from leave on the night of the 21st-22nd) *wounded and missing.*

Attached to the 71st Brigade Headquarters: Lieutenant J. O. Vessey, M.C., Assistant Signalling Officer, *missing;* Second-Lieutenant T. C. A. Clarke, Gas Officer, *missing.*

The following came out of the line with the Battalion on March 23rd: Lieutenant-Colonel F. Latham, D.S.O.; Captains R. N. Davis, H. W. J. Brooker and F. Taylor; Captain S. T. Hartshorne was the only company officer, and he rejoined, wounded, on the afternoon of March 23rd.

Of the other ranks, 30 were killed, 113 were wounded and 316 were missing.

The casualties incurred in the 6th Division during the forty-eight hours' fighting of March 21st-23rd, amounted to some 3,900 out of rather over 5,000 engaged, and out of a trench strength of under 5,000 infantry; while on the morning of the 23rd the 71st Infantry Brigade could muster no more than 11 officers and 279 non-commissioned officers and men out of a trench strength on the morning of March 21st of just over 1,800 all ranks !

The chief point noticeable during the foregoing operations was the inadequacy of the means of communication. During the whole of the 22nd, after the Battalion moved from Vaulx, only one message was received by the Battalion from the Brigade, and this, sent out at 9.45 a.m., was not received until 2.18, by which time the orders it contained had ceased to apply to the situation as then existing. No message was received from any other companies on the right of the Lagnicourt—Maricourt Wood road, all the orderlies having become casualties, while no reliable information was obtainable as to the situation on either flank, either from the flanks themselves or through from the rear.

The following is the report furnished by Captain S. T. Hartshorne, commanding "A" Company of the Battalion, on the events of March 21st-23rd :—

"21st March. 12.30 a.m. Message arrived from Battalion H.Q. warning the Company to stand-to in battle positions by 5.30 a.m. The Company was then in dug-outs as follows : Company H.Q. and Nos. 2 and 3 Platoons in the four Sunken Cross Roads, Nos. 1 and 4 in front of the village of Morchies.

"5.30 a.m. The Company stood-to—No. 3 Platoon in the Strong Point at the Report Centre; Company H.Q. and Nos. 1, 2 and 4 Platoons in the Vaulx—Morchies line near the Crucifix.

"2 p.m. The Strong Point at the Report Centre was captured by the enemy, Second-Lieutenant Fidoe, O.C. No. 3 Platoon, being killed and most of the Platoon becoming casualties. The rest of the Company had about 12 casualties.

"2.45 p.m. 'D' Company was observed retiring from the left front—Lagnicourt—down the Lagnicourt—Morchies road under Company Sergeant-Major Carter, all the officers being then casualties. This Company was commandeered by the O.C. 'A' Company and occupied part of the Vaulx—Morchies line astride the Report Centre—Crucifix Road. To occupy this part of the line the Company had to move in extended order over the open and it was necessary to drive out some of the enemy who were in possession of it—one prisoner was taken. Second-Lieutenant Frampton, 71st Brigade L.T.M. Battery, took over command of 'D' Company at this time.

"6.30 p.m. The remnants of the 2nd Sherwood Foresters and the 9th Norfolk Regiment arrived in the V—M line, having withdrawn from their original positions in the front line. Lieutenant-Colonel Prior* took charge of this portion of the line.

"7.30 p.m. 'C' Company 1st Leicestershire Regiment, by order of the O.C. 9th Norfolk Regiment, withdrew from the Sunken Road and took up a position in the V—M line.

"22nd March. About 3 a.m. O.C. 1st Leicestershire Regiment arrived and soon after the 2nd Foresters withdrew to a position in rear, leaving in the V—M line the following: 'A' Company—1 officer and 60 O.R., 'C' Company—1 officer and 37 O.R., and 'D' Company—3 officers and 100 O.R., and also a company of the 11th Leicestershire who were holding a few bays on each side of the Lagnicourt—Morchies road. Rations and water came up at night.

* Commanding 9th Battalion The Norfolk Regiment.

" 7.30 a.m. The enemy attacked in fairly large numbers at two points : in front of ' D ' Company astride the Report Centre—Crucifix Road and in front of 'A' Company. Both were beaten off by rifle and machine-gun and Lewis gun fire. The day was exceedingly foggy, our wire being only indistinctly seen. Although the attacks were beaten off, hostile snipers located themselves on the edge of our wire and were a source of great annoyance throughout the day, causing many casualties. They could not be dislodged, as no rifle bombs or Stokes' mortars were available. It was suspected that these men, under cover of the mist, attempted to cut our wire.

" 8.10 a.m. Two more attempts were made by the enemy to get through our wire—both were frustrated. During the morning we stood-to at intervals and opened a rapid fire at parties who approached our wire; when the mist cleared many enemy dead were seen lying out on the edge of the wire.

" 2.45 p.m. The enemy was seen advancing over the ridge on our left from the direction of the Report Centre—Maricourt Wood Road, and a message was at once sent to the O.C. 11th Essex telling him the following :—

" 1. That the enemy was on the ridge to the left.

" 2. That our artillery had been and was firing short.

" 3. Asking for instructions.

" This message was not delivered, but the orderly passed the information on to the batteries behind, who up till then did not know where the enemy was. The attack developed on the company of the 2nd South Lancs, on the left of ' D ' Company, who were forced out of their trench, leaving our left in the air. The enemy apparently occupied the V—M line for a considerable distance to the left. The enemy began bombing down the trench held by ' D ' Company, who were almost helpless as the supply of hand-grenades was very small.

" 3.15 p.m. A message was sent to the O.C. 9th Norfolks with the following information :—

" 1. That the enemy was in the V—M line in force.

" 2. Asking him to counter-attack.

" 3. Telling him that our intention was to help by hanging on as long as possible.

" The situation at this time was rather critical; the enemy was behind us, and was firing into our backs and was bombing down the trench, forcing our men before him.

" 3.30 p.m. About this time the enemy left the V—M line and began advancing on us from the rear. ' D ' Company took up a position along the sunken part of the road, Report Centre—Crucifix, firing to the rear, but the enemy was only held up temporarily, the trench at the road—an acute angle with the line ' D ' Company was holding—was forced, and ' D ' Company fell back again into the V—M line.

" 3.45 p.m. The enemy attacked the V—M line on our right, held by the 18th Brigade. This part was occupied by the enemy, and we were now subjected to very heavy machine-gun fire from the front, both flanks and left rear. Our men had gradually crowded down the trench towards the Crucifix end; several hasty blocks had been made in the trench, but these formed no real

F

obstacle to the enemy, as we had no bombs. It was impossible to send any men out of the trench to form any sort of a defensive flank, owing to the intensity of the machine-gun fire, and there were no trenches leading to the rear. At this time a strong attack developed from the front, but as soon as the men lined the parapet they were shot down by machine-gun bullets from the rear.

"4.10 p.m. The enemy by this time had advanced about 150 yards from the V—M line on our right towards the village of Morchies, our only line of retreat, and it was then decided to vacate the trench. The only way to do this was by filing out of the trench on the Lagnicourt—Morchies Road near the Crucifix, and this spot was covered by several enemy machine guns. In the rush that followed many men were mowed down by these and many more fell in Morchies cemetery. As the remnants withdrew over the ridge, behind Morchies, a 4·2 barrage fell on them, and crept along to the top of the ridge. The remnants got to the valley between Morchies and Beugny, and these were organized as far as possible in shell holes."

The crisis had been very serious and was as yet by no means over, for even on April 11th, Field-Marshal Sir Douglas Haig found it necessary to publish the following Order of the Day, addressed to "all ranks of the British Army in France and Flanders." :—

"*We are again at a crisis in the war. The enemy has collected on this front every available division, and is aiming at the destruction of the British Army. We have already inflicted on the enemy in the course of the last two days very heavy loss, and the French are sending troops as quickly as possible to our support. I feel that everyone in the Army, fully realizing how much depends on the exertions and steadfastness of each one of us, will do his utmost to prevent the enemy from attaining his object.*"

The Battalion was in camp near Bihucourt, where, on the evening of the 23rd, a warning order was promulgated stating that the Battalion would move next day by march route to Puisieux-au-Mont, and thence by rail via Doullens to Proven, the 6th Division being about to join General Plumer's Second Army in the north.

Leaving camp at 11.15 on the morning of the 24th, the Battalion—strength, including transport, 9 officers and 320 other ranks—reached Proven on the early morning of the 26th, was put up for the night in a camp near the Convent of St. Sixte, and then moved on next day to Winnezeele, where all settled down comfortably by midday. Here the 1st Leicestershire Regiment was quickly brought up to a strength of 24 officers and 688 non-commissioned officers and men by drafts, amongst others, of 99 men from the III. and V. Corps Cyclists and 40 transfers from other battalions.

The Brigadier communicated to the battalions concerned the following tribute, paid to the fighting power of the 71st Infantry Brigade, which he had received from the General Officer Commanding 6th Division :—

"*I have read with the greatest interest your report on the operations of the 71st Infantry Brigade on 21st and 22nd March.*

"*Please convey to the 1st Leicestershire Regiment, 2nd Sherwood*

Foresters and 9th Norfolk Regiment and 71st T.M. Battery, my admiration of the splendid fight they made against overwhelming forces of the enemy.

" While deeply deploring the losses, all ranks must feel that their sacrifices have not been in vain, as they stemmed the German advance for forty-eight hours. The courage and tenacity of the Leicesters, Sherwood Foresters and Norfolks have added undying fame to the records of the fine regiments of which they form a part."

The following is the text of the Brigadier's covering letter :—

" It gives me great pleasure to forward you the attached communication which I have received from the G.O.C. 6th Division.

" Will you please have the Major-General's letter, containing such high terms of praise, read to the men under your command on parade and also published in orders. I should also like you to tell them that, should the occasion again arise in the near future, I feel sure they will behave with the same gallantry and stoutness of heart as on the 21st and 22nd March, and that those who have lately joined the Brigade will worthily uphold the fine fighting traditions of their battalions."

Then when the 6th Division left the Third Army to join the Second, General Sir Julian Byng sent the following farewell letter to Major-General Marden :—

" I cannot allow the 6th Division to leave the Third Army without expressing my appreciation of their splendid conduct during the first stages of the great battle now in progress.

" By their devotion and courage they have broken up overwhelming attacks and prevented the enemy gaining his object, namely, a decisive victory.

" I wish them every possible good luck."

Finally, as proof of the intense anxiety and interest with which His Majesty the King and the British Cabinet were following the course of events on the Western Front, we may quote letters, dated March 23rd, addressed to the Commander-in-Chief of the British Army in France and Flanders.

From the Prime Minister :—

" The British Cabinet wishes to express to the Army the thanks of the Nation for its splendid defence. The whole Empire is thrilled with pride as it watches the heroic resistance offered by its brave troops to overwhelming odds. Knowing their steadfastness and courage whenever the honour of the Country depends on their valour, the Empire awaits with confidence the result of this struggle to defeat the enemy's last desperate efforts to trample down the free nations of the world. At home we are prepared to do all in our power to help in the true spirit of comradeship. The men necessary to replace all casualties, and the guns and machine guns required to make good those lost, are either now in France or already on their way, and still further reinforcements of men and guns are ready to be thrown into the battle."

F 2

From His Majesty the King :—

" I can assure you that the fortitude, courage and self-sacrifice with which the troops under your command are so heroically resisting greatly superior numbers is realized by Me and My people. The Empire stands calm and confident in its soldiers. May God bless and give them strength in their hour of trial."

The recent heavy fighting which had been and was still in progress did not prevent His Majesty the King from paying a long-contemplated visit to his troops during the last few days of March and the beginning of April. On March 29th he inspected representatives of the 6th Division in the square at Steenvoorde, and spoke to many of the surviving officers and men regarding the recent fighting. The 1st Battalion The Leicestershire Regiment was represented by Lieutenant-Colonel F. Latham, D.S.O., Captain S. T. Hartshorne, No. 5706 Company Sergeant-Major E. Battersby, No. 10419 Sergeant G. Foster, No. 10869 Corporal A. Cox, and Private Tipton.

In connection with this royal visit Major-General Marden published the following Order of the Day :—

" His Majesty the King this afternoon paid a visit to the 6th Division and talked to officers and men who had taken part in the recent fighting. On his departure the King asked the Divisional Commander to let the Division know how much he appreciated their magnificent defence on the 21st and 22nd instant. He wished them all good luck and was sure that he could depend on them to fight as well again.

" The Divisional Commander is sure that all ranks will proudly remember the honour done them by this special visit of His Majesty, and is confident that they will uphold in future actions the splendid reputation for fighting which they have won throughout the war, and added to in the recent battles of Cambrai and Bapaume."

On April 23rd His Majesty's visit came to an end and he returned to England, whence he addressed the following letter to Sir Douglas Haig :—

" My dear Field-Marshal.

" My short visit to the battle-front gave Me an exceptional opportunity of seeing you and some of your Generals engaged in the fierce battle still raging, and I thus obtained personal testimony to the indomitable courage and unflinching tenacity with which My splendid troops have withstood the supreme effort of the greater part of the enemy's fighting power.

" I was also fortunate enough to see units recently withdrawn from the front line, and listened with wonder as officers and men narrated the thrilling events of a week's stubborn fighting.

" I was present at the entraining of fresh troops to reinforce their comrades.

" In a large casualty clearing station I realized what can be accomplished by good organization in promptly dealing with every variety of casualty of greater or less severity, and passing on by trains to the base hospitals those fit to travel.

" The patient cheerfulness of the wounded was only equalled by the care and gentleness of those ministering to their wants.

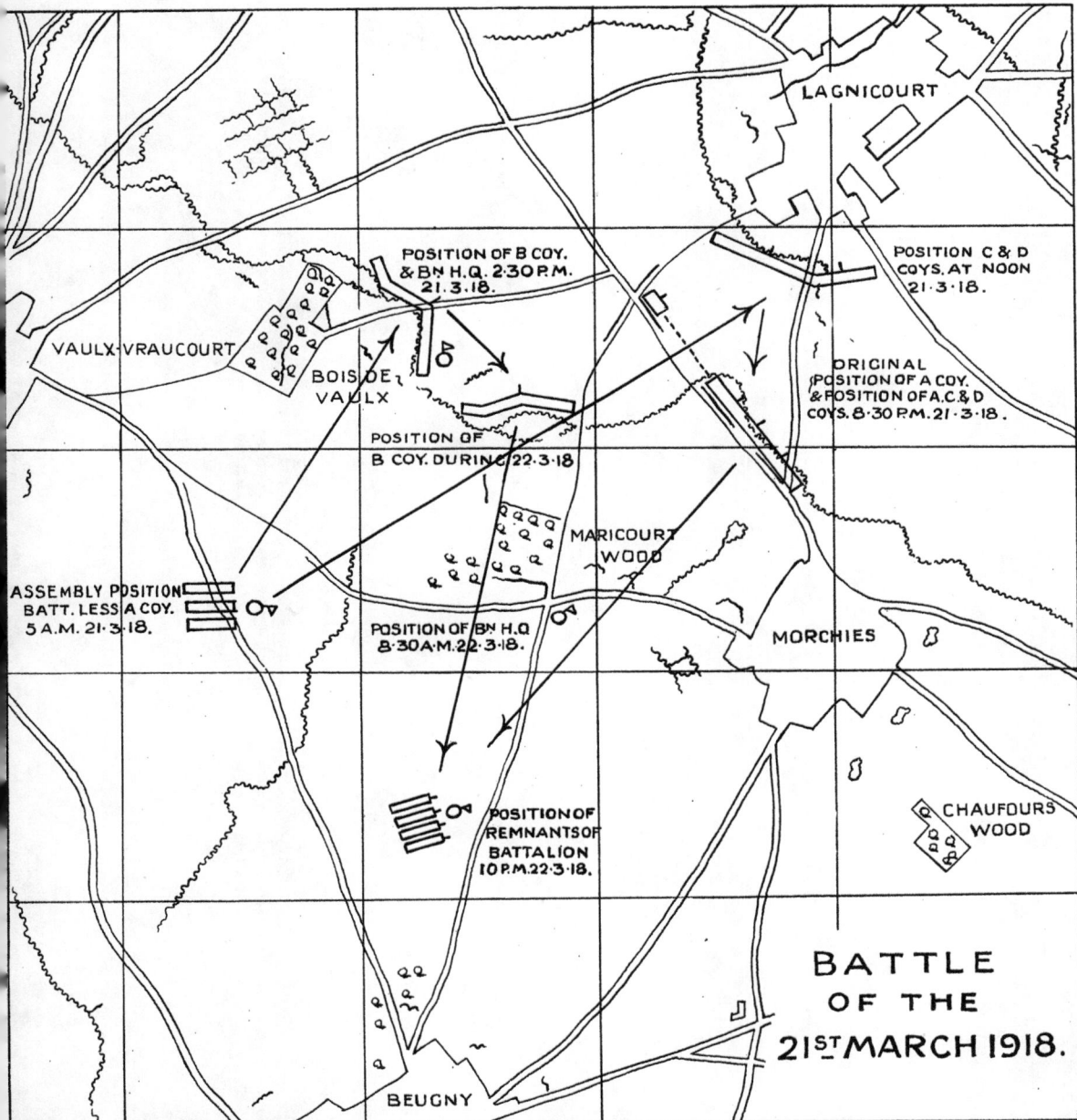

LAGNICOURT

POSITION OF B COY.
& BN H.Q. 2·30 P.M.
21·3·18.

POSITION C & D
COYS. AT NOON
21·3·18.

VAULX-VRAUCOURT

BOIS DE
VAULX

ORIGINAL
POSITION OF A COY.
& POSITION OF A, C & D
COYS. 8·30 P.M. 21·3·18.

POSITION OF
B COY. DURING 22·3·18.

MARICOURT
WOOD

ASSEMBLY POSITION
BATT. LESS A COY.
5 A.M. 21·3·18.

POSITION OF BN H.Q.
8·30 A.M. 22·3·18.

MORCHIES

CHAUFOURS
WOOD

POSITION OF
REMNANTS OF
BATTALION
10 P.M. 22·3·18.

BEUGNY

BATTLE
OF THE
21ST MARCH 1918.

YARDS 1000   500   0   1000   2000   3000 YARDS

" *With these experiences, short but vivid, I feel that the whole Empire will join with Me in expressing the gratitude due to you and your Army for the skilful, unswerving manner in which this formidable attack has been, and continues to be, dealt with.*

" *Though for the moment our troops have been obliged by sheer weight of numbers to give some ground, the impression left on My mind is that no army could be in better heart, braver or more confident than that which you have the honour to command.*

" *Anyone privileged to share these experiences would feel, with Me, proud of the British race and of that unconquerable spirit which will, please God, bring us through our present trials.*

" *We at home must ensure that the man-power is adequately maintained and that our workers—men and women—will continue nobly to meet the demands for all the necessities of war. Thus may you be relieved from any anxiety as to the means by which, with the support of our faithful and brave allies, your heroic Army shall justify the inspiring determination which I found permeated all ranks.*

" *Believe Me,*
" *Very sincerely yours,*
(Sd.) " *George, R.I.*"

The fighting on the Somme front came to an end on April 5th, but there were indications that the enemy intended to renew his attack north of the La Bassée Canal, a front which had been lately rather denuded of troops in order to replace or strengthen the divisions exhausted in the Somme fighting.

" The general situation now was that the Flanders front was held by tired and decimated divisions withdrawn from the big battle in the south. These had been brought up to a respectable strength by drafts from all sources .... many of whom had received no training in infantry weapons or methods of fighting. Officers and men were new to each other, and there was no chance to train, as the whole of every division was in the trenches.

" Against these forces the Germans now opened a determined offensive from Zandvoorde southwards."*

* " Short History of the 6th Division," p. 53.

CHAPTER VI.

1918.

April to November—The End of the Great War.

THE Battalion did not remain more than a very few days at Winnezeele, the 71st Brigade being required to take over trenches in the Ypres Salient from the 147th Brigade. On April 2nd, therefore, the Battalion marched to Godewaersvelde and there entrained, having been inspected on the march by the Corps Commander, and detrained early in the afternoon at the Asylum, Ypres, marching thence to the Belgian Château Camp. By the evening of the 3rd the Battalion had taken over front line trenches in the Reutel sub-sector, described as " apparently a quiet sector of the line. Chief features—duckboard tracks, shell holes, mud and water : no deep dug-outs, much work to be done to make the trenches passable and continuous, the line being held by a series of posts which were not connected by a trench system."

Here, on the 10th, a deserter came in and surrendered on the front occupied by " B " Company, stating that the 7th Division, to which his regiment belonged, was to attack early the following morning on the front south of the Becelaere—Menin road in two waves, infantry in the leading wave and machine guns in the second. No attack, however, developed, and it was surmised that the deserter had invented his story in order to make himself more popular, and the Battalion was relieved on the night of the 10th by the 2nd Durham Light Infantry and went back into a camp in rear at Belgian Battery Corner near Dranoutre; but the pressure of events further north was very soon to take the 71st Brigade elsewhere.

The German attack upon the British front in Flanders had opened on the morning of April 9th, following upon a thirty-six hours' bombardment along the whole line from Lens to Armentières, and by the evening of the 11th the enemy had forced back our line until it ran from Givenchy to Locon, west of Merville, west of Neuf Berquin, north of Steenwerck and Nieppe, east of Neuve Eglise and Wulverghem, west of Messines and along the ridge covering Wytschaete. So far the enemy had attacked with sixteen divisions only, but now having, somewhat unexpectedly, obtained a considerable measure of success over our weakened thirteen divisions, the German Commander resolved upon attempting the capture of the Channel ports, and threw in division after division until some eight and twenty were engaged, and the situation on the 13th, so far as the British were concerned, became very critical. More British troops— mainly Australians—were certainly arriving, but they could only come slowly and gradually into line.

On April 14th, General Foch assumed supreme command of the Allied Armies.

" On the afternoon of the 12th April sharp fighting had taken place in the neighbourhood of Neuve Eglise, and during the night the enemy's pressure in this sector had been maintained and extended. By the morning of the 13th his troops had forced their way into the village, but before noon were driven out by troops of the 33rd and 49th Divisions in a most successful counter-attack. . . . . In the evening further attacks developed . . . . at Neuve Eglise "*; and it was in consequence of these successful assaults by the enemy that on April 13th the 71st Infantry Brigade, then in Divisional Reserve at Dranoutre, was suddenly ordered to proceed to join the 49th Division of the IX. Corps, on the Neuve Eglise front.

The warning order was received at 12.45 p.m. and the Battalion left by bus shortly after three o'clock, " debussing " at Locrehof Farm, between Locre and Dranoutre, and being accommodated for the night in trenches south-east of Dranoutre. It was in the first instance informed that it would be required to proceed to the front line during the night, but these instructions were cancelled later, and the Battalion moved into the support line shortly after midnight. Here the Battalion was on the right and the 2nd Sherwood Foresters on the left, the two battalions being in support to the 103rd Infantry Brigade in front.

The general situation here seems to have been anything but clear, either as regards the movements of the enemy or the disposition of the troops on either flank of the 71st Brigade. A patrol sent out before noon on the 14th, under Second-Lieutenant W. E. Stimson, returned reporting that information received from the Officer Commanding 2nd Worcester Regiment was to the effect that Neuve Eglise had been cleared of the enemy by a recent counter-attack, and that a party of the Highland Light Infantry was sweeping forward from the left flank to complete the clearance of the ridge, but that reinforcements were urgently needed to occupy certain high ground which would enable the village to be securely held. A patrol sent out later—about 3.30 p.m., under Second-Lieutenant D. H. Sims—established the fact that the ridge west of Neuve Eglise was held by the enemy.

At 4 p.m. a heavy bombardment of the position occupied by the 71st Brigade opened, and the enemy was seen advancing down the slopes of this ridge, and our guns, in response to an appeal sent them, began firing, but the barrage was too close to the British line and no means existed for notifying this fact to our gunners. The enemy began bringing forward machine guns, but did not approach very closely, and, though a line of rifle pits held by troops of other units between the right and right-centre company of the Battalion was evacuated under the heavy shell fire, the Battalion front remained intact. About 7 p.m. the enemy gun-fire began to diminish in intensity, and the situation again became normal.

About eleven o'clock at night the Brigade front became the front line and was occupied as follows : one company 9th Norfolks, 1st Leicestershire, 2nd Foresters—two companies of the 9th Norfolks being held in reserve for counter-

* Despatch of July 28th, 1918.

attack purposes, and the rest of the night passed quietly, as did the early part of the 15th.

About 1.30 p.m., however, very heavy shelling of the Battalion area began, gradually increasing in intensity and reaching its climax about 3 p.m. The telephone line fortunately remained intact, and it was learnt that the Norfolk companies on the right of the Battalion had been attacked and driven back, and though a very fine counter-attack had temporarily restored the situation, the troops there available were not sufficient in number to hold the line. This made the position of the right company—"A"—of the Battalion somewhat precarious, but they managed to hold on generally, though evacuating certain of their trenches. A defensive flank was formed by a platoon of "B" Company and Battalion Headquarters; at 4.30, however, "A" Company was compelled to fall back by reason of very heavy shelling, and in order to conform to the line of the Norfolks on the right, who had withdrawn to the neighbourhood of the railway.

At five o'clock the enemy managed to bring up a field gun to within a very few hundred yards of the Battalion front line, firing point blank at the trenches.

As night came on the pressure increased on the front, "A" Company being especially pressed, while "B" Company also reported that the enemy was concentrating for attack, and asked for more men to help hold the line. All available servants and orderlies were sent forward, and eventually enough men were collected to hold a continuous line, when the British guns reopened effectively and the enemy attack came to nothing.

At 2 a.m. on the 16th other troops began to relieve the 71st Brigade, which was clear of the line by 4.15, withdrawing to a position in the valley to the west of Mount Kemmel, the Battalion being under the natural cover of ridges and sunken roads, but digging in also where necessary for protection against the shelling—chiefly by 5·9's—which was continuous throughout the morning.

At four o'clock in the afternoon, however, the Brigade moved forward again in support of the left sector of the 49th Division front, held by troops under General Wyatt, the front line boundaries of which were Dranoutre—Neuve Eglise road on the right to the Donegal Farm on the left. While moving forward, an aeroplane, showing British colours, flew over the valley by which the Battalion was marching, and heavy shelling of the exact route traversed at once commenced. "C" Company suffered many casualties, of one platoon only three men remaining unhit. On arriving at the position told off, the 1st Leicestershire was informed that the whole Battalion would be used for counter-attack should the enemy gain a foothold on the lower slopes of Mount Kemmel; six machine guns were placed on the left flank to fire to the front and to bring a plunging fire to bear on the valleys on the right; No. 7 Motor Machine Gun Battery was also attached to the Battalion.

The 17th was a day of heavy shelling, much moving forward of companies to threatened portions of the line, and also, unfortunately, of many casualties, "C" Company suffering especially; but the line was held, and at 4.15 in the afternoon French troops began to move forward in large numbers, advancing in extended order across the open from Locrehof Farm. "They belonged to the

99th Regiment," so we read in the War Diary, "and had a quiet journey forward, as hostile shelling had died away to nothing. They moved up to the front and support lines and commenced to dig themselves in in broad daylight. They appeared to be without any definite orders, and application made as far back as the Division for instructions only produced the answer that nothing was known of them !"

The line was now very strongly held, though the troops of the two nations were much intermingled, and all attacks henceforth made by the enemy were easily and bloodily repulsed.

On the morning of the 18th a warning order was received that the 49th Division, and the 71st Brigade attached, would be relieved that night by the troops of the 34th French Division, the 71st Infantry Brigade by the 3rd Battalion 83rd Regiment; and by the afternoon of the 20th the Brigade was back again with its own Division, the 1st Leicestershire being accommodated in Vancouver Camp, Vlamertinghe.

Here the following congratulatory messages were received :—

" *The Divisional Commander has very great pleasure in communicating the following wire which he has received from the General Officer Commanding 49th Division :—*

" ' *Wish to record my very warm appreciation of the services of the 71st Infantry Brigade whilst under my command. All ranks did splendidly.*'

" *The Divisional Commander congratulates you and all ranks of your Brigade on the conduct which has earned this appreciation from the Divisional Commander under whom you were at the time serving.*"

In forwarding the above to his battalions the Brigadier added :—

" *The Brigadier-General Commanding has great pleasure in communicating the above letter received from H.Q. 6th Division, and feels sure all ranks will appreciate the high terms of praise regarding the Brigade from the G.O.C. 49th Division. In addition he wishes to thank one and all for their untiring devotion to duty and steadiness under very trying conditions during the week the Brigade was detached from the Division, and he is certain that whatever the future may have in store for us the same high reputation of the 71st Infantry Brigade will be maintained.*"

The casualties during this week had been heavy, 3 officers—Lieutenants G. M. Walker and J. A. Hill and Second-Lieutenant L. Faulks—and 28 other ranks were killed, Second-Lieutenants A. H. Muggeridge and W. Clancey and 162 other ranks were wounded, and 23 men were missing; and though the Battalion was not especially actively engaged during the remaining three weeks of the month, the total casualty list rose to 32 killed, 189 wounded, 23 missing, and 71 men to hospital. On the 29th of the month six officers were wounded, four with the Battalion, and two—the Commanding Officer and the Transport Officer—at the transport lines; these were Lieutenant-Colonel F. Latham, D.S.O., Captain H. W. Brooker, Lieutenant D. F. M. Hackett, Second-Lieutenants A. E. Cooke, W. H. Halls and A. W. F. Williams.

After the return of the 71st Brigade to the 6th Division, the enemy succeeded in possessing himself of Mount Kemmel and the village of that name, and of the effect of this success the Commander-in-Chief said that it "seriously threatened our position in the Ypres Salient, the communications and southern defences of which were now under direct observation by the enemy; while his continued progress to the north-west in the Voormezeele sector would make the extrication of troops east of Ypres most hazardous. A further readjustment of our line in the Salient was accordingly carried out on the night of April 26th-27th, our troops withdrawing to the general line Pilckem—Wieltje—west end of Zillebeke Lake—Voormezeele. . . . . The month closed with the enemy definitely held on both the southern and northern battle fronts. . . . . In the six weeks of almost constant fighting, from the 21st March to the 30th April, a total of 55 British infantry divisions and three cavalry divisions was employed on the battle fronts against a force of 109 different German divisions. During this period a total of 141 different German divisions was engaged against the combined British and French forces."

" Incessant work on the new defences and heavy shelling, particularly gas-shelling of Ypres, were the only incidents for some time on the actual front of the Division, though heavy attacks on the 29th April on the division on the right, and the enemy's unsuccessful attack on Ridgewood on the 8th May, kept it on the alert. The Division was on the edge of the battle, and stood-to on several occasions for an attack on its own front."* Then on May 11th the 6th Division began to move southwards to relieve the 19th Division, joining the II. Corps under Lieutenant-General Sir C. Jacob. The move, so far as the Battalion was concerned, was not, however, completed until the 15th, when it was disposed in a ravine running south-west from Belgian Battery Corner in order from the right— " A," " D," " B " and " C " Companies; a platoon of " A " Company joining on to the 60th French Infantry Regiment of the 14th Division. Here a good deal of sickness developed in the Battalion, 4 officers and 35 other ranks being admitted to hospital between the 16th and 31st of the month, during the course of which 5 men were killed, 54 wounded (including Second-Lieutenants W. E. Stimson and T. Pollard), while one man was missing.

The 6th Division remained some three weeks in this area, one brigade being at Dirty Bucket Camp engaged on the rearward defences, one was training in the St. Jan-ter-Bierzen area, while the third was, when it could be spared, at Cormette, near Tilques, engaged in musketry.

At the end of the last week in June the Division was again transferred, this time to the XIX. Corps (Lieutenant-General Sir H. E. Watts), but prior to the move the Battalion carried out a raid, on the night of the 4th-5th, by 3 officers and 30 other ranks of " D " Company. The object of the raid was, as usual, to obtain identifications, to examine certain derelict trenches reported as occasionally occupied by the enemy, and to obtain proof of the fact, previously reported, of the poor physique and low *morale* of the opposing infantry. The enemy did not, however, put up much of a resistance, retreating on the approach of the raiders, who secured no prisoners and suffered two casualties.

* " Short History of the 6th Division," p. 54.

On the 25th the Battalion marched to St. Omer and proceeded thence by train to Wendinghem, marching from there to Rainsford Camp, near Watou, the 6th Division being under orders to relieve the 46th French Division in the Dickebusch sector, " on a very unpleasant front, where the dominating position of the enemy on Kemmel Hill made movement, even in the rear lines, impossible by day, and practically all work, of which there was plenty, had to be done by night." Here the 71st Brigade was at first in Divisional reserve, relieving the 15th Regiment of Chasseurs Alpins in the Hagebaert area, south-east of Poperinghe.

During June the Battalion had one officer killed, Second-Lieutenant F. E. Burford.

The 71st Infantry Brigade took no part in the successful operations carried out in July by the other brigades of the Division about Ridge Wood and Elzenwelle; while in August the battalions of the Brigade had regiments of the 27th Division of United States Infantry attached to them for instruction and training, the 2nd Battalion 105th Regiment being attached to the 71st Brigade, companies being affiliated, two at a time, to each British front line battalion. Later in the month the 107th Regiment was similarly attached to the 1st Leicestershire.

The American infantry was then considered sufficiently instructed and experienced to take over the front line, and, accordingly, on August 21st and 22nd the 27th New York Division relieved the 6th British Division, the Battalion then marching to Wellington Junction, near Ouderdom, " where the Battalion entrained in the light railway at 2.30 a.m. 23rd. A few 5'9 shells dropped unpleasantly close as the train moved off, but fortunately no casualties were sustained." Moving on by rail and road via Winnezeele and St. Momelin, Tilques was reached at 12.30 the same afternoon, and here all settled down in good but rather scattered billets.

Training now set in with more than usual severity, special attention being paid to the practice of advances in rear of a barrage, attacks on strong points, and—perhaps most significant of all of the approaching end of the war—" practice in marshalling and escorting of prisoners !"

On leaving the XIX. Corps, Lieutenant-General Watts sent to the 6th Division his " warmest thanks for and appreciation of the excellent service rendered " while under his command.

" Originally destined to take part in a projected attack for the recapture of Kemmel Hill and village, the Division suddenly received orders at the end of August, to the delight of all, to move southwards at very short notice. During September 1st, 2nd and 3rd the move southwards was carried out by rail, the Division, less artillery, detraining at Corbie, Heilly and Méricourt. On the 4th the Divisional artillery followed, and the whole division was concentrated in the area Heilly—Ribémont—Franvillers, on the River Ancre, in G.H.Q. Reserve. The next few days were devoted to a continuation of the training in open warfare commenced in the Wizernes area.

" The Germans, forced back in July and August from the high-water mark of their advance in March and April, had stood on the line of the Somme and the Péronne—Arras road. In the southern sector of the British front the Somme defences had been turned by the brilliant capture of Mont St. Quentin (to the north of and guarding Péronne) by the Australian Corps. The retreating enemy had been pursued across the Somme by the 32nd Division, which had been attached temporarily to the Australians. This Division now became part of the newly constituted IX. Corps (Lieutenant-General Sir W. Braithwaite," of General Rawlinson's Fourth Army, " which was to bear such a glorious part in the concluding chapter of the war, and which consisted of the 1st, 6th, 32nd, and 46th Divisions."*

The Field-Marshal Commanding the British Forces in the West has written as follows of the situation at the present time : †" The 1st September marks the close of the second stage in the British offensive. Having in the first stage freed Amiens by our brilliant success east of that town, in the second stage the troops of the Third and Fourth Armies, comprising 23 British divisions, by skilful leading, hard fighting and relentless and unremitting pursuit, in ten days had driven 35 German divisions from one side of the old Somme battlefield to the other, thereby turning the line of the River Somme. In so doing they had inflicted upon the enemy the heaviest losses in killed and wounded, and had taken from him over 35,000 prisoners and 270 guns. . . . . In the obstinate fighting of the past few days the enemy had been pressed back to the line of the Somme River and the high ground about Rocquigny and Beugny, where he had shown an intention to stand for a time. Thereafter his probable plan was to retire slowly, when forced to do so, from one intermediary position to another, until he could shelter his battered divisions behind the Hindenburg defences. . . . . A sudden and successful blow, of weight sufficient to break through the northern hinge of the defences to which it was his design to fall back, might produce results of great importance. At this date . . . . our troops were already in position to deliver such a stroke."

Orders for the move were received by the Battalion early on the morning of September 1st, and the same afternoon all marched by Mentque to St. Omer, which was left by train at 3.15 p.m. and detrained at daylight next morning at Corbie, whence the Battalion marched to Franvillers. " Breakfasts were served *en route* and Franvillers was reached about 10 a.m. Billets quite good, the village having been left practically untouched, though within two or three miles of the recent front line. Very few civilians in the village, so there was plenty of accommodation."

The next few days were spent continuing the form of training already sedulously practised elsewhere, and a certain amount of sport was also indulged in during such intervals of spare time as were available, the Battalion winning the Championship Cup presented by the Brigadier for the Brigade Cross-Country Run.

On September 11th the Battalion left Franvillers and moved to Daours, where orders were received stating that the 6th Division was to relieve the 32nd in the right section of the IX. Corps front. The 71st Infantry Brigade marched

* " Short History of the 6th Division," p. 58.
† Despatch of December 21st, 1918.

on the 14th, and by the early afternoon of this day the Battalion was settled down in bivouacs and shelters just east of the village of Monchy-la-Gache, the total strength of the Battalion now being 32 officers and 802 other ranks.

The 6th Division now relieved the 32nd in the Holnon Wood area, three and a half miles west of St. Quentin, having the 1st Division on the left and the 34th French Division on the right. The 1st and 2nd British and 34th French Divisions were on the 18th to attempt the capture of the heights commanding St. Quentin to the west and south, making this line a starting point for the attack on the Hindenburg Line which ran from just outside St. Quentin to the canal at Bellenglise.

The following were the orders issued on the night of September 16th :—

" The 6th British Division, in conjunction with the 1st British Division on the left and the 34th French Division on the right, will attack on the morning of 18th September to gain the Green and Red objectives shown on attached map. To make good the jumping-off line for this attack the 18th Infantry Brigade and the 34th French Division are attacking on the morning of the 17th to secure the general line—high ground in M.25.d. and S.3.a. Round Hill—Bois de Savy. For the attack on the 18th the 71st Infantry Brigade will be on the right, the 16th on the left, and the 18th in support behind the 71st. . . . The 71st Infantry Brigade will attack with the 2nd Sherwood Foresters and the 9th Norfolk Regiment; the 1st Leicestershire Regiment will be in reserve. The 2nd Sherwood Foresters will take the Green Line, the 9th Norfolks the Red Line. Both objectives will be consolidated in depth. Half a battalion of the 1st West Yorks is moving forward one hour before zero to a position in Trout Copse, and one company is at the call of the 2nd Sherwood Foresters to fill a gap between their right and the French left. . . . The French regiment on our right is the 59th. . . . . Two tanks are working with the Brigade; they will not be used forward of the Green Line."

The operations of the 17th were, however, only partially successful, the French attack failing, while the village of Holnon, through which the line was to have passed, was not completely cleared of the enemy. " The situation was therefore unsatisfactory on the right, but it was impossible to put off the general attack, and arrangements had to be improvised. Another unsatisfactory feature was that Holnon Wood covered practically the whole 2,500 yards frontage of the Division, and was so drenched with gas shells, and the tracks so bad, that both the 16th and 71st Brigades had to make a detour north and south of the wood respectively to reach their assembly positions, and this naturally fatigued the troops and hindered communication and supply.

" Standing on the east edge of the wood, a bare glacis-slope devoid of cover except for two or three shell-trap copses, stretched away for 3,000 yards to the high ground overlooking St. Quentin. There was no sign of life and very few trenches could be seen, though it was known that they were there, as the Fifth Army had held the position in March, 1918. It was found afterwards that the Germans had camouflaged their trenches with thistles, which had covered the ground to a height in many places of eighteen inches. At the highest point, about the centre of the Divisional area of attack, was a network of trenches known later as 'the Quadrilateral'—a name of bad omen to the 6th Division—and which, like its namesake on the Somme, could be reinforced under cover from the back slopes of the hill.   An examination of the battlefield after September 24th also revealed several narrow sunken roads filled with wire.   The position was one of great natural strength, and in addition the whole of the right was dominated by heights in the area to be attacked by the French.   Lastly, adequate time could not be given to brigades for reconnaissance owing to the imperative necessity of pushing on to guard the flank of the corps further north.   The troops had not seen the ground they had to attack over, and rain and smoke obscured the few landmarks existing on the 18th September.

" On that morning the Division attacked at 5.30 a.m. with the 71st Infantry Brigade on the right, its left directed on the Quadrilateral and its right on Holnon and Selency. . . . . Six tanks were allotted to the Division, but met with various mishaps or were knocked out and were not of much use.   The attack met with most determined opposition at once, especially on the right, where the difficulties of the 71st Brigade were increased by the failure of the French to take Round and Manchester Hills."*

So far the general account of the events of September 18th.

For the reasons already stated the attack of the 6th Division did not meet with the success hoped for, and the 1st Leicestershire was not called upon to take part in the assault, but had some 50 casualties while moving up to the concentration area.   During the night of the 18th-19th the following orders were issued for the renewal of the attack :—

" The enemy still holds the Quadrilateral Strong Point and is reported to be in Holnon Village.   The 6th Division is to attack to-morrow to capture these two places.   Selency, which is included in the objective, completely dominates Holnon, and it is hoped that when the former is captured the enemy will probably evacuate the latter village, if he still holds it.   The 6th Division will attack to-morrow with the 16th Infantry Brigade on the left and the 71st Infantry Brigade on the right.

" The 71st Infantry Brigade will attack with 9th Norfolk Regiment on left, 1st Leicestershire Regiment in centre and 1st West Yorkshire Regiment on right, the latter being attached to the 71st Brigade for this operation."

Owing to the very short notice given, preparations were very hurried, but the companies of the Battalion had all moved off to the assembly positions by 4.45 a.m. on the 19th, zero hour being at 5.30.   The companies were thus disposed : " A " Company, Lieutenant S. M. Geddes, right front; " C " Company, Captain J. Herring-Cooper, left front; " B " Company, Captain P. R. Milner, in support of and 300 yards in rear of " A "; and " D " Company, Captain H. H. Duvall, in support of and the same distance behind " C ".   The objective of the Battalion was some trenches in and about Epicure Alley and Etretat Trench, shown in green on the map issued.

The attack was launched at the appointed hour and the companies reached the first line of the objective, but were able to make no further progress owing

* " Short History of the 6th Division," pp. 59-61.

to the many casualties incurred and the great strength of the enemy wire in front; while communication was very difficult and for many hours no news was obtainable of the whereabouts and doings of "A" and "D" Companies. During the night the Brigade front was reorganized, the 1st Leicestershire taking the centre of the line, while reinforcements of 6 officers and 53 other ranks came up from the rear in replacement to some extent of the losses so far met with, which amounted, approximately, to 10 officers and 280 non-commissioned officers and men.

Rations were brought up also, but under great difficulties, the transport coming under heavy shell fire when within 50 yards of Battalion Headquarters, three out of six horses being killed and one wounded. Sergeant Camp, in charge of the transport, did exceptionally smart work on this night, delivering his rations and then getting his three limbers away by using two officers' chargers in the shafts and towing one of the limbers.

During the night, too, the Battalion was temporarily reorganized into two companies, "A" and "C" making one company under Captain Herring-Cooper, and "B" and "D" another under Captain Milner, M.C., and these then occupied trenches which were held throughout the 20th, during which the enemy shelled all the ground in the Battalion area, while the first line system being searched by machine guns, all movement was rendered impossible. That night the Battalion was relieved and withdrawn from the front line to the shelter of a quarry in rear. Here 6 officers and 75 other ranks came up on the 21st from the nucleus at the transport lines, the strength of the Battalion now being 19 officers and 361 other ranks.

The following was received by the General Officer Commanding the Division from the Army Commander :—

"*Please convey to the 6th Division my congratulations and warm thanks for their success of yesterday. Though all objectives were not attained they carried through a difficult operation with great gallantry and determination. I offer to all ranks my warm thanks and congratulations.*"

It was now decided to make a fresh attack upon the Quadrilateral—Selency position, to be launched on the morning of the 24th, the 18th Brigade, strengthened by the 1st Leicestershire Regiment, attacking on the right, and the 16th Brigade on the left of the Division; the French were to attack at the same time on the right flank, while on the left the 1st British Division was to attempt the capture of Fresnoy and Gricourt.

The night of the 23rd-24th passed quietly, and at 5 a.m. on the 24th the bombardment opened and the attack commenced. News was very slow in coming through as to the progress of the attack, but it was finally established that the French had seized Round Hill and Manchester Hill on the right, and the 16th Brigade had reached Argonne Trench, North Alley and Breton Alley; the 18th Brigade, however, had not been equally successful, having experienced exceptionally strong opposition, and, though a footing had been obtained by one of its battalions in the Quadrilateral and by another in Douai Trench, but little real progress had been made. A certain amount of further progress was gained by the 16th Brigade, but it was slow work.

At 10.30 a.m. two companies of the Battalion were pushed forward to support the 2nd Durham Light Infantry, which had suffered heavily, and it was then decided that a further attack must be made to connect the 1st West Yorkshire Regiment with the French, and the 1st Leicestershire Regiment was deputed to carry out this attack later in the evening, the written orders in connection therewith being received at 7.30 p.m., and these ran as follows : " Douai Trench, from within 50 yards of the Roman Road, Holnon—St. Quentin to within 100 yards of the Sunken Road at S.9.a.5. will be assaulted at 10.30 p.m. on the evening of the 24th September by the 1st Leicestershire Regiment, which will attack with two companies in depth.

" The 1st Leicestershire Regiment will form up the two assaulting companies along the eastern outskirts of Holnon Village, moving as close up to the barrage as possible when it comes down, preparatory to rushing the trench at 10.50 p.m.

" The 1st Leicestershire Regiment, after making good Douai Trench, will establish a post in the Sunken Road north of Selency, and if possible push posts out into Selency Village, gaining touch with the French at about the Cross Roads at S.9.c."

The assaulting companies were " B " (Captain P. R. Milner, M.C.) and " C " (Captain W. Wilson, D.C.M.), " B " being on the left and " C " on the right. The attack was duly launched, and, " delivered with great gallantry," was successful, and many enemy were killed in the trench, which was found to be strongly held. The success was largely due to the fact that the attackers followed the barrage so closely that they reached the parapet at the same moment that it lifted from the trench, and consequently the enemy had no time to recover and bring up his machine guns. About 25 Germans were killed in or about the trenches, the remainder bolting, and the captures included 8 gunners, 14 machine guns, 2 Lewis guns and one dart machine, at a cost to the Battalion of 1 officer (Captain Milner) wounded, and 47 other casualties.

A company of the 11th (Pioneer) Battalion of the Regiment now came up, and " by midnight of the 25th-26th September the 16th and 18th Infantry Brigades," assisted by the Battalion, " had completed the capture of the Quadrilateral, a position of such unusual natural strength that captured German officers admitted that they had fully expected to be able to hold it indefinitely. For this very fine performance, a remarkable instance of grit and determination and of intelligent initiative by regimental officers of all ranks, to whom the successful results were entirely due, the Division received the congratulations of the Army and Corps Commanders and G.O.C. 1st Division. The message telephoned on behalf of the Army Commander contained the following passage, ' He fully realizes the difficulties they have had to contend with, and admires the tenacity with which they have stuck to it and completed their task.' "*

The Battalion was relieved by the 2nd Durham Light Infantry during the night of the 26th-27th and went back to its own Brigade, being placed in reserve in the Fresnoy sector, where 4 officers and 126 other ranks joined during the morning, and, later in the day, 96 more non-commissioned officers and men, bringing the total strength up to 18 officers and 631 other ranks.

* " Short History of the 6th Division," pp. 63, 64.

" The enemy's resistance now broke down," to quote the Divisional History, " and during the 26th, 27th and 28th September patrols were able gradually to gain further ground, so that by the time the Division was relieved by the 4th French Division on the 29th-30th, posts had been established round three sides of the village of Fayet. . . . . The captures during the period were 10 officers, 372 other ranks, 4 guns, 15 trench mortars and 53 machine guns."

The Battalion moved on the night of September 29th by a long and tiring march in the dark to the Bouvincourt—Vraignes area, settling down under a heavy downpour of rain in trench shelters and bivouacs.

The casualties during September had again been serious : one officer— Lieutenant S. M. Geddes—and 50 other ranks were killed, 12 officers—Captains H. W. J. Brooker, H. H. Duvall and P. R. Milner, M.C., Lieutenants G. C. Coleman, T. O. Risden, and D. V. Webb, M.C., Second-Lieutenants R. J. Croker, G. Clark, D.C.M., F. W. Sisson, R. Shaw, G. Stevenson, O. M. Norman and W. Clancey—and 303 non-commissioned officers and men were wounded, and Second-Lieutenant C. A. Smith, D.C.M., and 30 men were missing—a total of little short of 400 casualties !

On October 4th the Battalion proceeded by bus and march route to Magny-la-Fosse and was billeted in trenches round the eastern edge of the village ; the German aircraft were very busy during the journey by day and during the night which followed, and here, on the 5th, orders were received for a fresh move.

While the 6th Division had been engaged in rear in reorganization and in absorbing such reinforcements as had reached its shattered units, the remaining divisions of the IX. Corps had broken the enemy resistance on the Hindenburg Line, but in so doing had encountered considerable opposition and sustained severe losses, requiring relief in their turn. The 6th Division was therefore brought forward with orders to attack on October 8th in the direction of Bohain. " The 30th American Division was on the right and about 2,000 yards ahead, connected to the 6th Division by a series of posts along the railway. This curious position entailed a very complicated creeping barrage, which, however, was successfully put in operation on the day of the attack. On the right was the French 42nd Division, slightly in rear, having followed the Germans through St. Quentin and met with strong resistance beyond it. The position to be attacked consisted of high rolling downs with deep transverse valleys, giving good cover for support and forward guns, and on the right a broad longitudinal valley closed by a ridge on which stood the village of Méricourt. . . . . The Divisional Commander decided to leave the valley severely alone to start with, merely smoking by guns and bombs from aeroplanes the Méricourt Ridge and attacking all along the high ground on the north."

The 6th Division was to attack with the 16th Brigade on the right and the 71st on the left next to the Americans, in the 71st Brigade the 2nd Sherwood Foresters and 9th Norfolks being on the right and left respectively and the 1st Leicestershire in reserve ; and this last was ordered to be " concentrated in the area H.17 a. and b. by zero *minus* two minutes on the day of attack, moving forward at zero *plus* 15 to the Sunken Road and consolidating in posts. Two companies then to push forward into the valley, full advantage being taken of

G

the cover afforded by the Sunken Road in that area. The remaining two companies to await relief by a battalion of the 18th Brigade, then joining the other two companies of the Battalion."

The Battalion advanced "according to plan" on the morning of October 8th and gained the positions pointed out to it in the Sunken Road and about Doon Mill, encountering a certain amount of opposition and sustaining losses amounting to 4 officers and about 100 other ranks; these positions were held during the rest of the day. Then, on the morning of the 9th, the 1st Leicestershire moved up to the front, relieving the 2nd Foresters and becoming the southern battalion of the Brigade, and the companies being disposed as follows : " A " on the right supported by " B," and " C " on the left supported by " D." " All the companies except ' D ' got off immediately behind the barrage and gained their final objective, ' D ' arriving 20 minutes later. The morning was particularly misty, but, none the less, direction was well maintained, and ' A ' and ' B ' Companies advanced on and passed through Gonnecourt Farm, while ' C ' moved direct to the high ground north-east of it. This objective also was gained and consolidated, and here an anti-tank gun was captured."

A platoon from each of the advanced companies then went over the ground in front as far as the railway line, the limit allotted, and about 2 p.m. news came to hand that the 9th Norfolks had secured the railway to the north, near Bohain, and that British cavalry was moving forward. " C " Company now advanced under the personal leadership of the Commanding Officer, but met with much opposition from enemy machine guns, upon which, while the Second-in-Command with a Lewis gun section endeavoured to outflank the enemy from the east, the Commanding Officer, with a captured light machine gun, tried to do the same from the west, and " C " Company was thus enabled to make an advance of some 200 yards to an embankment. The Adjutant had been sent to direct " A " Company to work up the railway from the south, but unfortunately the Adjutant was killed and the receipt of the order by " A " Company was belated. The whole line indicated to the Battalion was in its possession by dusk, and the captures made included 2 heavy and 3 light machine guns, one dart machine and 10 prisoners, while several enemy dead were found. Unfortunately the enemy had a covered line of retreat, up which about a hundred of them fell back, thus avoiding capture.

The advance was continued on the 10th, very little opposition being met with, while " A " Company secured 8 prisoners belonging to the 142nd Regiment. All objectives were again taken, but a defensive flank had to be made on the right where the 138th Brigade, 46th Division, had not advanced quite so far as was hoped. The Battalion was now in touch with the 138th Brigade on the right and the 2nd Foresters on the left.

Moving forward again at daybreak on the 11th—the three units of the Brigade in line and the Battalion on the right—it was found that the enemy resistance appeared to have stiffened and the advance was checked by very heavy machine-gun fire all along the front, and after some 400 yards the Brigade had to dig in, the German machine guns continuing very active all day. At night the 18th Brigade relieved the 71st, and the Battalion—all greatly exhausted—withdrew to huts north of Bohain, where two clear days were devoted to cleaning up and reorganization.

The following messages were received by the General Officer Commanding 6th Division regarding the operations carried out during the preceding days by those under his command :—

From the Army Commander :—

" *Will you please convey to the 6th Division my warm thanks and hearty congratulations on their success. They have done admirable work, and I wish them all good luck.*"

From the Corps Commander :—

" *Well done 6th Division! So glad casualties so light considering what the Division has accomplished.*"

On the 14th, the 71st Brigade returned to the same front, where it was early reported that the enemy had retired, but patrols pushed forward established the fact that, while the Germans had withdrawn from the lower slopes of the ridge they had been occupying, they were still holding the high ground, and no change had been effected in the situation when the 47th Division relieved the 6th again on the 17th.

Frontal attacks upon the enemy positions having so far proved fruitless, the General Officer Commanding IX. Corps now decided to move two of his divisions—the 6th and 46th—to the north flank and attack from the south-east and east respectively.

On the early morning of the 20th the 71st Brigade rendezvoused at Brancourt, where buses were in waiting, and, passing through Vaux Andigny and La Haie Manneresse, reached St. Souplet about three o'clock in the afternoon. From here the Battalion moved up to the line, meeting guides at Le Quennelet Grange, and occupied trenches in the vicinity of the Basuel—Ors road, having the 9th Norfolks on the right and the 21st Manchesters on the left. All remained here in readiness for the attack to be carried out on the 23rd, when the 71st Brigade was to advance through the dense country north-east of Basuel, the 1st Leicestershire on the left, the 9th Norfolks on the right and the 2nd Foresters in support. The right of the Brigade objective was the Basuel—Ors road, the left was a track running to the north through the Bois de l'Eveque.

Soon after midnight on the 22nd the Battalion was formed up, " C " and " D " Companies in front, " A " following to " mop up " and " B " in reserve, but the advance at once experienced great difficulties. Immediately in front of the forward companies were small orchards with thick hedges reinforced by wire, and, though billhooks were used, the wire and the hedges soon caused the attacking lines to miss direction, they lost touch with the accompanying tanks in the fog and failed to keep up with the barrage, and the whole line was eventually held up little more than 400 yards from its starting point; casualties, too, had been heavy, particularly in officers.

The line remained thus stationary until shortly after midday on the 23rd, when it was reported that the enemy was retiring across the Sambre Canal, and

G 2

the Battalion line was then pushed well forward, and in so doing Lieutenant Mee and his company effected the capture of an anti-tank gun, the sights of which had been removed, and of four of its crew.

During the night of the 23rd-24th the 71st Brigade was relieved by the 16th, which renewed the attack; German opposition had by this time begun to weaken, and good progress was made on this and succeeding days all along the 6th Division front, until by the night of the 28th a bridge-head had been established on the canal at Ors, while posts on the west bank commanded the whole line of the canal.

While temporarily out of the line the Battalion was in billets in St. Souplet, where the companies were reorganized, vacancies in the establishments of warrant and non-commissioned officers were filled up, Lewis gun teams completed, while Lieutenant-Colonel J. H. Martin, D.S.O., M.C., of the King's Own Lancaster Regiment, arrived at Battalion Headquarters and assumed command of the Battalion.

During the month of October the Battalion lost two officers and 36 other ranks killed or died of wounds, 12 officers and 228 non-commissioned officers and men wounded and 12 men missing. The names of the officers were as follows: killed or died of wounds, Captain D. V. Webb, M.C., and Second-Lieutenant A. E. Brown; wounded, Captain F. H. Jeeps, Lieutenants J. A. Thomas, G. Colborne Smith, S. F. Mackay and W. J. Collis, Second-Lieutenants A. E. W. Paterson, W. Marshall, R. H. Nixon, D. H. Sims, M.C., T. Pollard, F. S. Dennis, and S. T. Heath.

On the night of October 30th-31st the relief of the 6th Division by the 32nd was completed, and it withdrew from St. Souplet to Fresnoy-le-Grand, moving again to Bohain on November 6th, by which date the IX. Corps had, in seven weeks of fighting, advanced fifty miles, capturing 318 guns and not far short of 17,000 prisoners; while the 6th Division itself, during the same period, had sustained over 6,000 casualties.

On the night of November 4th-5th the Germans began to fall back practically all along the front, and by the 9th the enemy was everywhere in full retreat.

The German leaders now admitted defeat and realized the hopelessness of any further prolongation of the struggle, for their country was in the throes of revolution, the High Seas Fleet had mutinied and the Kaiser and Crown Prince had fled the country. On the evening of Thursday, November 7th, German delegates presented themselves at the headquarters of Marshal Foch, and early on the morning of the 11th they signed the terms which the allied governments had determined upon. These were that all allied prisoners were at once to be surrendered, the left bank of the Rhine was to be occupied, 5,000 guns, 3,000 machine guns and 2,000 aeroplanes were at once to be surrendered, while all submarines and a large portion of the German Fleet were to be handed over to the charge of the Allies.

The situation on the British front on the morning of November 11th is thus stated in Sir Douglas Haig's despatch of December 21st, 1918: " In the fighting since the 1st November our troops had broken the enemy's resistance beyond possibility of recovery, and had forced on him a disorderly retreat along the whole front of the British Armies. Thereafter the enemy was capable neither of accepting nor refusing battle. The utter confusion of his troops, the state of his railways, congested with abandoned trains, the capture of huge quantities of rolling stock and material, all showed that our attack had been decisive. . . . . A continuance of hostilities could only have meant disaster to the German armies and armed invasion of Germany."

The Battalion was in billets in and near the Rue de Vaux in the eastern part of the town of Bohain when, very shortly after 11 a.m. on November 11th, the following message was circulated to all the units of the 6th Division :—

" G. 861. 11th.

" Hostilities ceased at 11.00 hours this morning.

" 6th Div. H.Q.   (sd.) T. T. Grove, Lt.-Colonel,
" General Staff."

The strength of the Battalion this day was 21 officers and 657 non-commissioned officers and men, the following being the officers present on this Day of Days : Lieutenant-Colonel J. H. Martin, D.S.O., M.C., Captains G. N. Wykes and R. N. Davis, M.C. (Adjutant), Lieutenants P. W. Bennett (Assistant Adjutant) and J. Featherstone, M.C. (Signalling Officer), Second-Lieutenants L. G. Arnold (Lewis Gun Officer), and W. Priestley (Transport Officer); Major and Quartermaster J. H. Greasley, M.C.; and Captain E. H. Granger, R.A.M.C. (Medical Officer).

"A" Company : Captain G. Delmer, M.C., Second-Lieutenants B. W. Sadler and A. Stewart, M.M.

"B" Company : Second-Lieutenants W. Cooper, R. V. Burns and J. H. Raynes.

"C" Company : Captain C. A. Dodson, Second-Lieutenants R. E. F. Richards and W. Burton.

"D" Company : Captain G. W. Grossmith, M.C., Second-Lieutenants A. W. J. Watts, G. S. V. West and D. G. Passmore.

Also, Regimental Sergeant-Major Gamble, Regimental Quartermaster-Sergeant Bolland, Company Sergeant-Major Billingham, Company Quarter-master-Sergeant Smith, Company Sergeant-Major Faulkner, Company Sergeant-Major Bennett and Company Quartermaster-Sergeant Dodd.

The following had served with the Battalion throughout the war, from embarkation to the Armistice : Captain (now Major) and Quartermaster J. H. Greasley, M.C., Sergeant H. T. Whitcher and Private McAllister.

To his soldiers of all ranks His Majesty the King sent the following words of praise, gratitude and congratulation through their leader :—

" No words can express My feelings of admiration for the glorious British Army whose splendid bravery under your leadership has now achieved this magnificent success over the enemy. You have fought without ceasing for the past four years. My warmest congratulations to you and your undaunted

Army, where all ranks, with mutual confidence in each other, have faced hardship and danger with dogged resolution and have fought with an irresistible determination which has now resulted in this final and overwhelming victory."

In making known to the nation, through Parliament, the terms of the Armistice concluded with the Central Powers, the Prime Minister spoke as follows :—

" Thus at 11 o'clock this morning came to an end the cruellest and most terrible war that has ever scourged mankind. I hope we may say that thus, this fateful morning, came to an end all wars. This is no time for words. Our hearts are too full of gratitude to which no tongue can give adequate expression. I will therefore move that the House do immediately adjourn until this time tomorrow, and that we, the House of Commons, proceed to St. Margaret's to give humble and renewed thanks for the great deliverance of the world from its great peril."

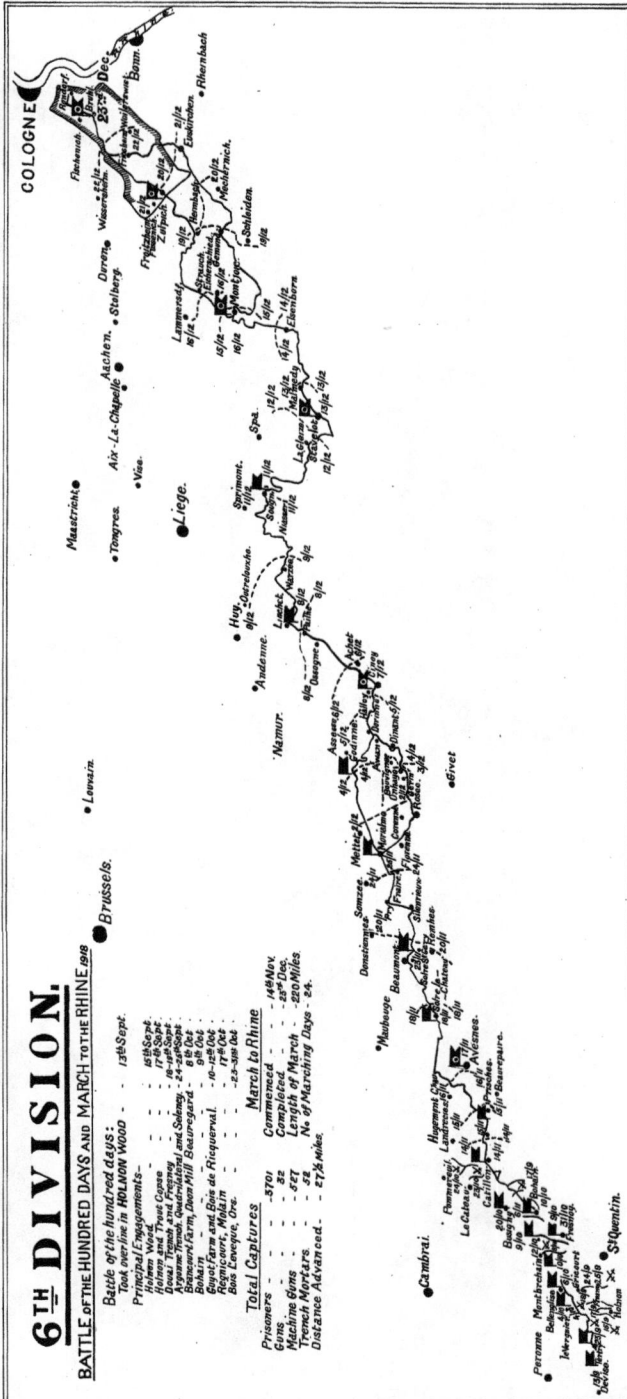

6TH DIVISION.
BATTLE OF THE HUNDRED DAYS AND MARCH TO THE RHINE 1918

Battle of the hundred days:

Took over line in HOLNON WOOD - - 13th Sept.

Principal Engagements—
Holnon Wood - - -	18th Sept.
Holnon and Trout Copse - -	17th Sept.
Holnon Trench and Fresnoy -	18-19th Sept.
Argoeuve Trench, Quadrilateral and Sidney -	24-24th Sept.
Beaucamp Farm, Deon Mill Beauregard	8th Oct.
Bohain - - -	9th Oct.
Guyot Farm and Bois de Riqueval -	10-12th Oct.
Regnicourt, Molain -	17th Oct.
Bois Eveque, Ors. -	23-3rd Oct.

Total Captures:
Prisoners - - -	5701
Guns - - -	82
Machine Guns - -	587
Trench Mortars - -	58
Distance Advanced -	27¼ Miles

March to Rhine
Commenced -	14th Nov.
Completed -	23rd Dec.
Length of March -	220 Miles
No of Marching Days -	24.

COLOGNE

Maastricht. Tongres. Aix-La-Chapelle. Aachen. Stolberg. Duren. Wassenberg. Bonn. Rheinbach. Eschweiler.

Spa. Liege. Louvain. Brussels. Huy. Andenne. Namur. Givet. Cambrai. Peronne. St. Quentin.

CHAPTER VII.

1918-1927.

DEMOBILIZATION AND THE YEARS OF PEACE.

On the day following the announcement of the signing of the armistice a warning order was received to the effect that the 6th Division would move at once to the Catillon area, preparatory to the march into and occupation by the Allies of the western provinces of Germany, for the IX. Corps was now to be transferred to the Second Army, commanded by General Sir H. Plumer, to whom had been assigned the charge of the British Army of Occupation.

The Battalion marched from the neighbourhood of Bohain on November 14th, the units of the 6th Division being speeded on their way by the following farewell order from General Sir H. Rawlinson, the Commander of the Fourth Army :—

"*Now that the 6th Division is passing to the command of another Army, I desire to place on record my sincere appreciation and warm thanks for the valuable services rendered by you since you joined the Fourth Army in September last.*

"*The Division has passed through strenuous times and has seen some heavy fighting, especially in September between Holnon Wood and the Canal, and at Bohain and Vaux Andigny in October, where the gallantry and determination of all ranks filled me with admiration.*

"*I congratulate most heartily you all on the victories you have won, and trust that at some future time I may again find the Division under my command.*"

The Division moved forward in three Infantry Brigade Groups and one Divisional Troops Group, the Battalion being with the 71st Infantry Brigade Group; and, marching by Catillon, Prisches, Dompierre, Wattignies, Solre-le-Château and Solre-St. Gery, Silenrieux was reached on the 24th, the 71st Brigade halting here for several days and the Battalion being accommodated in billets described as " not very clean, but otherwise comfortable, consisting chiefly of small rooms in houses in the western end of the village." On the 19th, Major G. N. Wykes and a party left the line of march and proceeded to England to fetch the Colours, returning with them on November 29th and rejoining the Battalion at Silenrieux.

The march was not resumed until December 2nd, on which day the 1st Battalion started on its march to the Rhine; the route lay by way of Florennes, Onhaye, Spontin, Schaltin, Pailhe, Ouffet, Aywaille, Stoumont and

Francorchamps, leaving which place the frontier was crossed into Germany and all arrived at the big German camp at Elsenborn on December 15th.

"The march from the neighbourhood of Dinant across the Ardennes and along the lovely valley of the River Amblève, will always stand out as a most delightful reminiscence. All ranks worked hard at their equipment, and the transport was so smart as to be thought by the Belgians to be new. It was a proud and splendid Division which marched, with drums beating and Colours flying, across the German frontier into the little town of Malmédy between the 13th and 16th December. Marching generally by only one road, the length of the Division, when billeted, varied from ten to twenty-five miles. It was particularly interesting for Brigades to occupy the German huts at Elsenborn Camp of exercise, where large numbers of the enemy had assembled in the end of July, 1914, for the conquest of Belgium."*

The Battalion continued its march on the 15th, and, halting at Katzerherberg, Konzen, Heimbach, Zulpich, Lechenich and Rondorf, on December 27th the final stage of the 220-mile march to the Rhine was reached, the Leicestershire halting at Wesseling, a town some seven miles south of Cologne on the banks of the Rhine.

The marches had been long and at the outset some of the halts had been protracted, the delay being due to the difficulty experienced in rationing the leading divisions of the Army of Occupation, the necessity in some cases of feeding the French and Belgian population, the destruction caused by the enemy to the roads and railways, and also in some degree to the fact that the retirement of the German Army was not always carried out as had been agreed upon.

On the conclusion of this long march the General Commanding the 6th Division issued an order congratulating all ranks on " their steady marching, excellent turn-out and high standard of march-discipline."

The area allotted to the Division was a strip of country almost rectangular in shape, with a maximum length of twenty miles and a maximum breadth of twelve miles, and lying to the immediate south-west of Cologne. The northwest border ran along the ring of forts encircling the city, and these were later also included in the divisional area.

On December 28th the first man to be demobilized left the Battalion; this was No. 7826 Sergeant W. Birch.

For the demobilization of the units of the British Army which everywhere commenced in this month, preparations had been elaborated comparatively early in the war, for as soon as the huge scale upon which the war was to be conducted was appreciated, it was at the same time realized that much would have to be done, when peace was finally proclaimed, to ease the distress and confusion which would almost certainly be occasioned were many hundreds of thousands of men to be suddenly returned to civil life before labour had sufficiently recovered from the war to provide employment enough for all who were likely to need it. So early as January, 1915, a scheme was evolved and presented to

---

* " Short History of the 6th Division," p. 78.

the Cabinet, which contained proposals for meeting all the very many difficulties which had been foreseen when the *personnel* of our huge army should be ready to return to civil life. The suggestions therein made were provisionally approved, but as there seemed at the time no immediate prospect of their materializing, they were laid aside to be taken up again when the need for carrying them into effect should arise.

As the war progressed and drew nearer to its inevitable conclusion, committees were appointed to deal with demobilization in greater detail, and eventually it was decided to offer each soldier on leaving the Army :—

1. A furlough, with pay and separation allowances for four weeks from the date of demobilization.
2. A railway warrant to his home.
3. A twelve-months' policy of insurance against unemployment.
4. A money gratuity *in addition* to the ordinary Service gratuity.

Several alternative methods of dispersal were considered, and at first the principle was accepted and followed of granting men release from Army service in order of priority, determined by individual qualifications, the idea of an early reconstruction of a peace-time army being carefully kept in view—that is to say, the army was to be dispersed in accordance with the requirements of the recon-struction of industry, and by individuals rather than by units.

The scheme, as in the beginning administered, met with no small amount of opposition, while a system of " special releases," forming no part or parcel of the original plan, was justly open to the charge of " favouritism "; serving soldiers could not readily understand why other men should be considered to have stronger claims for early discharge than they; hopes were raised which it was not found possible to gratify; and very considerable difficulty was experienced in making men, unavoidably retained with the Colours, realize that a state of war still existed, and that for some time to come an army of no inconsiderable size must remain in the field ready for possible emergencies. As a result of the many representations made, Army Order No. 55 of 1919 was issued, and this abolished the principle of demobilization on industrial grounds, and substituted that of release on grounds of age and length of Army service.

After settling down at Wesseling " Demobilization " provided a subject of many lectures delivered to the non-commissioned officers and men of the Battalion, as did also that of " Educational Training," a subject which had received much consideration in the higher circles of the Army when it was realized that the war was really coming to an end. Briefly, the idea was to ascertain in the first place exactly what point of education had been reached by each soldier, and what was his particular branch or subject in which he was chiefly interested; and then, it being discovered what available talent for instruction there might be latent among officers and other ranks, to form groups or classes for the study of such subjects. Immediately after the Armistice was concluded the scheme was developed, and to each battalion an Education Officer was appointed to co-ordinate the work, under the guidance and supervision of

Brigade and Divisional Education Officers. Captain P. W. Bennett was appointed Education Officer to the Battalion, with Acting Quartermaster Sergeant Chesterfield and Sergeant Cross as assistant instructors. The classes were from the outset very well attended, nearly 200 men presenting themselves for preliminary examination.

By the end of January, 1919, 201 other ranks had joined the Battalion as reinforcements—mostly men discharged from hospital or returning from leave; 53 had re-enlisted for the *post-bellum* army; while one officer and 173 non-commissioned officers and men had been demobilized, leaving the total strength of the Battalion at 42 officers and 777 other ranks.

By the end of February the total number of men demobilized had risen to two officers and 305 other ranks; while by March 26th the process of demobilization had reduced the strength of the Battalion—now at Bruhl, to which town it had moved two days previously—to no more than 9 officers and 126 non-commissioned officers and men.

Orders had already been received that the 6th Division, as such, would cease to exist as from March 16th, and farewell remarks were now the order of the day.

From Brigadier-General P. W. Brown, D.S.O., Commanding 71st Brigade, came the following :—

" Now that the demobilization of the greater part of the British Expeditionary Force, and the reforming of our peace garrisons at home and abroad necessitate the breaking up of the 71st Infantry Brigade, I desire to place on record my very high appreciation of the services of all ranks, from the highest to the lowest, and to thank all from the bottom of my heart for their unfailing support, cheerful endurance of hardship, and marked devotion to duty on every occasion.

" I have now had the honour and pleasure of commanding the Brigade for 19 months, and during that time we have had our share of hard knocks. The milestones of the period were the victorious attacks at Cambrai on 20th November, 1917, followed ten days later by the enemy's counter-attack, when the steadiness of the Brigade north of Marcoing—all troops on their right having temporarily been driven back—was most marked; the enemy's offensive on 21st and 22nd March, 1918, when the Brigade suffered such heavy casualties, but maintained its position in the Corps line until relieved on the evening of the latter date; the enemy's offensive against the Channel Ports in April, 1918, when the Brigade, composed mainly of new drafts, fought with its usual gallantry south of Mont Kemmel, earning the special thanks of the Commander of the Division to which it was attached; and lastly, the victorious advance from September 18th to October 30th, which resulted in the enemy suing for an armistice.

" Between these different dates were the discomforts and hardships of the seemingly never-ending trench warfare, demanding almost as high a standard of valour and determination as the more active phases.

"*We all deplore the loss of many gallant friends, who so worthily upheld the fine traditions of their regiments, and who will never be forgotten. Those who are left may with certainty look back with pride in years to come on the parts they played in the 71st Infantry Brigade.*

"*Once again I thank you for the support you have at all times given me, and, whatever the future may hold for you, I wish you all the very best of luck, good-bye and Godspeed.*"

In General Marden's farewell message he reviewed at length the services of the 6th Division from the beginning to the close of the war, and concluded by saying :—

"*Few of the original members of the 6th Division now remain with it, but I am sure that all those who, like myself, have been associated with the Division for any length of time, will always cherish proud and happy memories of the time spent with it.*

"*The 6th Division has never gone to a new command without a hearty welcome, nor left a command without an expression of thanks for services rendered and of regret that it was being transferred.*

"*I wish all ranks the best of luck in life, whatever fate may have for them in the future.*"

On March 15th the Battalion, now under the command of Captain and Brevet Major (Temporary Lieutenant-Colonel) F. Latham, D.S.O., handed over all transport and stores to the 51st (Young Soldiers) Battalion The Leicestershire Regiment, which was at the time at Wesseling, near Cologne, commanded by Captain (Temporary Lieutenant-Colonel) A. T. Le M. Utterson, D.S.O.; and on April 1st the Cadre consisted of eleven officers and 129 non-commissioned officers and men, the officers then present being Lieutenant-Colonel F. Latham, D.S.O., Captain R. N. Davis, M.C. (Adjutant), Lieutenant R. V. Burns (Demobilization Officer), Second-Lieutenants A. Stewart, M.M., C. J. Steele, V. G. Matthews and D. S. Cox, Major J. H. Greasley, M.C. (Quartermaster) and Lieutenant H. Bolland (Quartermaster). Lieutenant A. B. Gould was on leave and Lieutenant J. V. Tailby, M.C., was on command.

On April 6th the Battalion Cadre moved from Wesseling by train via Cologne to Ath, where two days later the strength was again reduced to nine officers and 94 other ranks; and on the 23rd information was received that the Cadre would in all probability be sent home via Antwerp about May 6th; but on this date the O.C. was told that the departure had been postponed until the 10th and that the destination of the Cadre was Lichfield.

At 3.15 p.m. on the date specified the remnant of the 1st Battalion The Leicestershire Regiment—6 officers and 35 other ranks composing the Cadre, and the Band and Drums making a further number of 41 non-commissioned officers and men—left Ath, reached Dunkirk early on the morning of the 11th, and on detraining was accommodated in No. 2 Embarkation Camp, remaining here for some 48 hours.

Then at 7 a.m. on the 13th the final move took place, the Cadre—6 officers and 74 other ranks—marching down to the quay and sailing for England in the s.s. *Margilief;* Southampton was reached next day, and from here the Cadre was at once dispatched by train to Lichfield, where a few days were spent before the Cadre was sent on to the Regimental Depot at South Wigston, where it arrived on May 19th.

The following account of the Civic Reception of the Cadre of the 1st Battalion of the Regiment at Leicester is extracted from the *Leicester Mail* of May 20th, 1919 :—

" Enthusiastic scenes marked the welcome home of the ' Cadre ' of the 1st Leicestershire Regiment, which arrived in the county town yesterday. We believe this is the first official appearance of the 1st Batt. of the ' Tigers ' in the Territorial centre, although one company was present at the unveiling of the Boer War Memorial, and formed the Guard of Honour on that occasion. The ' Cadre,' which is really the nucleus of the post-war reformation of the Battalion, was greeted as the worthy representative of that famous Regiment which has taken a memorable share in the greatest of our victories, and has added eternal lustre to the record of the ' Tigers.'

"The ' Cadre,' commanded by Col. Latham, D.S.O., arrived at the Midland station about a quarter past two. The men formed up on the platform, and their officers were greeted by the Mayor (Councillor J. Lovell), who was accompanied by the Mayoress, Miss Winnie Lovell, and Mr. W. H. Lovell. Amongst those present were the Rev. W. Williamson, C.F. (Presbyterian Chaplain for No. 3 Area), Captain Simpson, and many interested spectators. Among the officers who arrived with the party were Major Bacchus (in command of Glen Parva), Major Greasley (Quartermaster of Battalion) and Captain Davis (Adjutant).

" After a brief delay the men commenced their march to the Municipal Buildings. The ' Cadre ' was headed by the band of the 1st Leicestershire, discoursing lively music, and in the midst of the party the Battalion Colours, uncased and borne by 2/Lt. Stewart and 2/Lt. Burns, waved their silken folds, resplendent in colour and with their embroidered gold thread glittering in the sunlight. In the station yard were assembled a large number of wounded men now at local hospitals, who greeted their comrades with the restrained warmth of those who have ' been through it.' Outside was no restraint, and the progress down Granby Street was a veritable triumphal procession. The men cheered, the women waved handkerchiefs and shouted shrill greetings, and every window *en route* was alive with welcoming faces. Many were the recognitions of old comrades, especially among the demobilized men, who had assembled in good force to witness the official return of their old unit. The soldiers were pelted with confetti and good wishes, and the police on duty had hard work to keep the road clear for the procession through the dense crowd which extended as far as Horsefair Street.

" At the Municipal Buildings the men formed up in front of the main entrance, where Major Sergeantson, O.B.E. (Secretary of the Leicestershire Territorial Association), the Territorial veteran, Col. Sarson, and Major Evan Barlow, awaited the civic party. The Mayor, in his address of welcome, said : ' Officers, non-commissioned officers, and men of the "Tigers," I am exceedingly pleased to be in this position, and to have the opportunity of welcoming back from the fields of war this " Cadre " of The Leicestershire Regiment. I do so most heartily. The Leicestershire Regiment has always had a proud record. You have worthily maintained that record, and the deeds you have performed, when we read of them in the Press, have filled us with wonder and admiration. The gratitude of Leicester people—of all English people—is due to the Leicesters for the way in which they have conducted themselves. We in the good old town of Leicester have done our best to back you up. Not only have we subscribed towards carrying on this war to a successful end in which you have participated, but we have attended to your wounded who were sent home, and thousands of people have given their charitable efforts in the relief of suffering. We have had a quiet time industrially. No man has raised his voice or by action sought to hinder the work you have done so nobly and so well. Therefore it gives us great pleasure to welcome you. We know you are reduced in numbers, but your spirit has remained firm. There are many who went out with you who, alas, will never return. We mourn for them. Only last week I took part in a large joint meeting of the town and county at which a resolution was passed that a fitting memorial to those men should be raised. That is as it should be. I am sure the whole of Leicester will support that effort. I thank you on behalf of the town whose name you so nobly bear for the services you have so gallantly rendered.'

" The Mayor read the following telegram from the Duke of Rutland : ' Regret I cannot possibly be at Leicester when the Cadre of 1st Leicestershire Regiment arrives. Please offer to them all my most hearty greetings on their return home from the war in which they so greatly distinguished themselves. I bid them sincerely welcome.'

" Three hearty cheers were then given for the ' Tigers,' and three more for the Mayor.

" Col. Latham responded and thanked the Mayor for his kind words and the people of Leicester for the welcome which had been accorded the ' Cadre ' of the 1st Leicestershire Regiment, which he had had the honour to command in the field. He was delighted to have seen so many well known faces of men who had fought gallantly with the Battalion. These men no doubt were proud of having fought with their County Regiment in a just cause, and having assisted the Battalion in gaining a glorious finish to the war. The men in the ranks had no doubt borne the brunt of the war, and the manner in which they maintained their courage, their cheerfulness, and their discipline amidst dangers and difficulties, which could not be understood by any who had not been through them, had been marvellous, and they deserved the highest praise. He only hoped that now they would carry back to civil life the old maxim of the Army—*mutual support;* they could not get on without it. He took the opportunity of expressing sympathy with the relatives of those who had fallen whilst gallantly fighting with their Battalion, and also hoped that those men who were still suffering from wounds or sickness might soon be well enough to carry on their part in civil life. He also thanked those who had kindly looked after their interests and welfare, especially the proprietors of the local daily newspapers, which meant so much to the men, and also those who had made or purchased articles to assist them through the winter, and the committee that arranged the distribution.'

" The officers and men were entertained to tea at the Town Hall, and afterwards marched to Glen Parva, amid renewed scenes of enthusiasm, the Mayor and Mayoress, in their motor car, heading the procession down Aylestone Road.

" There was a heartiness and beautiful simplicity about the welcome extended to the ' Cadre ' of the 1st Leicestershire, yesterday, by the County Town, which was deeply appreciated by the officers and men. Perhaps the writer may be allowed to say a few words about the civic hospitality. The officers sat down to a cold collation in the ante-room of the Council Chamber, and were afterwards conducted over the Town Hall by their host and hostess. The non-commissioned officers' tea party in another part of the building was truly a remarkable one. All present wore one or more decorations; and all, with one exception, had been through the entire campaign. The men sat down to a good spread in the Police-muster room."

At this time the 3rd (Special Reserve) Battalion of the Regiment was at Sniggery Camp, Hightown, Liverpool, engaged, under command of Colonel C. H. D. Palmer, in carrying out its demobilization; and, on August 3rd, 1919, Lieutenant-Colonel E. L. Challenor, C.B., C.M.G., D.S.O., took over command of what was left of this Battalion, which was joined on August 11th by the Cadre from the Depot, and the 1st Battalion was then reformed from the Cadre and the remnants of the 3rd Battalion, its very first duty being to assist in keeping the peace in Liverpool, where serious trouble had broken out, described as follows in the *Annual Register* for this year : " On August 2nd and 3rd extensive rioting took place in Liverpool owing to the police strike, and considerable damage was done to property. The military were called out and bayonet charges were made, as a result of which the outbreak of anarchy was brought under control. Further disorganization was caused by the action of the tramwaymen in going on strike, while a similar course was considered by the dockers and railwaymen, who referred the question to their Executives."

For some little time past the Battalion had been under orders to proceed to Lichfield, there to be stationed, but these instructions were suddenly cancelled, and on January 17th, 1920, the Battalion was hurriedly sent over to Ireland, and, after disembarkation, was taken by rail to Athlone, where it was accommodated in Victoria Barracks and in the Workhouse.

During the preceding months the state of affairs in Ireland had been steadily growing from bad to worse, causing almost greater anxiety than had ever before been experienced in the history of that country. In the course of the winter of 1919-1920 there were numerous raids made by armed men on post offices all over the country, undertaken with the object of obtaining money; there were several murderous attacks upon the police and constabulary; and a reign of terror gradually became established in Ireland, where it was computed that from early in 1916 until the end of 1919 there had taken place no fewer than 18 murders, 77 armed attacks, numerous assaults upon policemen, soldiers and civilians, 20 raids made for the purpose of obtaining arms and ammunition, 70 incendiary fires and very many other offences, amounting in all to 1,529 criminal offences of this kind. It was confidently hoped that the Home Rule Bill, then about to be introduced in Parliament, would bring about what was with undue optimism described as " harmonious action between the Parliaments of Southern and Northern Ireland "; its reception, however, by the Nationalist party was the reverse of cordial, if not indeed fiercely antagonistic. One Irish paper denounced it as " a scheme for the plunder and partition of Ireland," and as " a betrayal of every principle that was ever professed regarding democracy and nationality!" In February and March, 1920, the state of Ireland grew worse rather than better; almost daily were fresh murders reported, and soldiers and policemen were attacked and even killed in all parts of the country.

The 1st Battalion The Leicestershire Regiment was afforded early experience of the hostility of a section of the people among whom they had been set down, when in February Lance-Corporal Markillie was severely wounded by a bomb thrown by Sinn Feiners into a railway carriage, the corporal eventually losing his arm by reason of the injuries received.

At Athlone the Battalion formed part of the 13th Infantry Brigade, commanded by Brigadier-General T. S. Lambert, C.B., C.M.G., of the 5th Division under Major-General Sir H. S. Jeudwine, K.C.B.

On March 29th " D " Company was sent to Galway on detachment, but rejoined Headquarters in July, in which month " C " Company went on detachment to Roscommon.

The condition of affairs during June became even worse than before; early in that month a very daring raid was carried out in Dublin by a band of armed men nearly one hundred strong; the same night attempts were made to capture three police barracks, two in King's County and a third in County Tipperary; while fresh difficulties were caused by the refusal of Irish railwaymen to handle munitions, and others declined to take charge of a train carrying a party of thirty soldiers. Then at the end of the month three Army officers of high rank were kidnapped while out fishing, one of the three being seriously wounded when trying to escape. In July disorders continued to be rampant, murderous tactics were adopted by adherents of Sinn Fein, and several particularly brutal outrages were perpetrated in the south of Ireland, particularly in the Cork district; several attempts were also made to induce British soldiers to sell their arms and ammunition; and the roads in the vicinity of British garrisons were repeatedly found to have had trenches dug across them. In September the " Curfew Order " was brought into force at Athlone, under which no civilian was permitted to be out of doors between 11 p.m. and 5 a.m.

In October, " B " Company relieved " C " Company at Roscommon, and in the same month a party of the Battalion was ambushed near Lough Rea, when Lieutenant St. J. Hodson and Private Bradley were wounded. In this affair Lance-Corporal H. R. Cantrill, of The Leicestershire Regiment, behaved with special gallantry, and the announcement of its recognition appeared in the *London Gazette* of February 18th, 1921, where we read :—

" The King has been graciously pleased to approve of the award of the Medal of the Military Division of the Most Excellent Order of the British Empire to the undermentioned, in recognition of gallant conduct in the performance of military duties:—

" To be dated 17th January, 1921.

" The Leicestershire Regiment.

" No. 4850180 Lance-Corporal Herbert Roger Cantrill."

Early in December, 1920, Martial Law was proclaimed in the following districts :—

The County of Cork (East Riding and West Riding),

The County of the City of Cork,

The County of Tipperary (North Riding and South Riding),

The County of Limerick,

The County of the City of Limerick,

The County of Kerry;

while " the generals or other officers " commanding the infantry brigades stationed in these districts were appointed Military Governors, the proclamation ending on the somewhat belated note that " The Forces of the Crown are hereby declared to be on active service " ! The effect of the proclamation of Martial Law was for a time good; certain of the more troubled districts showed signs of quieting down, many of the officers of the Irish Republican Army were said to be " on the run," and there was a general reluctance to fill their places. The military continued to search all suspected houses and possible hiding-places, and considerable stores of ammunition and explosives were found in small quantities all over the country.

Outrages of all kinds continued during the early half of 1921; thus in March, Private Redding was wounded in an ambush at Drumcondra; in April, Lance-Corporal Freakley was ambushed and wounded at Hunston House; while in June there was a succession of such ambushes, Corporal Jaggar and Private Marks being wounded at Roscommon, while Mrs. Challenor, the wife of the Commanding Officer of the Battalion, was ambushed and wounded outside Athlone. Brigadier-General T. S. Lambert was severely wounded on the same occasion and died that evening.

On June 22nd, 1921, His Majesty the King opened the Northern Ireland Parliament in Belfast and appealed to all Irishmen to combine together in the endeavour to secure peace; while later the Prime Minister invited the heads of the Government of Northern Ireland and the leaders of Sinn Fein to meet and discuss matters at a joint conference in London. An agreement as a basis of discussion was drawn up, and on July 11th a truce was proclaimed between the Supreme Government and Dail Eireann, all operations against the rebels coming to an end on that date; the truce was, however, not religiously observed by Sinn Fein, for in the same month Lance-Corporal Weldon of the Battalion was murdered in the streets of Castlerea.

The negotiations which now commenced were at least once broken off, and their continuation was on another occasion seriously imperilled by the injudicious utterances of de Valera; but finally, on December 6th, an agreement was arrived at and Southern Ireland was constituted a Free State under the British Crown.

On January 10th, 1922, " A " Company was sent to Naas on detachment, and "D" Company to the Curragh, while "B" Company rejoined Headquarters from Roscommon. Headquarters and " B " and " C " remained on at Athlone until March 1st, when, having handed over the barracks to the Free State troops, the two companies of the Battalion went to the Curragh, Headquarters proceeding first to Naas and a week later to the Curragh.

In May the married families of the Battalion were sent to Aldershot, and on the 15th of that month, the Curragh Camp having been made over to the troops of the Irish Free State, the Battalion was sent for a time to a camp at Phœnix Park, Dublin, and then on September 28th to the barracks of the Royal Irish Constabulary in the city. By this time the British troops had commenced to evacuate Ireland, and on December 12th the 1st Leicestershire embarked for England at North Wall, Dublin, being one of the four last battalions of British troops to leave Southern Ireland.

Aldershot was reached on December 18th, when the Battalion marched into and occupied Badajos Barracks.

On June 18th, 1923, His Majesty the King visited Aldershot, when he was received by a Guard of Honour furnished by the Battalion; and on August 3rd Lieutenant-Colonel F. H. Edwards, D.S.O., M.C., assumed command of the 1st Battalion, vice Lieutenant-Colonel E. L. Challenor, C.B., C.M.G., C.B.E., D.S.O., whose period of command had now come to a close.

In February, 1924, notification appeared in Army Orders that the Battalion would move to Egypt during the trooping season of 1924-25, and on January 6th, 1925, it embarked at Southampton in the hired transport City of Marseilles, reached Port Said on the 16th of the same month, and proceeded to camp at Moascar, near Ismailia, sending " D " Company to Cyprus on detachment a few days later. By the middle of October the bulk of the Battalion was concentrated at Alexandria, in Mustapha Barracks, " D " Company rejoining in December from Cyprus.

H

While quartered in Egypt the Battalion won the following sporting events :
The Officers' team won the Alexandria Junior Polo Cup.

The Battalion won the Command Rugby Football Cup.

In October, 1927, the Battalion took second place at the Command Rifle meeting, winning 15 Cups and 29 Medals in Individual and Team Events.

In July, 1927, the Battalion was placed under orders for service in India, on August 2nd Lieutenant-Colonel Edwards' command came to an end, and on October 18th Lieutenant-Colonel C. S. Davies, C.M.G., D.S.O., assumed command of the 1st Battalion The Leicestershire Regiment in his place.

It was not, however, until November 16th that the Battalion, on relief by the 1st Bn. Durham Light Infantry, embarked at Alexandria, for India, reaching Bombay on the 28th of the same month and proceeding thence by rail to Kamptee, where it arrived on November 30th and took the place of the 1st Bn. Wiltshire Regiment in Argaum Barracks.

THE 2nd BATTALION

2ND BATTALION

CHAPTER I.

1914

BATTLE OF LA BASSÉE—BATTLE OF FESTUBERT.

AT the time when the Great War broke out there were no fewer than 52 battalions of British infantry quartered in India and Burma, and of these 17 were stationed in Bengal, 14 in the Punjab, 12 in Bombay, 6 in Madras and 3 in Burma, and, as has been said in an earlier chapter, the immediate anxiety of the War Councils held in London when war seemed imminent was to bring home as expeditiously as possible all the British portion of the Indian garrison that could be spared, replacing it by units of the Territorial Force which were now asked to volunteer for Indian service.

Before the end of September ten battalions of British infantry had left India, some of these proceeding direct to France with the two divisions of the Indian Army Corps, others voyaging to England to join those divisions which were being organized at home; by the end of the year 1914 fifteen more British battalions had sailed for other theatres of the world war; and by the beginning of the year 1915 there were rather less than a dozen British infantry battalions remaining in India. Actually, as the war went on the following denudations of the British Establishment in India took place :—

> 7 Cavalry Regiments out of 9 were sent overseas;
> 44 Infantry Battalions out of 52 were sent overseas;
> 43 Batteries out of 56 were sent overseas;

while in the place of these there were received from England 29 batteries of Territorial artillery and 35 battalions of Territorial infantry; but before these arrived in the country the British garrison of India had been reduced by 15,000 men.

The Indian portion of the normal garrison was also heavily drawn upon, for 20 out of 39 regiments of Indian cavalry and 98 out of 138 infantry battalions were sent overseas during the progress of the war.

By the end of 1914 six expeditionary forces had been dispatched overseas (exclusive of the operations against German Tsingtao in North China), comprising the following formations :—

> 3 Infantry Divisions,
> 8 Infantry Brigades,

1 Mixed force, including 3 Infantry Battalions,
2 Cavalry Divisions,
1 Cavalry Brigade,

with their full complements of attached troops, administrative services and reinforcements, as well as 4 field artillery brigades in excess of the normal Indian allotment.

" In addition, 32 Regular British infantry battalions and the bulk of the Regular horse, field and heavy batteries were sent to England.

" By the early spring of 1915 two more infantry brigades were dispatched from India to form, with a brigade already overseas, a new division, and also another cavalry brigade, thus bringing India's total initial effort up to :—

2 Indian Army Corps,
7 Infantry Brigades,
1 Mixed force, including 3 Infantry Battalions,
2 Cavalry Divisions,
2 Cavalry Brigades,

plus corps, divisional, attached troops, administrative services and reinforcements."*

It was at eleven o'clock on the morning of August 9th, 1914, that a telegram from the Brigade Major, Bareilly Brigade, reached the Headquarters of the 2nd Battalion The Leicestershire Regiment at Ranikhet—" Mobilize War 7th Division." The necessary orders were at once issued, " C " Company at Delhi was directed to rejoin with all possible dispatch, the Battalion was medically inspected, bayonets were sharpened and the boots of all ranks were hobnailed.

" C " Company was relieved at Delhi by a company of the 3rd Battalion King's Royal Rifles from Meerut, and by the evening of the 11th the Battalion, completed for service so far as was possible at its peace station, was ready to leave Ranikhet for the plains, *en route* to the port of embarkation.

Next day, the 12th, the Battalion marched out of Ranikhet and started on its 52-mile march to railhead, and, moving by Ratighat, Bhowali and Jeolikote, Kathgodam was reached on the 15th; here the Battalion was entrained by wings, and arrived at Bareilly at 5 and 6 p.m. the same day. There was, however, still to be some delay before any further and final move was to take place, and the opportunity may here be taken of describing briefly the nature and composition of the contingent which India was to send to the European theatre of war.

India's contribution then consisted primarily of two divisions, later increased to an Army Corps with the necessary additional troops and staff, and the divisions selected were those the headquarters of which were at Lahore and Meerut. Each division was composed of three brigades and each of these contained four infantry battalions—one British and three Indian. The Meerut Division, to which the 2nd Battalion The Leicestershire Regiment belonged,

* " India's Contribution to the Great War," pp. 76, 77.

had been known in India as the 7th Division, while the brigade of which it formed part was the 20th, but in order, no doubt, to avoid any possible confusion with the divisions and brigades of the British Expeditionary Force bearing the same numbers, it was decided that the Indian units should be known for the future, not by numbers, but by the names of their headquarters in India. Thus the 2nd Battalion The Leicestershire Regiment now belonged to the Garhwal Brigade of the Meerut Division, this last being composed as under :—

Meerut Division—Commander, Lieutenant-General C. A. Anderson, C.B.
Dehra Dun Brigade—Brigadier-General C. E. Johnson.
1st Battalion The Seaforth Highlanders,
1st Battalion 9th Gurkha Rifles,
2nd Battalion 2nd Gurkha Rifles,
6th Jat Light Infantry.

Garhwal Brigade—Major-General H. D'U. Keary, C.B., D.S.O.
2nd Battalion The Leicestershire Regiment,
2nd Battalion 3rd Gurkha Rifles,
1st Battalion 39th Garhwal Rifles,
2nd Battalion 39th Garhwal Rifles.

Bareilly Brigade—Major-General F. Macbean, C.V.O., C.B.
2nd Battalion The Black Watch,
41st Dogras,
58th Rifles (Frontier Force),
2nd Battalion 8th Gurkha Rifles.

The Indian Army Corps was completed by four brigades of Royal Field Artillery, one heavy battery, a regiment of Indian cavalry, two companies Royal Engineers, with an Indian infantry battalion per division, while the Army Corps Commander was Lieutenant-General Sir James Willcocks.

There was, however, to be some considerable delay before the units composing the Indian Army Corps were sufficiently equipped with all the many items considered necessary for active service in a European theatre of war; and actually, though the 2nd Battalion The Leicestershire Regiment had quitted its peace station in the hills at only 69 hours' notice and had arrived at Brigade Headquarters in the plains only four days later, and though all the necessary requisitions had at once been sent in to the responsible Ordnance and Clothing authorities in India, it took exactly five weeks to get the Battalion on board ship; so that had it for any reason been necessary to expedite embarkation the Battalion must have set out on its voyage to France no more than partially equipped.

It was not until September 3rd that the Battalion received telegraphic orders to leave Bareilly for Karachi, the port selected for embarkation, on the 5th, and early on the morning of that day it left in two trains, arriving in Karachi on the morning of the 8th and being quartered for a week in the Rest Camp.

Then at long last, at 10 a.m. on September 15th, Headquarters and " C " and " D " Companies embarked in the *Devanha*, strength 10 officers and 437

other ranks, while exactly twenty-four hours later " A " and " B " Companies—
9 officers and 417 non-commissioned officers and men—were put on board the
Elephanta, the whole then sailing under escort on the 21st.   The following were
the officers accompanying the Battalion : Lieutenant-Colonel C. G. Blackader,
D.S.O.; Majors H. Gordon and R. N. Knatchbull, D.S.O.; Captains H. A.
Grant, F. H. Romilly, L. B. C. Tristram, F. Latham (Adjutant), and D. L.
Weir; Lieutenants R. Le Fanu, M. K. Wardle, C. Chudleigh, R. H. Ames,
G. P. de A. G. Tunks and R. A. N. Lowther; Second-Lieutenants T. R.
Grylls, G. A. Quayle, M. W. Seton-Browne, H. M. Raleigh and E. L.
Wateridge, with Lieutenant and Quartermaster H. C. Brodie.

Major J. R. A. H. Paul, D.S.O., and Second-Lieutenant E. H.
Pakenham were left sick in India, while Second-Lieutenant G. C. Dickinson
remained behind in charge of details.

The voyage westward was prosecuted without the slightest interruption or
mishap—indeed, it may here be stated that none of the transports, conveying
British troops to the different seats of war from every part of the world, were in
any way interfered with by the German naval forces.   Port Said was reached
on October 4th, and on the 12th the 2nd Battalion The Leicestershire Regiment
disembarked at Marseilles and moved to La Valentine Camp.

With the arrival in France of the Meerut Division the Indian Army Corps
was tolerably complete; two brigades of the Lahore Division had disembarked
at Marseilles by the end of September, Lieutenant-General Sir James Willcocks
arriving much about the same time with the Corps Staff; one infantry brigade
of the Lahore Division had been detained in Egypt to reinforce the garrison and
to guard the Canal pending the arrival of Territorial troops.   By October 11th
the Meerut Division was also disembarking, to be followed very shortly by the
Indian Cavalry Corps; but it was not until practically the end of November
that the whole Corps was complete in France, while " the situation was such
when the Lahore Division arrived, that several battalions were at once taken
from their brigades and thrown in anyhow with cavalry and infantry to help
stem the German rush between Ypres and La Bassée."*

Something over a week did the Battalion remain at Marseilles, moving on to
Orleans on the 21st, and here the Indian divisions were equipped with mechanical
and horse transport, moving on thence on October 26th to Lillers and on the
28th to Calonne, the Battalion relieving the 3rd Battalion Worcestershire
Regiment in the trenches up in the firing line.

By this date the Indian Corps—*less* the Sirhind Brigade remaining temporarily in Egypt, and *plus* certain troops lent from the British Expeditionary
Force—had taken over the front previously held by the II. Army Corps; this
was about eight miles in length from north of Givenchy on the right, passing
east of Festubert and Richebourg L'Avoué, west of Neuve Chapelle, past
Mauquissart and then bending round to Rouges Bancs on the left.   The Meerut
Division held the southern portion of the trenches in the following order,

---

* Willcocks, " With the Indians in France," p. 24.

commencing from Givenchy—Bareilly Brigade—Garhwal Brigade—Dehra Dun Brigade, with the Jullundur Brigade of the Lahore Division on the left.

In the sector now taken over by the 2nd Battalion The Leicestershire Regiment, the trenches had been much battered by German high explosive shells, and considerable work was required to put them into anything approaching a satisfactory state of repair; there was no adequate head cover against enemy fire or even against the weather, while in the front, so far as the eye could reach, there stretched a sea of mud over which rapid movement was impossible, and the heavy rain which set in on the night of October 29th converted the fire trenches into ditches full of mud and the communication trenches into streams of filthy water; it was through bogs, ditches and darkness that the relieving troops tramped to their first battle positions.

Here the greater part of the 2nd Battalion remained upwards of three weeks, doing what they could, with the insufficient materials at command, to repair the trenches and keep them in tolerable order, making raids upon the enemy in their front and repelling such as were by the Germans directed against them—always under heavy shell fire, to which, at that period of the war, our guns were quite unable to make any really effective reply.

Captain L. B. C. Tristram was killed the very first night in the trenches.

On the night of November 17th-18th "B" and "C" Companies were relieved by two companies of the 1st Seaforth Highlanders of the Dehra Dun Brigade, but it was not until some days later—on the evening of November 22nd—that the 1st Manchesters replaced "A" and "D" Companies of The Leicestershire Regiment in the trenches, when the whole Battalion was concentrated in billets at La Couture.

During this tour in the trenches, taking part in the operations connected with the Battle of La Bassée, the casualties in the Battalion had amounted to Lieutenant E. L. Wateridge and 14 non-commissioned officers and men killed, Lieutenants R. Le Fanu and M. K. Wardle and 73 other ranks wounded.

During the same period a very gallant action, performed on November 20th by No. 9139 Private Garton of the Regiment, was brought to notice in the following letter from Lieutenant B. H. Waller, 107th Pioneers, of the Divisional Troops of the Meerut Division :—

" SIR,

" *I beg to bring to your good notice the following incident which occurred this morning about 9.30 a.m. A mortar bomb from the German trenches dropped right into a portion of the trench occupied by the 107th Pioneers and exploded, throwing one man right out of the trench on to the rampart. This was unnoticed by the men of the section, who were at the moment working on a communication trench 20 yards behind. But one of the men of the Leicesters saw the occurrence. He ran down and reported. I went up the trench with him and heard the man moaning the other side. The man of the Leicesters was No. 9139 Pte. Garton, ' D ' Company. Pte. Garton said, ' I am going for him,' jumped out of the trench and dragged the man in. This all took place within*

70 yards of the enemy's trenches and was done so quickly that the enemy had no time to fire.   I consider it a brave act.

(Sd.)   " B. H. Waller, *Lt.*,

" 107th *Pioneers.*"

" 20.11.14.

This was followed by the letters here given :—

" *I concur in considering this act a meritorious one, as it was not incumbent on Pte. Garton to retrieve this wounded man.   I desire to bring this act to your favourable notice.*

(Sd.)   " H. P. Keelan, *Major,*

" *Comdg. Half Bn.* 107th *Pioneers.*"

" *In Left Centre Trenches.*

" 20.11.14."

" '*To Brigade Major, Garhwal Brigade.*

" *I beg to forward the accompanying report from O.C. Half Bn.* 107th *Pioneers.   In my opinion the act of Pte. Garton was a brave one, when one considers that even a movement in our trenches brings down the fire of the enemy.   I recommend Pte. Garton,* *of the Battalion under my command, to the favourable notice of the G.O.C.*

(Sd.)   " C. G. Blackader, *Lt.-Col.,*

" *Comdg. 2nd Leicestershire Regiment.*"

The Battalion had, however, enjoyed the rest and comparative quiet of La Couture for something less than 24 hours, when at about 3.30 on the afternoon of November 23rd orders were received to move at once to the Headquarters of the Bareilly Brigade at Gorre.   This was reached two hours later, and here the Battalion was given fresh orders to move on and report to Brigadier-General R. M. Egerton, commanding the Ferozepore Brigade of the Indian Corps near Festubert.   The reason for these orders and the movements and fighting which followed on their receipt are stated as follows in " With the Indians in France," pp. 119 *et seq.:—*

" The Army Corps was now on the eve of its first considerable fight.   Signs were not wanting that the Germans meant to break into, or through, a portion of our line, and the fighting that followed was confined to the Corps alone. . . . . on this solitary occasion we had it all to ourselves, and although it was a purely defensive action the results were highly satisfactory. . . . . On this night, 22nd-23rd November, in accordance with orders, the Meerut Division was in process of relief by the Lahore Division, *plus* a portion of the Secunderabad Cavalry Brigade.   By the morning of the 23rd November the relief had been partially completed, the result being that five units of the Lahore Division and two battalions of the Meerut were now in the line. . . . . By 7.45 a.m. the O.C. Centre Section reported that the Germans had broken his line. . . . . Half an hour later General Macbean was informed that part of the 58th Rifles had also

* Private—then Lance-Corporal—Garton was awarded the D.C.M. in the *London Gazette* of February 18th, 1915.

been driven from their trenches, and this repeated retirement of our troops was rendering our hold precarious. . . . . By noon the situation appeared more serious, as the 34th Pioneers and 9th Bhopals had been forced from all their trenches, and this, added to the gap caused by portions of the 58th Rifles retiring, left a long line of front trenches in possession of the enemy."

It was in consequence of the above that the 2nd Battalion Leicestershire Regiment had been ordered up at such short notice, and on reporting to General Egerton, who was now in command of this portion of the Corps front, he launched from his right flank an attack composed of " B " and " C " Companies of the Regiment and two of the 107th Pioneers. The two companies of the Battalion were those which had been longest at rest, and the following is an account by Major H. Gordon of the part which they played in this attack.

" About 4 p.m. 24th November I took ' B ' and ' C ' Companies up the communicating trench to a point about 70 yards from the part of the fire trench occupied by the Germans; this fire trench was in prolongation of the trench held by the 107th Pioneers. This Regiment had been sent up to attack and recapture the part of the trench held by the enemy—this was the right of the German trench. Unknown to us, the 1st Bn. 39th Garhwalis had been sent to attack the left, and subsequently it appeared they entered the left part of the trench. At about 5 p.m. Brig.-General Egerton ordered one company 2nd Leicestershire Regiment to attack the trench in flank and one company 107th Pioneers to extend to our left, while one company of each regiment was to be in reserve. I ordered ' B ' Company to lead and put ' C ' Company in support. ' B ' Company got out in good order and gained their position by moving along a natural ditch parallel to and about 15 yards in rear of the fire trench. The company of Pioneers which was to form on our left, also got into position, but when the advance began, instead of prolonging to our left, the Pioneers closed in on ' B ' Company of ours and rather hampered their movements.

" Captain H. A. Grant led his men into the enemy's trench, and here he and Second-Lieutenant M. W. Seton-Browne were killed.

" The enemy retired and we killed a number of them in their retirement. The Officer Commanding the Pioneer Company came back and reported that his men were unable to advance on account of heavy losses. I went forward and separated our men from the Pioneers and brought them along to where the leading men of ' B ' Company had established themselves in the enemy's trench. This took place about 6 a.m. [on the 25th] and by 7 a.m. I had got away all the wounded. Subsequently it transpired that the 1st/39th Garhwalis actually joined up to the part of the trench captured by us at about 6.30 a.m. At 8.30 a.m. I left Festubert with the two companies to proceed to billets at Gorre, where we came under shrapnel fire."

Of Major Gordon's attack General Willcocks wrote that " the Leicesters effected a lodgment in the enemy's trenches, but were hard pressed to retain it owing to heavy bombing, and the 107th Pioneers were repulsed, but their combined action without doubt considerably disconcerted the Germans and assisted the 39th Garhwalis who were advancing up the hostile trenches from the opposite direction." And later, specially mentioning The Leicestershire Regiment, he says : " The Leicesters in their counter-attack with the 107th Pioneers lost Captain H. Grant, killed whilst leading his company in the charge, and Second-Lieutenant M. Seton-Browne was also killed at the head of his platoon just as he had reached the enemy trench. No. 8224 Lance-Corporal G. Gray, Sergeant P. Foister and three men were brought to notice for their fine example. The latter received the D.C.M. Major H. Gordon was in command of the attack and received the D.S.O. Throughout the time the Leicesters served with me in France this splendid corps shared the brunt of every fight in which their Brigade was engaged. Its sterling grit was recognized by none more than the Indian soldiers."

The German attack was made by the 112th Infantry Regiment of the 29th Division of the XIV. Army Corps, supported by the 170th Infantry Regiment.

From Gorre the Battalion went back to its former billets at La Couture the same afternoon, but only for a very brief period of rest, since in the middle of the 28th a return was made to the trenches for another spell of 48 hours, the Battalion relieving the 2nd/39th Garhwalis in the trenches east of Festubert, where Lieutenant-Colonel Blackader assumed charge of the centre section, having under his command 500 of his own Battalion, 300 of the 58th Rifles, 230 of the 9th Bhopals and 100 men of the 34th Pioneers. Here " A," " B " and " D " and half " C " Company were in the firing line, with the remainder of " C " Company in rear in support.

During the 48 hours that this tour of the trenches lasted, the enemy was fairly active, sniping and bombing being frequent, particularly on that portion of the Battalion front held by " D " Company; on relief by the 1st Battalion 39th Garhwalis on the evening of the 30th The Leicestershire Regiment returned to billets at La Couture. The Battalion can hardly have more than reached here when it was announced that His Majesty the King had arrived to inspect his armies in France, and that he would see representatives of the different units composing the Indian Corps at 9 a.m. on December 1st at Locon.

There was little or no time for " cleaning up," and when " A " Company, made up to 100 strong by men from " D " Company, under Major R. N. Knatchbull, with Lieutenants C. A. E. Chudleigh and R. A. N. Lowther, paraded before His Majesty at Locon, all ranks presented an appearance which the King graciously—and appropriately—described as " looking war-worn " ! His Majesty spoke to several of the officers and other ranks, asking questions about work and conditions of life in the trenches, and that the King appreciated what he had been able to see of detachments of the Indian Corps is evident from a speech made later to the 2nd Battalion The Leicestershire Regiment by General Sir James Willcocks, who said :—

" I have been commanded by the King to express His Majesty's keen appreciation of the services rendered by the Battalion during the war, and of the fine work which they have done. His Majesty hopes that at the conclusion of the war he may have an early opportunity of seeing the Regiment again."

During the next fortnight or so the Battalion had another tour of trench duty, but of this there is nothing very special to record; on the 17th, however, the 2nd Battalion had only just relieved the 2nd Battalion 3rd Gurkhas in the trench line in front of the Rue des Berceaux, when this relief was ordered to be cancelled and The Leicestershire Regiment to be released, as it was required to take part in an attack upon a portion of the German trenches; this, and similar enterprises undertaken at this time, was in pursuance of orders lately issued by Sir John French that all corps were to make frequent attacks upon the enemy, taking all possible measures to consolidate and extend every success achieved.

On this date—December 18th—the Indian Corps was thus distributed: " The French on our right had their extreme left on the Bethune—La Bassée road. From this road the canal was held by the Connaught Rangers of the Ferozepore Brigade, and the remainder of this brigade held the trenches as far east as Givenchy. The Sirhind Brigade was on their left and extended the line, keeping parallel to the Festubert Road, up to within half a mile of the cross-roads at La Quinque Rue. This completed the front of the Lahore Division; and the Meerut Division, with the Seaforth Highlanders of the Dehra Dun Brigade on their extreme right, was distributed as follows: remainder of this brigade in position as far as the cross-roads of the Rue du Bois, the line passing through what was commonly then known as ' The Orchard.' The Garhwal Brigade was on the left of the Corps, and held trenches as far as the cross-roads south of Neuve Chapelle. . . . . The portion of German trench to be attacked by the Lahore Division was just opposite the junction of the Ferozepore and Sirhind Brigades, and the attacking troops consisted of one battalion from each brigade. The Meerut Division had selected as its objective the German trenches near ' The Orchard ' and opposite the 6th Jats of the Dehra Dun Brigade. The attacking troops consisted of one and a half battalions of the Garhwal Brigade.''*

These last-named attacking troops consisted of the 2nd Battalion The Leicestershire Regiment, a half battalion of the 2nd/3rd Gurkhas, one company of the 107th Pioneers and a party of Sappers and Miners; all were under the command of Lieutenant-Colonel C. G. Blackader, and we can hardly do better than set down the story of the attack as recorded by him in the Battalion War Diary.

" The Battalion, on relief from the trenches, rendezvoused at Battalion Headquarters, and at 12.30 a.m. on the 19th December proceeded to the Salient, known regimentally as ' " C " Company's Salient.' The plan was as follows :—

" A bombing party proceeded to the barricade up the ditch leading to the enemy, and relieved the 6th Jats. One company was to deploy from the ditch to the right outside the wire in front of our parapet and lie down; another company was to do the same on the left. As soon as the advance commenced, the remaining two companies were to do the same—one on each side of the ditch—and advance in support. At 3.15 a.m. the deployment was completed in absolute silence, and at 3.30 the advance commenced. The companies had

* " With the Indians in France," pp. 149, 150.

three platoons in the front line and one in support, the latter accompanied by a bombing party.

" As soon as the parties came up in line with the bombing party in the ditch, the latter jumped over the barricade, cut the wire, advanced to the enemy's barricade and bombed it. The left company had barely gone twenty yards when a Maxim opened on their right, then twenty more yards and they were stopped by a hedge with barbed wire in the ditch; this caused a few minutes' delay, but they got through and immediately a second Maxim opened. The Company then entered the trench under the fire of the two Maxims and captured it and the guns. Only one German was found in the trench, the rest having escaped during the delay at the hedge and ditch. This trench was very deep and narrow and about 60 yards long. The O.C. Company—Captain Romilly— concluded that there must be another trench in rear, and he accordingly got his men out of the trench and lined them up for a second advance. A Maxim gun immediately opened on his right and another behind this one and to his left. He determined to go for the latter and advanced on it, but got into the ditch in which it had been only to find it empty. The Company was now behind the Maxim that had opened on the right, and Captain Romilly reformed his Company to attack this. At this moment our batteries opened fire and shells commenced bursting over the Company and the enemy's trenches, when Captain Romilly, thinking he had gone too far, decided to return to the first German trench which he had taken; this he found occupied by the supporting company.

" Dawn was now breaking, so this trench was put into a state of defence, as also the natural ditch in front of it for a distance of some 200 yards.

" The company on the right had missed the first German trench in its advance, as it bore too much to its right. On passing this trench it was met by heavy Maxim and rifle fire, but all rushed forward and captured the trench, about 100 yards in length. This trench bore round to the right, and they advanced along it with the bombing party in front; it led into one of the enemy's main trenches, and when within 20 yards of it the whole of the bombing party, 8 in number, was put out of action—all except one. They also were met by a heavy enfilade rifle fire. The O.C. Company decided to erect a barricade at once, and this was accomplished under heavy rifle fire and hard bombing by the enemy. The trench was put into a state of defence. The company in support moved forward and reinforced this company, and I also sent a company of the 2nd/3rd Gurkhas with the same purpose. I regret I have not been able to find out what happened to this company under Major Dundas, but it evidently reinforced the Half Battalion 2nd/3rd Gurkha Rifles in reserve at daylight; nor is it possible to say what happened to the supporting company on the right, as Major Knatchbull was wounded, and Lieutenant Tooley missing, but it eventually joined up with the leading company.*

" Stock was taken of the position as soon as it was light enough. The Pioneer Company improved the communication trench, and as it could be

* What happened to Major Dundas' men and the part they played at this time and later in the action is recorded on p. 151 of General Willcocks' book.

seen that a main enemy trench flanked its right, I ordered it to be made into a fire trench as well and to be traversed. This work was excellently done by the Company, and they were of the greatest assistance.

"The captured trench on the right was also not only enfiladed by this trench, but commanded by it; there were no traverses in it, and, being very narrow, it was very hard to work in. It was not long before the enemy started on it with heavy bombs from mortars, and, bringing a Maxim up the trench, blew the barricade down, and we were steadily pushed back along it until finally we only held 30 yards of it. Captain Bamberger, R.E., was killed while gallantly directing the erection of the barricade. At the same time the two Maxims opened in front with the object of enfilading the communication trench, and the parapet had to be built up again and again to prevent this. The conclusion was now being forced upon me that, unless an attack was initiated on the right and the enemy's trench in that direction held, the position was untenable, and I reported accordingly, with the result that is already known. The retirement was well carried out and without loss. Finally, the net profits were 2 Maxim guns,* 4 prisoners, and I personally saw 5 dead Germans, but my officers report many more than this wounded and I consider more were killed. One of the killed was an officer, but it was impossible to get to him."

General Willcocks states that the following were brought to special notice during these operations: "Colonel Blackader, who led his Battalion and withdrew it skilfully; Major Knatchbull, Captain Romilly and Lieutenant Tooley, all of the Leicesters; No. 6725 Private Buckingham, for great gallantry [and it is pleasant to record that this brave soldier later in the war won the V.C.]; Sergeant Sutherland, Lance-Corporal Brake and Pte. Crisp; and if all the names of other brave Leicester officers and men were recorded here and whenever the Battalion was engaged, they would fill many pages."

The following message was received by Major-General Anderson from the Indian Army Corps Commander:—

"*G.O.C. Meerut Division.*

"*I congratulate you on the good work done last night, which shows what can be done by enterprise and care. Please send my hearty congratulations to Major-General Keary, the Leicesters and the 2nd/3rd Gurkhas for their gallant behaviour.*"

In forwarding the above message to the units concerned, General Anderson wrote:—

"*It gives me great pleasure to forward this appreciative message of the Corps Commander as regards the regiments mentioned. I feel sure that further information will show how well and ably the other units engaged supported the attack, the success of which is due to the gallantry of our officers and men and to the fact that the details of the attack were arranged after obtaining the valuable advice of yourself and the Commanding Officers of the units entrusted with its execution.*

"*To the G.O.C. Garhwal Brigade.*"

I 2   * These two Maxim guns are now outside the Officers' Mess of the 2nd Battalion.

The Meerut Division had now been relieved in the front line by troops of the I. Army Corps, and remained at the disposal of that Corps for a few days longer until a new alignment had been taken up, but was not called upon to make any further effort for the present.   For the few days that remained of this, the opening year of the war, the 2nd Battalion The Leicestershire Regiment had experience of several different billets, first at Richebourg St. Vaast, then at Lestrem, then at Robecq, and finally at Ecquedecques, where, on January 4th, 1915, the Battalion was inspected by General Sir James Willcocks, the Indian Army Corps Commander, who addressed officers and men as follows :—

" *Second Leicestershire Regiment.*

" *I am very glad to inspect you here to-day, and I heartily congratulate you on your invariable good work throughout the campaign.   Both in fighting and in discipline you have distinguished yourselves, and no other regiment has done better than you.   The Honours List which will shortly appear will contain the names of many of you, and a further List will be published later which deals with the battle after the 17th December.   Your Commanding Officer, Colonel Blackader, has been given the command of a Brigade, and from that you know that the Regiment has done well in everything.*"

Then on January 7th the Battalion was inspected by Field-Marshal Sir John French, the Commander-in-Chief of the British Expeditionary Force, who spoke as follows :—

" *Second Leicestershire Regiment.*

" *It gives me the greatest pleasure to inspect you here to-day and to see such a fine body of men.   I have heard of your gallantry with great satisfaction and I have heard nothing but good reports of your work.   You are a Regiment with fine traditions.   You have not only worthily maintained these, but you have added fresh lustre to them.   I wish personally to thank you for your good work, and I am very grateful to you.   I feel sure that I can depend upon you in the future as I have done in the past, and I am certain that you will gain still further honours until the campaign is completely finished.*"

Certain changes had now been made in the commands within the Indian Corps, Major-General Keary being promoted to the command of the Lahore Division, while Lieutenant-Colonel Blackader took his place at the head of the Garhwal Brigade.   Major-General Keary bade farewell to the Battalion in the following words :—

" *Officers, Non-Commissioned Officers and men of the 2nd Leicestershire.*

" *I am very sorry to be saying good-bye to you to-day.   It has been a great pleasure as well as a great honour to have had you under my command, and I cannot speak too highly of the work you have done.   Personally I am very grateful to you, as I feel it is in a great part owing to your good work that I have been placed in another and higher position in the Army Corps. I am very glad that your Commanding Officer has been appointed your Brigadier in my place, and I feel certain that you will continue to do as well as you have done under me. Though I am no longer in command of you, I shall not be far off, and I shall always take the greatest interest in your doings and in your welfare.*

" I wish good-bye to all of you."

Lieutenant-Colonel Blackader was succeeded in command of the Battalion by Major H. Gordon, D.S.O.

I

CHAPTER II.

1915

THE BATTLE OF NEUVE CHAPELLE.

THE months of January and February, 1915, went by without the occurrence of any events of special importance on the front guarded by the Indian Army Corps, but while the troops were not very actively engaged during this period, every opportunity was taken of filling up gaps—some 79 non-commissioned officers and men arriving as reinforcements for the 2nd Battalion The Leicestershire Regiment. Then also the troops were exercised in route-marching whenever " at rest " in rear, for it was realized that the constant soaking that all had undergone while on duty in the trenches and the comparatively inactive lives they had led, might have caused their marching powers to deteriorate and that their efficiency might be found to be impaired should at any time a prolonged advance become necessary. Further, every opportunity was taken of exercising all ranks in the handling and tactical use of trench mortars, rifle grenades and bombs—indeed, of all the weapons employed in the new warfare.

During these two opening months of the year heavy rain fell, accompanied by violent wind storms with falls of snow, the whole country became a wilderness of mud, and offensive operations on any large scale were impossible for either side; casualties, however, continued to mount up, and by the beginning of February the losses in the Indian Army Corps totalled 1,429 killed, 5,989 wounded and 2,335 missing, leaving the fighting strength of the Corps at about the same date at 20,736 rifles, 880 sabres, 114 guns and 4,000 artillery personnel.*

At the beginning of March the following was the general distribution of the troops along the northern portion of the line held by the Allies. The line from Dixmude southwards to the apex of the Ypres Salient was held by French troops with some British cavalry; to the South of these was the V. Corps, under General Plumer, in touch with whom was the II. Corps. The III. Corps, under General Pulteney, remained opposite Armentières, from where the line from Estaires to the west of Neuve Chapelle was held by the IV. Corps, under General Rawlinson. On his right the Indian Army Corps occupied the front as far as Givenchy, linking up here with the I. Corps under General Haig, who was in touch with the Tenth French Army across the La Bassée Canal.

* Merewether and Smith, " The Indian Corps in France," pp. 203, 204.

OFFICERS OF THE 2ND BATTALION THE LEICESTERSHIRE REGIMENT, JANUARY, 1915.

Back Row—2/Lt. W. Murphy. Lt. E. C. M. Cross. Lt. G. P. D'A. Tunks. Lt. T. R. Grylls. Lt. H. M. Raleigh. Lt. R. A. N. Lowther. Lt. A. S. MacIntyre.
Centre Row—M. St. Andre (Interpreter). Lt H. C. Brodie (Quartermaster). Capt. N. A. Morgan. Rev. R. Irwin (Chaplain). 2/Lt. V. Buxton. Capt. R. J. McIntyre.
2/Lt. H. L. Bayfield. 2/Lt. W. Picking. 2/Lt. J. Redwood. 2/Lt. Morgan (Interpreter).
Front Row—Capt. D. L. Weir. Capt. F. Latham (Adjutant). Major H. Gordon, D.S.O. (Comdg. Officer). Brig.-Gen. C. G. Blackader, D.S.O. (Comdg. Garhwal Brigade).
Capt. F Lewis. Capt. F. H. Romilly.

During the night of February 28th-March 1st a readjustment of the line of the Indian Army Corps had been carried out, and the front of the Corps then extended from Chocolat Menier Corner through Port Arthur to the La Bassée—Estaires road, and this was occupied by one brigade only of the Meerut Division, the other two brigades being in reserve, while the greater part of the Lahore Division was in Corps Reserve; but on March 7th the Lahore Division, moving forward, was concentrated in the area Calonne—Lestrem—Robecq, while the Meerut Division also moved forward so as to provide the necessary room and accommodation for the division in rear. Thus by March 9th the brigades of the Meerut Division were disposed as follows :—

Dehra Dun Brigade—La Couture.
Garhwal Brigade—Richebourg St. Vaast.
Bareilly Brigade—Holding the front line.

The strength of the Meerut Division in the first week in March amounted to 11,234 bayonets, and the Garhwal Brigade was composed as under :—

2nd Battalion The Leicestershire Regiment.
3rd Battalion The London Regiment (Territorial Force).
1st Battalion 39th Garhwal Rifles.
2nd Battalion 39th Garhwal Rifles.
2nd Battalion 3rd Gurkha Rifles.

The justification for and the object of the operations to be undertaken on this front early in March are described in Sir John French's despatch of April 5th, 1915, in which he wrote : " About the end of February many vital considerations induced me to believe that a vigorous offensive movement by the forces under my command should be planned and carried out at the earliest possible moment.

" Amongst the more important reasons which convinced me of the necessity were : the general aspect of the Allied situation throughout Europe, and particularly the marked success of the Russian Army in repelling the violent onslaughts of Marshal von Hindenburg; the apparent weakening of the enemy in my front, and the necessity for assisting our Russian allies to the utmost by holding as many hostile troops as possible in the Western theatre; the efforts to this end which were being made by the French forces at Arras and Champagne; and, perhaps the most weighty consideration of all, the need of fostering the offensive spirit in the troops under my command, after the trying and possibly enervating experiences which they had gone through of a severe winter in the trenches."

The part of the German line selected for the coming British offensive was that covering the village of Neuve Chapelle, in rear of which lay the Aubers Ridge and the city of Lille. Neuve Chapelle had already in the previous October been twice taken and lost by our troops, and since its final recapture by the enemy at the end of that month the British line had run well to the west of that village. The attack now projected was to be undertaken by the IV. and Indian Corps, the 8th Division of the former and the Meerut Division of the latter Corps supplying the assaulting troops.

On March 9th General Sir Douglas Haig, commanding the First Army, in which at this time the Indian Corps was included, issued the following order :—

" We are about to engage the enemy under very favourable conditions. Until now in the present campaign the British Army has, by its pluck and determination, gained victories against an enemy greatly superior both in men and guns. Reinforcements have made us stronger than the enemy in our front. Our guns are now both more numerous than the enemy's are, and also larger than any hitherto used by any army in the field. Our Flying Corps has driven the Germans from the air.

" On the Eastern Front and to the south of us, our Allies have made marked progress and caused enormous losses to the Germans, who are, moreover, harassed by internal troubles and shortage of supplies, so that there is little prospect at present of big reinforcements being sent against us here.

" In front of us we have only one German Corps, spread out on a front as large as that occupied by the whole of our First Army.

" We are now about to attack with about 48 battalions a locality in that front which is held by some three German battalions. It seems probable, also, that for the first day of the operations the Germans will not have more than four battalions available as reinforcements for the counter-attack. Quickness of movement is therefore of the first importance to enable us to forestall the enemy and thereby gain success without severe loss.

" At no time in the war has there been a more favourable moment for us, and I feel confident of success. The extent of that success must depend on the rapidity and determination with which we advance.

" Although fighting in France, let us remember that we are fighting to preserve the British Empire and to protect our homes against the organized savagery of the German Army. To ensure success, each one of us must play his part and fight like men for the Honour of Old England."

"The immediate objective was the enemy's trenches west of Neuve Chapelle, and the occupation of a line to the east of the diamond-shaped figure formed by the main road from Estaires to La Bassée, and the road by Fleurbaix to Armentières, and that which connects the two. In the northern angle of this diamond lies the village of Neuve Chapelle. The general object of the attack was to enable the IV. and Indian Corps to establish themselves on a more forward line to the east, the ultimate objective being the high ground on which are situated the villages of Aubers and Ligny-le-Grand, with the intention finally of cutting off that portion of the enemy's troops which held the line between Neuve Chapelle and La Bassée."*

The following extracts from the Operation Orders of Brigadier-General C. G. Blackader, commanding the Garhwal Brigade, give the general plan and objects of the attack :—

"The Indian and IV. Corps are to co-operate in an attack on Neuve Chapelle on the 10th March. The 8th Division is to attack from the IV. Corps front and the Meerut Division from that of the Indian Corps. The artillery of the

* The Indian Corps in France " p. 212.

two corps will bombard the area to be attacked for 35 minutes before the assault. This bombardment will commence at 7.30 a.m. and cease at 8.5 a.m., artillery fire continuing with increased fuse and range.

" The Garhwal Brigade (simultaneously with the 8th Division attack) will assault the enemy's trenches east of the Estaires—La Bassée road at 8.5 a.m., as follows, as detailed in Table A."

In this table the place of assembly of the 2nd Battalion The Leicestershire Regiment is given as " the trenches from Port Arthur Road Junction to 300 yards north-north-west along the La Bassée Road to the southern half of the front breastwork parallel to and 100 yards west of the Estaires—La Bassée Road," their onward route from the place of assembly being by Edward Road, Rue du Bois and Roomès Trench.

The objective of the Battalion was " the group of houses round the cross-roads at ' D,' on the Port Arthur—Neuve Chapelle Road; the limits of the zone of attack were—on the right, a line from the north-east exit of the Rue du Bois from Port Arthur, and on the left, the natural ditch running towards the enemy's lines from the Estaires—La Bassée road 300 yards from the Port Arthur cross-roads; finally, the line to be occupied and immediately consolidated was the road D—N at the crossing of the Rivière des Layes to O, and then to the road 100 yards north-east of the cross-roads at D inclusive."

Two machine guns were to accompany each assaulting battalion, which was also to be provided with 192 bombs; every man was to carry 150 rounds of ammunition, two sandbags, his emergency ration and the unexpended portion of the day's ration; while, in order to indicate to the artillery and to supporting units the points reached by the attacking troops, coloured flags (pink for flank battalions, light and dark blue for centre battalions) were directed to be placed on the British side of any enemy trenches or buildings captured.

In the attack by the Garhwal Brigade the 1st/39th Garhwal Rifles were on the right, the 2nd Leicestershire and 2nd/3rd Gurkha Rifles were on the right and left centre respectively, and the 2nd/39th Garhwal Rifles were on the left; the 3rd London Regiment was in support. Of the 2nd Leicestershire Regiment, " C " Company (Captain D. L. Weir) and " B " (Captain N. A. Morgan) were in the front line on right and left, with " D " and " A " Companies, under Lieutenant V. Buxton and Captain F. H. Romilly, in the same positions in support.

The following description of the ground may enable the reader to follow the course of the action with greater ease and clearness. " Eastwards from our front lay the village of Neuve Chapelle, in pre-war times a typical French townlet, with its centre street lined by estaminets, small shops and neat dwelling-houses, while on the outskirts were the villas of the better-to-do residents. The most prominent buildings were the white church on the left of the main street, the brewery in the south-east corner of the village, and a small château to the north-east of the church. The village was already in a half-ruined condition as the effect of the previous sanguinary fighting in October, 1914. . . . . Between our line and the village lay fields, intersected by deep ditches and cut up by hedges.

The going was terrible, as the recent heavy rains had converted the plough into holding bog. Further to the east, at a distance of about two miles south-west of Lille, commences a ridge which, running in a horse-shoe shape, connects the villages of Illies and Aubers, both of which were occupied by the enemy. Between the two villages is a plateau, the importance of which to us lay in the fact that its capture, while depriving the enemy of great advantages accruing from his possession of the high ground, would give us command of the approaches to the three great manufacturing centres of Lille, Roubaix and Tourcoing.

" Between Neuve Chapelle and the Aubers Ridge runs the stream known as the river des Layes, a tributary of the Lys, with a width of 6 to 10 feet, and a depth at that season of 3 to 4½ feet. The enemy had constructed a second line of defence along the eastern side of the stream, with strong bridge-heads. A large wood, consisting mainly of young trees with a thick undergrowth, called the Bois du Biez, lies to the southward of Neuve Chapelle."*

The night of March 9th-10th was intensely cold and some snow fell, but towards morning the weather conditions slightly improved and there was a mild frost which made the going rather better, and day broke on the 10th with mist and low-lying clouds. It had been confidently hoped that the attack would come upon the enemy as a complete surprise, but his patrols and aviators appear to have reported the British trenches as being packed with men, and very soon after 7 a.m. the German guns commenced a heavy bombardment of our trenches, " which caused a large number of casualties among the 2nd Leicesters. The 1st Battalion [39th Garhwal Rifles], who were also assembled at that spot, escaped with a few light shells, one of which did great damage, killing four signallers and destroying most of the Battalion telephones."†

To quote from the War Diary of the 2nd Battalion The Leicestershire Regiment :—

" 10th March. All in position by 5 a.m. At 7.30 a.m. the artillery bombardment commenced and at 7.45 ' C ' Company, followed by ' D,' moved up the communication trench to the northern portion of the eastern face of Port Arthur. At 8.5 a.m. ' B ' and ' C ' Companies advanced, each company having two platoons in the front line closely supported by the two other platoons in the second line. The advance was carried out at a steady double, the first line of enemy trenches was carried, and the advance was continued over several other enemy trenches, reaching the final objective at about 8.30. [This was the line P.O. to the road.] ' B ' Company occupied that portion of German trench extending from P to the line joining D and 5, and ' C ' Company on the right of ' B ' extended through O to the road. Two platoons from both ' A ' and ' D ' Companies had supported ' B ' and ' C ' in the third line. The platoons of ' D ' Company occupied the houses about D, covering ' C ' Company's rear, and finally moved up on ' C ' Company's right, connecting ' C ' Company with the road D.N. Meanwhile, owing to the 1st Bn. 39th Garhwalis edging off to their right, a gap of about 200 yards of the first German trench

* " The Indian Corps in France," pp. 213, 214.
† Evatt, " Historical Record of the 39th Royal Garhwal Rifles," p. 45.

had been unaccounted for, and this portion was still held by Germans who moved down the trench opposite our right.*

" The two companies endeavoured to dislodge them from the trench to the north of the Ruined House and from the house opposite our right, and one platoon from ' D ' Company of the reserve, under Captain Romilly, succeeded in bombing them back down the trench up to within 20 yards of the Ruined House; here a barricade was built, and was held with two reserve platoons of ' A ' Company until the Seaforth Highlanders, advancing from our left, took over the line." [About 5 p.m.]

" The companies in the front line at once commenced improving the German trench and reversed the parapet. About 5 p.m. the enemy endeavoured to retire north-eastwards, but, with the 1st Seaforths attacking from the west, the 3rd Londons from the south-west, and with the fire from ' A ' Company enfilading them, they raised the white flag and surrendered, about 80 prisoners being taken.

" About 3.40 p.m. orders had been received that the left of our advanced line was to swing round to P. and connect with the 2/3rd Gurkhas, but this had already been done. At 3.45 information was received that the Dehra Dun Brigade was going to pass through us and attack the Bois du Biez, and that the Garhwal Brigade would remain on the line T.P.O. and consolidate the position; and by 5.15 p.m. the front line of the Indian Army Corps from left to right was as follows : 2/39th Garhwalis—2/3rd Gurkhas—2nd Leicesters—1st Seaforths—3rd London—1/39th Garhwalis; up to this time the right flank of the forward line by the road had been in the air.

" About midnight, 10th-11th March, the 2/39th Garhwalis were withdrawn and attached to the Dehra Dun Brigade.

" Early on the 11th the Dehra Dun Brigade advanced as far as the Bois du Biez, but withdrew before dawn and dug themselves in—the 2/2nd Gurkhas digging a trench 100 yards in front of the 2/3rd Gurkhas' trench and the 2/39th Garhwalis coming into that portion of our line which was held by ' C ' and half ' D ' Companies of the Battalion. This trench dug by the 2/2nd Gurkhas, however, made 60 yards of trench on our left, occupied by ' B ' Company and facing north, of no account, as this particular part of the trench flanked the line held by the 2/3rd Gurkhas. The half of ' A ' Company in the front line was withdrawn to D at dusk, while during the night of the 11th-12th the 2/2nd Gurkhas were also withdrawn and the trench was left unoccupied."

On the morning of March 11th the following was circulated among the units which had been engaged in the fighting of the last two days :—

* This loss of direction is explained as follows on p. 48 of the 39th War History : " On the bombardment lifting, the first line, consisting of No. 2 Company (Dogras) and No. 4 Company (Garhwalis), went over the parapet. . . . The leading companies, unfortunately, at once took the wrong direction. In the case of No. 4 this was evidently due to the fact that the trench from which they jumped off did not exactly face in the direction of the objective. This explanation is, however, inexplicable in the case of No. 2 Company, and it can only be conjectured that the Dogras, being the younger in war, and relying greatly on the more experienced Garhwalis alongside, kept touch with, and even followed, them, instead of, as ordered, keeping their left flank on the 2nd Leicesters, who were to their left rear and out of sight." The 1/39th suffered here very heavy casualties, having six British officers killed and wounded.

" The following from General Haig begins: ' Field-Marshal Commanding-in-Chief wishes his heartiest congratulations to be conveyed to Corps Commanders and to all ranks of the First Army for the splendid success they have gained to-day.' Would you also kindly express my gratitude for the magnificent determination you and all ranks have displayed in executing my orders for to-day's battle. The enemy has been completely surprised, and I trust that to-morrow the effect of to-day's fighting will result in still greater success."

To resume quotation from the Battalion War Diary :—

" 12th March. The enemy artillery shelled Port Arthur. On the 12th at 5.15 a.m. the Germans counter-attacked and 'A' and 'D' Companies at D. were called up, but this counter-attack broke down on the right at 100 yards from our trenches. On the left they occupied the trench vacated by the 2/2nd Gurkhas, and advanced from there direct on the 2/3rd Gurkhas, but they were received with a frontal fire from the Gurkhas and were enfiladed by a machine gun and 'B' Company under Captain R. J. McIntyre, and few returned to their trench. Then at 9 a.m. a white flag was seen in this trench and at 9.30 a company of 1/4th Gurkhas advanced, and, there being no further movement by the enemy, a party under Second-Lieutenant A. S. McIntyre, under fire from the enemy behind white flags, rushed to the trench and assisted the Gurkhas in clearing it of the enemy, many of whom were killed and wounded, the remainder surrendering to the 1st Bn. Highland Light Infantry further north.

" Information was received at 11 a.m. that the Sirhind Brigade, supported by the Jullundur Brigade, was going to attack in an easterly direction, but no attack took place although troops were formed up behind the front line; but, owing to the open nature of the ground and lack of cover, they suffered somewhat heavily. At 3.37 p.m. received information that the Garhwal Brigade would remain in possession of the line, and the Ferozepur Brigade came up at six o'clock, but by 11 p.m. it was decided that the proposed attack would not take place, and the Jullundur and Ferozepur Brigades were withdrawn half an hour later."

On the morning of the 13th the situation—or so much of it as came under Battalion observation—was anything but clear. There was heavy shelling by the enemy, and his snipers were very active; there were reports that German troops were massing on portions of the line of the Rivière des Layes; while up to late in the afternoon appearances were in favour of an enemy attack. Orders were, however, issued for the relief of the line by the Sirhind Brigade, all necessary preparations were made, and the relief was completed by midnight on March 13th–14th, when all seemed quiet, and the 2nd Battalion The Leicestershire Regiment, its place in the line having been taken by the 1st Battalion 4th Gurkha Rifles, marched to L'Epinette via Rue des Berceaux, Queen Mary Road, La Couture, Zelobes and Locon Roads, reaching their billets at six o'clock on the morning of March 14th.

All ranks were thoroughly in need of rest; the Battalion stretcher bearers, whose work had been very heavy, had worked continuously from 8 a.m. on the 10th to midnight on the 11th-12th, while the Scouts and Pioneers had carried ammunition, rations and stores up to the company trenches every night, generally under fire. The casualties unhappily had been numerous, and amounted to 250 of all ranks killed and wounded. Of the officers engaged, Second-Lieutenant W. Murphy was killed, Lieutenant H. L. Bayfield died of wounds, while wounded were Captain N. A. Morgan, Lieutenants T. R. Grylls, H. M. Raleigh, G. C. Dickinson and V. Buxton.

Many gallant deeds had been performed by individual officers and men of the Battalion during these days of storm and stress, and the following is the account given of some of these by the historian of the Indian Army Corps* :—

" During this attack [of the 10th] and again on the 12th March, Private William Buckingham, 2nd Leicesters, on several occasions displayed the greatest bravery and devotion in rescuing and aiding wounded men. Time after time he went out under the heaviest fire and brought in those who would otherwise almost certainly have perished. In the performance of this noble work, Private Buckingham was severely wounded in the chest and arm. For his conspicuous valour he was awarded the Victoria Cross. This very valiant soldier was killed during the fighting on the Somme in September, 1916.

" The story of the 2nd Leicesters throughout the campaign is full of instances of bravery and self-devotion, of which it is unfortunately impossible, within the scope of this history, to mention more than a few. Amongst others of the Battalion who received the Distinguished Conduct Medal for services in this battle was Private G. Hill, who, during the attack of the 10th March, showed a supreme contempt for danger by continually carrying messages across the open under very heavy fire, the enemy being only a hundred yards away. Later in the day he was wounded by a bomb while engaged in clearing the Germans out of a trench.

" Corporal R. Keitley was granted the same decoration for displaying great courage and the utmost devotion to duty in removing the wounded from the firing line to the aid post during three whole days, without rest and with hardly any food. Throughout he was under very heavy fire. In this work he was assisted by Private C. Oakes, who also received the Distinguished Conduct Medal.

" Sergeant H. E. Ruckledge dressed the wounds of several men after being himself wounded in the leg. He then collected sandbags and took them to the firing line, being wounded in the wrist in the act. Next, he went to the aid of a seriously wounded officer. All these gallant actions were performed under heavy fire. Private J. Steeples voluntarily went out into the open with another man under severe close-range fire and carried a wounded officer under cover. In both cases the Distinguished Conduct Medal was awarded.

" These are a few instances of the spirit which inspired this splendid Battalion to the deeds which it performed."

* " The Indian Corps in France," pp. 231, 232.

The award of the Victoria Cross to Private Buckingham is thus recorded in the London Gazette of April 28th, 1915 :—

"*No. 6276 Private William Buckingham, 2nd Battalion The Leicestershire Regiment.*

"*For conspicuous acts of bravery and devotion to duty in rescuing and rendering aid to the wounded, whilst exposed to heavy fire, especially at Neuve Chapelle on 10th and 12th March, 1915.*"

But Private Buckingham did not confine his efforts to rescuing and rendering aid to his comrades or even his own countrymen only; "during the battle," he told a friend when at home convalescing from his wound, "I came upon a badly-wounded German soldier. One of his legs had been blown off. He was lying right in the fire zone. His piteous appeal for help—well, I rendered first-aid as well as I could and just carried him to a place of safety."

A fine instance, indeed, of that "Brotherhood which binds the Brave of all the Earth."

But in this History of The Leicestershire Regiment in the Great War, it is surely not out of place to put on record the gallantry of the officers and men of another regiment of the Indian Army Corps—the 1st Battalion 4th Gurkhas—who suffered heavy loss in the endeavour to bring in a man of the 2nd Leicestershire.

"About 2 p.m. on the 12th March," we read in "The Indian Corps in France," "a number of casualties occurred among the British officers of this Battalion in their endeavour to rescue a wounded private of the Leicesters, who was lying about 20 yards in front of the Gurkha parapet. Major Young, Jemadar Gangabir Gurung and Rifleman Wazir Sing Burathoki went out together to try to bring the wounded man in. In doing so, Major Young was mortally, and the Rifleman severely, wounded. Captains Hogg and McGann, without a moment's hesitation, rushed out to help, but both were at once hit. Captain McGann managed to crawl back unaided, and Jemadar Gangabir, with the help of some Gurkhas, eventually succeeded in bringing Captain Hogg back. For this gallantry and devotion, the Jemadar and the Rifleman received the Second Class of the Indian Order of Merit; the latter was also subsequently awarded the Russian Medal of St. George, 3rd Class.

"It is typical of the spirit of the Corps, and indeed of the British Army, that these three British officers and a number of Indian soldiers should have risked their lives to bring to safety a single private soldier of the Leicesters."

On March 16th the 2nd Battalion The Leicestershire Regiment was inspected by the Divisional Commander, Major-General Anderson, who made the following speech :—

"*Colonel Gordon, Officers, Non-Commissioned Officers and Men of The Leicestershire Regiment.*

"*First, I hope you all realize how deeply we all feel about all the good fellows you have lost. Some of them have gone back wounded, we hope to see*

PRIVATE W. BUCKINGHAM, V.C.

them again as good fellows as ever they were; the others who are gone died in a fight that is a credit even to The Leicestershire Regiment.

"*I know The Leicestershire Regiment; I knew them six and thirty years ago in Afghanistan, they were a magnificent Regiment then, you, their successors, are a magnificent Regiment now.*

"*I can't say more than that I am proud to command troops that contain such a corps as The Leicestershire Regiment. Wherever The Leicestershire Regiment is, I know that part of the line is safe and more than safe. Whatever they have to do, I know they will do all that is asked of them and more than could be hoped for.*

"*Colonel Gordon will, I am sure, have very many recommendations to make of those who have specially distinguished themselves, and I am sure that your old Colonel, General Blackader, will take jolly good care that they are sent in to me, and I can tell you that I will take jolly good care that they go on to the Corps. Colonel Gordon, I congratulate you on your command of so fine a Regiment.*"

On the following day—March 17th—there was an inspection by Sir James Willcocks, the Commander of the Indian Corps, who also addressed the Battalion in very flattering terms and in the following words :—

"*Leicestershire Regiment.*

"*You don't want a lot of talk; I have spoken to you before. I congratulate you and thank you most heartily for what you have done. You have fought now for five months and fought well. I am proud and thankful to have such a Battalion in my Corps, and bigger people than I think the same. I have had congratulatory messages from the Viceroy, from Sir John French, and from others at home.*

"*I thank you.*"

As General Willcocks rode off parade he remarked in loud tones to Brigadier-General Blackader : "By Jove! That Regiment fights well. Young fellows just coming out to join them ought to feel pretty proud of themselves !"

Nor were the Commander-in-Chief of the British Expeditionary Force and the General Commanding the First Army unappreciative of the services of the units composing the Indian Army Corps. In his despatch of April 5th of this year dealing with the conduct and the results of the Battle of Neuve Chapelle, the Field-Marshal wrote that :—

"*While the success attained was due to the magnificent bearing and indomitable courage displayed by the troops of the IV. and Indian Corps, I consider that the able and skilful dispositions which were made by the General Officer Commanding the First Army contributed largely to the defeat of the enemy and to the capture of his position*"; and in an Order of the Day issued to the First Army at the conclusion of the operations, the Field-Marshal expressed himself as follows :—

" I am anxious to express to you personally my warmest appreciation of the skilful manner in which you have carried out your orders, and my fervent and most heartfelt appreciation of the magnificent gallantry and devoted, tenacious courage displayed by all ranks whom you have ably led to success and victory. My warmest thanks to you all."

Finally, in the following order, General Sir Douglas Haig summed up the general results of the action and expressed his sense of the skill and courage by means of which success had been achieved :—

" I desire to express to all ranks of the First Army my great appreciation of the task accomplished by them in the past four days of severe fighting. The First Army has captured the German trenches on a front of two miles, including the whole village of Neuve Chapelle, and some strongly defended works. Very serious loss has been inflicted on the enemy, nearly 2,000 prisoners are in our hands, and his casualties in killed and wounded are estimated at about 16,000. I wish also to thank all concerned for the careful preparation made for the assault. Much depended on this thoroughness and secrecy. The attack was such a complete surprise to the enemy that he had neither a Corps nor an Army Reserve at hand and had to draw on the adjoining army for help.

" The absolute success of the operation of breaking through the German line on the first day is not only a tribute to the careful forethought and attention to detail on the part of the leaders, but it has proved beyond question that our forces can defeat the Germans where and when they choose, no matter what mechanical contrivances or elaborate defences are opposed to their advance.

" The results of the successful action just fought are not, however, confined to the material losses sustained by the enemy. The organization of the German forces from Ypres to far south of the La Bassée Canal has been thrown into a state of confusion. Reinforcements available to oppose the French in the battle which is taking place at Notre Dame de Lorette, or destined for other parts of the line, have been drawn into the fight opposite the First Army, and, in many cases, severely handled.

" The losses sustained by the First Army, though heavy, are fully compensated for by the results achieved, which have brought us one step forward in our efforts to end the war; and the British soldier has once more given the Germans a proof of his superiority in a fight, as well as of his pluck and determination to conquer. The spirit and energy shown by all ranks augur well for the future, and I feel confident that the success achieved by the First Army at Neuve Chapelle is the forerunner of still greater victories which must be gained in order to bring the war to a successful conclusion."

Sir Douglas Haig spoke no less than the truth when he described as "heavy" the losses sustained by the First Army at the Battle of Neuve Chapelle, for these were as under :—

Killed, 190 officers and 2,337 other ranks.

Wounded, 359 officers and 8,174 other ranks.

Missing, 23 officers and 1,728 other ranks.

Total casualties, 12,811.

In the Indian Army Corps these—included in the above—amounted to :—

> Killed, 41 British officers, 22 Indian officers, 364 British and 408 Indian other ranks.
>
> Wounded, 91 British officers, 36 Indian officers, 1,461 British and 1,495 Indian other ranks.
>
> Missing, 1 British officer, 2 Indian officers, 87 British and 225 Indian other ranks.
>
> Total, 133 British officers, 60 Indian officers, 1,912 British and 2,128 Indian other ranks.

Or in all 4,233 officers, non-commissioned officers and men, British and Indian, killed, wounded and missing.

The following brief account of the Battle of Neuve Chapelle is contributed by the officer then commanding the 2nd Battalion :—

" The 2nd Leicestershire Regiment, with the whole First Army, was on the tip-toe of excitement as the date of the Battle of Neuve Chapelle approached. This was the first occasion I remember, on which air photographs were used to help commanders of battalions to locate and recognize their objectives. The enemy's trenches were studied over the top and through periscopes for many days. That an attack was coming the Germans well knew, for, a day before, they had exhibited and placed in front of our trenches at Port Arthur a placard bearing the legend : ' Come on, we are ready for you.' The men were fit and well trained, and tales of our massed guns and terrific barrage, and the knowledge that the Boche was weak on our front, gave all ranks the feel of a certain coming victory. We had not the dreary dead feeling which the British Army often subsequently had on the eve of a big offensive. The wire in front of the enemy trenches was very thin and full of gaps. Our artillery for the first time was better than that of the enemy and our Royal Flying Corps dominated the air. Everyone felt full of hope for a certain break through. The day before the attack, the 2nd Leicesters were billeted in Richebourg l'Avoué along with other units of the Garhwal Brigade, and the houses were literally stuffed full of troops. At five o'clock in a drizzling cold rain we marched up to Port Arthur and had to squeeze into a very small space till the artillery had finished its preliminary barrage. At 7.30 a.m. it began, and for the first time in their lives the soldiers of the British Army experienced the roar of a barrage. As far as I remember the enemy did not reply heavily till much later in the day, but all the same we suffered a few casualties before the advance. Among them was poor Captain Noel Morgan, who got a big bit of German shell in his chest and has a tube in his body to this day. He was a fine Company Commander, devoted to his duty and had a splendidly trained company.

" At 8.5 a.m. our leading waves advanced, and within half an hour we had gained our various objectives with little opposition and very few casualties. The whole country in front was open to us—no wire—no enemy in sight and certainly a big enough gap to push through a mass of men and cavalry. Later in the day, when the Dehra Dun Brigade went through us, they got to the

Bois du Biez without opposition—and there was nothing to stop them even then. I have talked to very many who were present on that day, and no one who was actually in the battle had the slightest doubt that we could have been in Lille in a few hours. But 'slow' was the order, the Dehra Dun Brigade was called back behind the river, troops were to be relieved, sections of the front taken over, and all the usual staff work gone through, occupying hours and hours of time, and the golden opportunity was missed. There was a lack of ammunition, but in German war diaries we read that the enemy were in similar plight and had exhausted nearly all their artillery ammunition too—they were packing up in Lille and preparing for a hurried retreat. A like chance never presented itself again. On our next attack on May 9th, the Boche was prepared and masses of wire held us up all along the front.

"At about ten o'clock on the morning of the battle, I went and examined our positions and gave orders for consolidating them and found the men full of fight and keen to go on. In the afternoon we discovered that a trench, in front of Port Arthur and between our Headquarters and our advanced position, was full of Germans who had moved to their right when the 1st Garhwalis lost direction. They were causing us many casualties.

"An attack by another regiment had failed to dislodge them. I sent Romilly with a platoon to turn them out and supported him with a machine gun to keep the enemy heads down. Romilly was the keenest man I have ever met in a battle and bombs were a hobby to him. And in these early days it was not all joy handling a bomb! Under cover of the machine gun he rushed the north end of the trench and established himself there. And then began the most beautiful bit of trench fighting I have ever seen, and, indeed, it became a model for a bombing attack.

"Romilly, having thought out his task, had taken with him a quantity of bombs, and, with bayonet men in front and behind him, he himself advanced up the trench, throwing his bombs into the succeeding traverses.

"At last Romilly got tired of this slow progress, and the exhilarating sight was seen of this determined officer jumping up on the top of the trench, followed by his runner with a supply of bombs, and thus moving up the trench throwing his bombs at the cowering enemy below. In a few minutes it was over, and Romilly brought back about 80 prisoners and cleared the front of this nest of hidden enemy. It was a magnificent feat and won Romilly a well-deserved D.S.O. This method of attack was used at Festubert by the 1/39th Garhwal on 24th November, and was followed and perfected by Romilly's affair at Neuve Chapelle.

"A very curious incident came under my observation on the first day of the battle. I was dictating orders to my Adjutant and a signaller was sitting beside me. Suddenly a shell came very close to us, and I looked round to say something to the signaller and found him as white as a sheet and stone dead. He had not been touched, but his heart stopped from the shock of the shell."

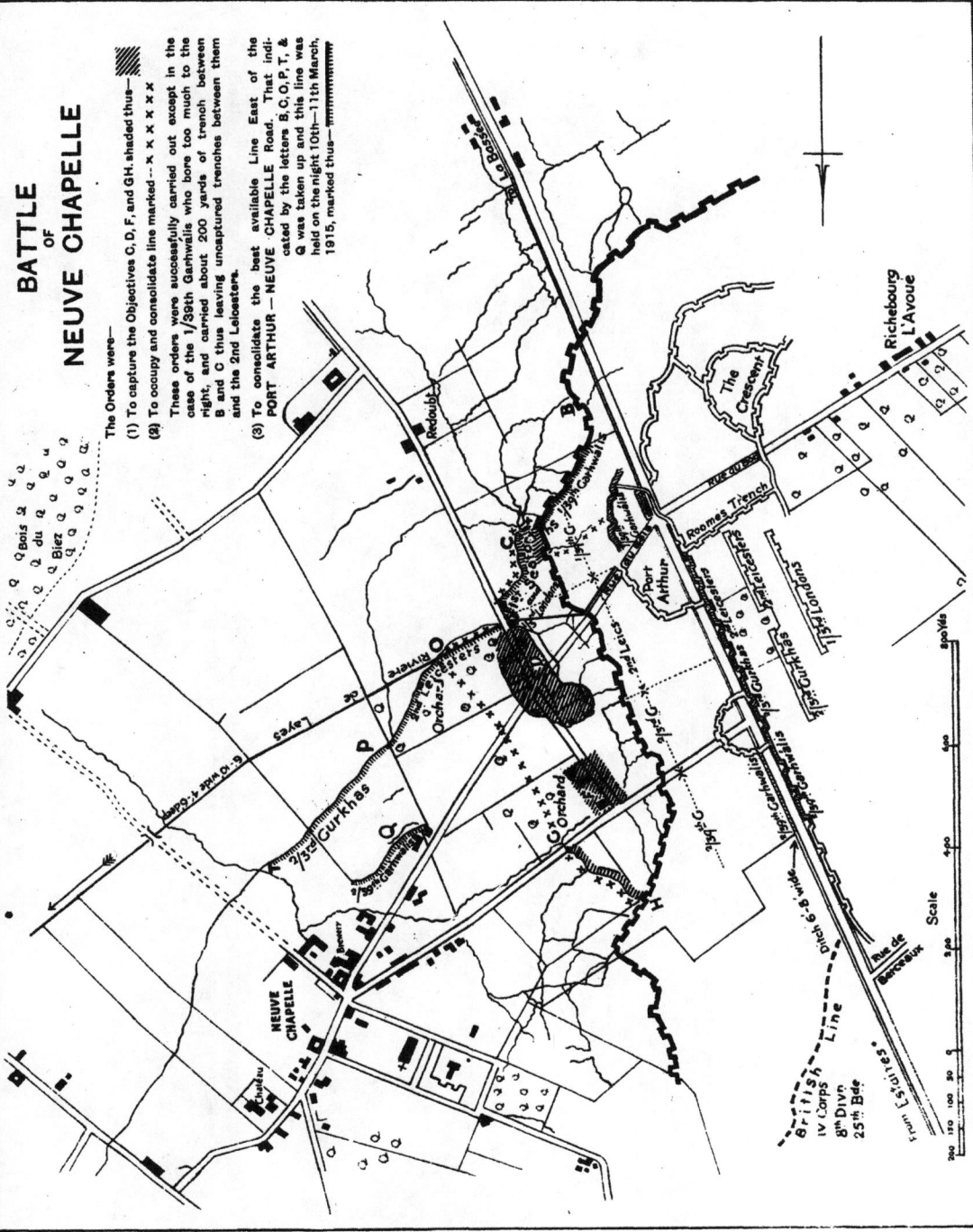

BATTLE
OF
NEUVE CHAPELLE

The Orders were—

(1) To capture the Objectives C, D, F, and GH. shaded thus—

(2) To occupy and consolidate line marked—x x x x x x

These orders were successfully carried out except in the case of the 1/39th Garhwalis who bore too much to the right, and carried about 200 yards of trench between B and C thus leaving uncaptured trenches between them and the 2nd Leicesters.

(3) To consolidate the best available Line East of the PORT ARTHUR — NEUVE CHAPELLE Road. That indicated by the letters B, C, O, P, T, & Q was taken up and this line was held on the night 10th—11th March, 1915, marked thus—ⱳⱳⱳⱳⱳⱳ

British — — — — Line
IV Corps
8ᵗʰ Divn
25ᵗʰ Bde

Scale

CHAPTER III.

1915

AT the end of March there was a general reorganization of the brigades of the Indian Army Corps, when the Garhwal Brigade was made up as follows :—

2nd Battalion The Leicestershire Regiment,
3rd London Regiment (Territorial Force),
The Garhwal Rifles,
2nd Battalion 3rd Gurkhas,
2nd Battalion 8th Gurkhas,

the 1st and 2nd Battalions Garhwal Rifles having, owing to their heavy losses in the recent battle, been amalgamated into one battalion.

The Indian Army Corps as a whole took no part in the Second Battle of Ypres of the early part of this year, the Lahore Division only being engaged; and it was not until May that the Meerut Division was called upon again for offensive operations on a large scale, the reasons for undertaking which are set forth as under in the despatch of Sir John French of June 15th, wherein he wrote :—

" In pursuance of a promise which I made to the French Commander-in-Chief to support an attack which his troops were making on the 9th May between the right of my line and Arras, I directed Sir Douglas Haig to carry out on that date an attack on the German trenches in the neighbourhood of Rouges Bancs (north-west of Fromelles) by the IV. Corps, and between Neuve Chapelle and Givenchy by the I. and Indian Corps."

The general instructions for the attack were that the First Army was to break through the enemy's line and gain the La Bassée—Lille road between La Bassée and Fournes, the I. Corps, with its right on Givenchy, attacking from about Richebourg l'Avoué, advancing on the line Rue du Marais—Illies; the Indian Corps, covering the left of the I., was to capture the Ferme du Biez, its onward movement thence being directed on Ligny le Grand and La Cliqueterie Farm; while the IV. Corps was to break through the German line near Rouges Bancs with the double object of organizing a defensive flank from La Cordonnerie Farm to Fromelles and of turning the Aubers defences from the north-east.

" On the 18th April secret orders were issued by Sir James Willcocks for the operations of the Indian Corps. The Meerut Division was to attack on a front of 600 yards, reinforced by the artillery of the Lahore Division, and by any other guns which might be placed at the disposal of the Corps, the line being held by the Lahore Division, of which one brigade would be in Corps Reserve. . . . . The assault on the first objective, the enemy's trenches opposite to them, was to be delivered by the Dehra Dun Brigade on a three-battalion front, the Bareilly Brigade being in support, and the Garhwal Brigade [less the Garhwal Rifles and 2/8th Gurkhas, which were detailed for another object], was to be in Divisional Reserve." *

The attack was to have been delivered on the 8th, but was postponed until the following day, and in Lieutenant-Colonel Gordon's operation orders it was laid down that " the Battalion will be formed up in quarter column facing south on ground by the track leading from Croix Barbée "—where the 2nd Leicestershire Regiment was then occupying billets—" to Richebourg St. Vaast by 1.30 a.m. in the following order—Headquarters, ' A,' ' D,' ' C ' and ' B ' Companies. The Battalion will occupy trenches 300 yards south of the Croix Barbée—La Couture—Richebourg Road, companies moving to positions allotted to them on receiving orders to do so."

On the 6th, 7th and 8th the whole ground between Croix Barbée and Lansdowne Post was reconnoitred and alternative routes laid out, while bridges were placed over the many ditches and streams which cut up the country, and on the 9th—the day of the attack—the battalions of the Garhwal Brigade were held in reserve at certain breastworks to the south of Croix Barbée.

The attack by the Dehra Dun Brigade failed in face of the very heavy fire met with from the German rifles and machine guns, and at 1.45 p.m. the Battalion left its trenches and advanced to breastworks at the Rue des Berceaux on a front of one company in eight small columns in file at 150 yards between companies. This advance was made under enemy fire, which became heavier as the Battalion approached Lansdowne Post, but the casualties fortunately were very trifling, greatly due to the extreme accuracy of the enemy barrage, which allowed the Battalion to move forward relying on the exact burst of each shell.

On arrival at the Rue des Berceaux breastwork, the companies closed in on their left and advanced up the Crescent Communication Trench, which was found, however, to be badly blocked by wounded and other men moving down it, for experience had not yet taught the need for many such trenches ; but the Battalion managed to reach the head of this trench by 3 p.m., about which time Captain A. W. S. Brock was hit in the arm by shrapnel, while Captain M. K. Wardle, who was acting as Staff Captain to the Brigade, was also wounded while bringing a message from the Brigadier to the Commanding Officer. At 4 p.m. the Bareilly Brigade attacked, but this attack was also unsuccessful, and during the night of May 9th-10th the Battalion took over certain trenches, " A " and half " D " Companies being in the front line, the remainder of " D " and " C " Companies being in support in Crescent Trench,

* " The Indian Corps in France," pp. 343, 344.

while "B" Company was in reserve; the whole moved on the following night into a breastwork north of the Rue du Bois, and was tolerably heavily shelled during the 11th and 12th by the German guns.

On the morning of May 13th instructions were received from the First Army for operations on the 14th, the general plan of the main attack being as follows :—

"(1) To continue pressing forward towards Violaines and Beau Puits, establishing a defensive flank along the La Bassée Road on the left and maintaining the right at Givenchy.

"(2) The line to be established in the first instance, if possible, on the general line of the road Festubert—La Quinque Rue—La Tourelle Cross-roads—Port Arthur. This position to be consolidated, the troops reformed, and communication established.

"(3) During this process a bombardment on the whole front would continue, with fire specially directed on the next objectives, the Rue d'Ouvert—Rue du Marais, after which a fresh advance on this line would take place.

"The assault to be carried out simultaneously by the Indian Corps and the 1st Division, commencing at 11.30 p.m. on the 14th May. The attacking troops of the Indian Corps were to be the Meerut Division, less the Dehra Dun Brigade, whose place was taken by the Sirhind Brigade. The Lahore Division was to continue to hold its front and to assist with rifle and gunfire."*

At 8.15 p.m. on May 13th the 2nd Battalion The Leicestershire Regiment left the breastworks north of the Rue du Bois and moved forward, the companies then being distributed as follows : 3 platoons of "C" Company in the front line west of the Orchard front trench; 1 platoon of "C" and the whole of "B" Company in the Guards' trenches; "D" Company and Battalion Headquarters in a breastwork immediately north of the Rue du Bois; and "A" Company in another breastwork just 60 yards north of this. Then later in the evening, when the shelling by the enemy had to some extent diminished, the Battalion went forward to Lansdowne Post, all being settled in by 10.30 p.m., and here the whole of the 15th was spent.

Moving off again at 8.30 p.m. on this day the Battalion took over the front line from which the assault was to be made, and the Garhwal Brigade was now disposed with the 2nd Leicestershire on the right, the Garhwal Rifles on the left, the 3rd London Regiment and two companies of the 2/3rd Gurkhas in support, the remainder of the 2/3rd being in Brigade Reserve : the 2nd Division was on the right of the Garhwal Brigade. Eleven bridges had been placed over the stream running parallel to and from 20 to 30 yards in front of it, so that these, with the four bridges already existing, made a total of 15 on the Battalion front alone. More bridges would have been placed in position had this been possible, but the stream had been widened at many points by the holes made by heavy shells, while the trunks of fallen trees also blocked many places where a bridge or bridges might usefully have been thrown across the water. The work of getting these bridges into position had been an operation of great

K * "The Indian Corps in France," pp. 357, 358.

difficulty and of no small danger, by reason of the flares sent up by the enemy and the constant bursts of fire from his trenches, but it was accomplished with no more than two or three casualties.

At 10.45 two platoons crossed over to the far side of the stream, while four more were formed up in the trenches ready to go forward in support should such be called for; the rest of the Battalion formed up lying down in rear in close column of platoons, ready to advance on the word being given.

The leading platoons, closely followed by the second line, went forward to the assault at 11.30 p.m., when the enemy at once opened a very fierce fire with rifles and machine guns, while trench mortars and shrapnel searched the stream and the ground on either bank; grenades were also hurled from the German parapets, and these, bursting on impact, illuminated the ground, literally turning night into day.

The leading men pushed gallantly on, but only a few reached the enemy trenches, and as each successive line came under this heavy fire the bridges became blocked, and the many obstacles so impeded progress that effective support was impossible; thus the impetus of the assault was broken before it had really got under way. The enemy breastwork was fully manned, and such was the intensity and accuracy of the fire from it that no fewer than 8 officer platoon commanders were killed or wounded.

About midnight it was realized that the attack could not possibly reach the German line, and orders were accordingly issued for withdrawal, upon receipt of which the Battalion, at 2 in the morning of the 16th, moved back to the Guards' and Reserve Trenches north of the Rue du Bois, and thence the same evening to Croix Barbée.

In this attack, and during the operations immediately preceding it, the losses of the Battalion amounted to: killed or died of wounds, Lieutenant G. W. M. Crosse, Second-Lieutenants H. T. Dooley,* G. J. Gandy, J. G. Tayler and H. A. Browne and 24 other ranks; Captains A. W. S. Brock, M. K. Wardle, and 220 non-commissioned officers and men were wounded, while 5 men were missing.

The attack was renewed on this day by the two battalions of the Garhwal Brigade which had been in support or reserve on the 15th; but though this, and other attacks which followed, were equally unsuccessful, they were continued in pursuance of orders which had been received to the effect that the "Indian Army Corps was to carry on continuous hostilities with a view to harassing the enemy and wearing down his resistance." That these operations were not carried on without very serious wastage in a Corps the units of which could not be easily and adequately reinforced, is proved by the fact that the losses of the Corps after the May fighting amounted to 3,620 all ranks killed, 17,484 wounded and 4,321 missing, or 25,424 casualties in all.†

In his despatch of June 15th, 1915, the Field-Marshal thus summed up the results of the Battle of Festubert: "In the battle the enemy was driven from a

---

* Second-Lieutenant Dooley was killed on May 1st being buried with his orderly in his dug-out.
† "With the Indians in France," p. 294.

position which was strongly entrenched and fortified, and ground was won on a front of four miles to an average depth of 600 yards. The enemy is known to have suffered very heavy losses, and in the course of the battle 785 prisoners and 10 machine guns were captured. A number of machine guns were also destroyed by our fire."

The end of May and the beginning of June were spent by the 2nd Leicestershire in billets to the south of Paradis; and then about June 7th trenches in the front line and situated astride the Albert Road were taken over from the 1st Battalion Seaforth Highlanders. During this tour the enemy shelling was tolerably constant and effective, as may be realized by extracts from the War Diary :—

" 12th June. Second-Lieutenant C. G. Woodburn, 3rd Battalion, joined. Farm Corner was breached in three places and a bombing party at the head of the trench was cut off. Captain Wilson at once built up the breaches and sent Second-Lieutenant Wilkinson with a telephone to the advanced post. Our front line had about 120 big shells into it to-day, with only one casualty. By night all damage was repaired.

" 13th. Our snipers shot three Germans to-day. Enemy shelled our communication trenches and Headquarters with shrapnel. Our patrols from ' C ' and ' D ' Companies did useful work in locating the enemy's wire and working parties. New trench dug parallel to Farm Corner.

" 14th. Farm Corner Trench breached by enemy's heavy guns in two places. While working at wire in front to-night numerous enemy flares disclosed our position and heavy rifle and machine-gun fire was opened. Second-Lieutenant Sanders was seriously wounded, and Captain Romilly, assisted by Private Page of ' D ' Company, went out and carried him in. 'A' Company was moved up closer to the trench on south side of the Rue du Bois.

" 15th. Operations on a large scale by the corps on our right, and a minor operation by the Lahore Division on our left, began at 6 p.m. Enemy replied to our bombardment and our trenches were heavily shelled. Our machine guns under Captain Le Fanu were co-operating in the attack by the H.L.I. on our left."

Trench fever now claimed many victims and the number of men admitted to hospital grew daily larger. On the 16th, Captain Latham, the Adjutant, was wounded; on the following day Captain Rolph rejoined the Battalion, bringing a draft of 55 men; while on the 18th, the day before relief in the trenches took the Battalion back to Brigade Reserve between Richebourg and La Couture, Captain Le Fanu just removed his maxims and ammunition in time to prevent their destruction by enemy shells. On the 27th, Second-Lieutenant Woodburn, who had only joined as recently as the 12th, was wounded while out with a working party.

During the greater part of July the Battalion was in billets at Vieille Chapelle and near Merville, and later near Bout de Ville, during which time H.R.H. the Prince of Wales inspected part of the Battalion on parade, having breakfast afterwards with the Commanding Officer. In July three officers joined—Lieutenant H. H. Phillips, Second-Lieutenants M. W. Brown and G. W. Tanner—and a draft of 40 non-commissioned officers and men came out from home.

From July 15th to August 1st the Battalion was attached to the Sirhind Brigade, under Brigadier-General W. G. Walker, V.C., C.B., and on rejoining its own Brigade that officer wrote to Lieutenant-Colonel Gordon, commanding the 2nd Leicestershire Regiment, as under :—

" I wanted to bid you au revoir and to tell you how much I have appreciated the honour of having your Battalion under my command, even for so short a time. I have been very pleased with the way the men have worked, and with your general Bandobust in the trenches, which is as good as any I have seen. Would you please convey my appreciation to your officers and men."

During the first fortnight of August the Battalion was back at La Gorgue, engaged in war training of all kinds, and on the 16th the Garhwal Brigade relieved the Bareilly Brigade in an especially lively section of the front, extending from the Fauquissart—Aubers road to a point 750 yards south of it, and here the companies were distributed as follows in that portion of the line occupied by the Battalion : " A " Company (under Captain W. C. Wilson) in the firing line, " B " Company (Second-Lieutenant D. Sutherland), and half " C " Company (Lieutenant H. H. Phillips) in support, while in reserve was the other half of " C " (Captain D. L. Weir) in Wangerie Post, and " D " Company (Second-Lieutenant W. T. Pickin) in Road Bend Post. In this sub-section there was some very useful patrol work done, Lieutenant Brown and Second-Lieutenant Tanner being particularly active. The enemy also showed a hostile spirit on the night of the 22nd, some of them creeping close up to a listening post, into which they threw two hand grenades and then hurriedly withdrew. By the explosion of the grenade Private Mitchell, of the Battalion, was killed, a private of the 6th Battalion Wiltshire Regiment, attached for instruction, was mortally wounded, and two other men of the post were hit.

Private Davis, one of the group, who escaped unhurt, showed great courage and devotion to duty by remaining on guard at his post until reinforcements arrived; while Sergeant Bentley, from whose platoon the post was furnished, also displayed fine courage by going up alone to the post on hearing the explosion of the grenades. Captain E. C. Deane, R.A.M.C., the Medical Officer of the Battalion, at once climbed over the parapet and ran across the open under fire to aid the wounded men.

In this month Second-Lieutenants V. E. Ellingham and W. Wilson joined the Battalion, and on the 31st the strength return shows 24 officers and 848 other ranks.

During the greater part of September the Battalion was in billets at Bout de Ville, and on the 20th, near La Gorgue, the Meerut Division was inspected by Field-Marshal Earl Kitchener of Khartoum, Secretary of State for War, who was accompanied by the Commanders of the First Army, of the Indian Army Corps and of the Meerut Division; the 2nd Battalion The Leicestershire Regiment paraded 570 strong, including officers. Lord Kitchener told the Battalion that " he had heard very good reports of it and was very pleased to see the men on parade, as he had heard so much about their good work. He complimented the Battalion on their soldier-like appearance."

Of the reasons for and objects of the fresh operations which were now about to take place and in which the 2nd Battalion The Leicestershire Regiment was to play an important part, the following account is given in the Field-Marshal's despatch of October 15th, 1915 :—

" It was arranged that we should make a combined attack from certain points of the Allied line during the last week in September. The reinforcements I have received enabled me to comply with several requests which General Joffre has made that I should take over additional portions of the French line. In fulfilment of the rôle assigned to it in these operations the Army under my command attacked the enemy on the morning of the 25th September.

" The main attack was delivered by the I. and IV. Corps between the La Bassée Canal on the north and a point of the enemy's line opposite the village of Grenay on the south. At the same time a secondary attack, designed with the object of distracting the enemy's attention and holding his troops to their ground, was made by the V. Corps on Bellewaarde Farm, situated to the east of Ypres. Subsidiary attacks with similar objects were delivered by the III. and Indian Corps north of the La Bassée Canal and along the whole front of the Second Army."

The Indian Army Corps had, however, already fought its last battle under the Commander who had brought it from India to France, for on September 6th General Sir James Willcocks vacated his high office, which was assumed by Lieutenant-General Sir C. Anderson, the Commander of the Meerut Division, who was succeeded in that command by Major-General C. W. Jacob, the leader of the Dehra Dun Brigade.

" In the coming attack three objectives were assigned to the Indian Army Corps :—

" (1) To attack the enemy's line between the Sunken Road and Winchester Road, and to establish our line along the road running from Mauquissart to the Duck's Bill.

" (2) To press on, with the left in front, until the high ground between Haut Pommereau and La Cliqueterie Farm was gained.

" (3) To continue the advance from that point in a south-easterly direction, in order to assist our main offensive in the south by turning the La Bassée defences from the north."

The attack was to be delivered by the Meerut Division, the 19th and the Lahore Divisions holding the whole of the front except that portion from which the Meerut Division was to advance. The 20th Division of the III. Corps, on the left, was to co-operate with the Lahore Division by covering the flank of the Meerut Division with its fire.

" The assault was to be preceded by four days' deliberate bombardment by artillery and trench mortars, the enemy at the same time being prevented, by rifle, rifle-grenade and machine-gun fire, from repairing the damage done to his obstacles and defences; by the explosion of a mine under the enemy's parapet, opposite the left of our attack, two minutes before the gas and smoke commenced; by a gas and smoke attack immediately before the assault; and by the formation of thick smoke barrages on each flank of the assaulting troops.

" The Garhwal Brigade was detailed for the right assault, the Bareilly Brigade for the left, with the Dehra Dun Brigade in Divisional Reserve, each assaulting brigade having three battalions in the front line and two in reserve.

" From right to left the assaulting troops were disposed as follows :—

" Garhwal Brigade : 2/3rd Gurkhas, 2nd Leicesters and 2/8th Gurkhas. " On the extreme right the 1/3rd Londons continued to hold the Duck's Bill, while the 39th Garhwal Rifles held the Home Counties Trench in rear of the centre of the Brigade."*

For a week prior to the commencement of the operations the 2nd Leicestershire had been working hard at strengthening the front line and preparing defences in rear; four very strong lines had been constructed, and these were fully capable of resisting the enemy's bombardment.

At 7.10 p.m. on September 24th the Battalion marched from the concentration area near Pont du Hem and moved up to the front and support lines in the position of assembly, the concentration being completed by ten o'clock, while by 5.30 on the morning of the 25th the Battalion was in position of readiness, drawn up in four lines opposite the objective, with bombing, sandbag and carrying parties all at hand.

At 5.48 a mine on the left of the British attack, charged with no less than one ton of gun-cotton, went up with a deafening roar, forming a crater 92 feet across and completely obliterating the German salient; two minutes later an intense bombardment opened by the British guns, doing enormous damage to the enemy parapets; and at 6 a.m. the infantry advanced under cover of a smoke barrage. Unfortunately the direction of the wind had changed during the night and the gas could not be turned on against the enemy as had been intended.

The first line of the Battalion got over the parapet, followed by the second, but the left had to form to the right in order to get into line with the right, the trench running back from a salient near the centre, and as the two first lines " went over," the third and fourth filed into the vacant positions in the firing line. The gas, which here and there had unfortunately been turned on, affected a good many men, while the density of the smoke barrage made direction anything but easy. Casualties began at once, and the third line was ordered to fill up the gaps; and, it seeming likely that gaps would equally occur on the flanks, the fourth line was moved forward at 6.7 a.m., with special instructions to keep in touch with the units on either flank. Within ten minutes of the start the left of the Battalion was over the German parapet and the flag could be seen

* " The Indian Corps in France" pp. 399, et seq.

waving over the enemy lines; but " A " Company, which was on the left of the assaulting line, had gone forward with such dash that it had outstripped the 2/8th Gurkhas and consequently came in for a good deal of rifle and machine-gun fire from the right front.

Undeterred, however, the men went on, got over the uncut wire and reached the road from Mauquissart to the Duck's Bill with parties of the 2/8th Gurkhas, thus gaining their objective. The right, however, had not fared so well; the men there went forward in a good line until held up by the uncut German wire, and a number of men collected here in the ditches in front of the wire, waiting further developments.

The general reports of happenings which filtered back to Battalion and Brigade Headquarters were very obscure and conflicting. At first it was stated and believed that the enemy's front line had been captured, but later this was found to be incorrect, and by about 7 a.m. it was discovered that the right of the Garhwal Brigade had been held up by the German wire, in which such few gaps as existed had been filled up by the enemy with rolls of French wire. On the left, however, as above stated, the 2/8th Gurkhas and the left of the 2nd Leicestershire had got through the front trenches, but unfortunately with very heavy losses, especially in officers.

" The progress of the action," to quote from " The Indian Corps in France," " cannot be recorded with accuracy, owing to the impossibility of observation from our front-line trenches, due to the impenetrable wall of smoke and gas, which was rendered even more opaque by the dampness of the air. Secondly, as reported by General Jacob, the heavy losses in officers, especially of those who would have been able to throw light on obscure points, prevents certainty as to the details. The main story, however, can be reconstructed without grave inaccuracy. As regards the Leicesters, the position remained unchanged throughout the day, until, at 4.30 p.m., orders were received for the survivors to get back to our trenches as opportunity offered. The Battalion had fought with all the bravery for which it was famous, and, had the wire in front of the right of the Garhwal Brigade been cut, there is little doubt that the whole of the enemy's first-line trenches would have been captured. As it was, the holding up of the right and right centre attacks exposed the right of the left flank and rendered its temporary success of no avail."

What was left of the 2nd Battalion The Leicestershire Regiment was relieved from the front line by the Garhwal Rifles at 6.30 p.m. and moved into support and local reserve just in rear, being again relieved at midday on the 26th by the 2/2nd Gurkhas and going into billets near La Gorgue, the last days of September and the opening days of October being spent at Paradis.

The losses in the Battalion had once again been terribly heavy. There were killed or died of wounds, or were missing and believed killed, 5 officers—Captains F. H. Romilly, D.S.O., and E. C. Deane, R.A.M.C.; Lieutenant W. T. Pickin; Second-Lieutenants M. W. Browne and R. E. S. Lodge—and 72 other ranks. Wounded, 11 officers—Lieutenant-Colonel H. Gordon, D.S.O.; Major F. Lewis; Captains D. L. Weir and W. C. Wilson; Lieutenant H. H.

Phillips; Second-Lieutenants G. W. Tanner, H. H. Hemphill, V. E. Ellingham, C. C. Bailey, G. W. Grossmith and C. G. Woodburn*—and 220 non-commissioned officers and men. Gassed, Second-Lieutenant W. Wilson and 42 men. Missing, Second-Lieutenants W. P. Wilkinson, E. A. Wilkinson and T. R. Longcroft and 96 other ranks, or a total of 20 officers and 430 men killed, wounded, missing or gassed.

A brother-officer contributes the following about the death of Romilly :—

" Romilly and I had been home together on a short leave of six days. When the gallant Latham was wounded I had made Romilly my Adjutant. His wife came to see him off at Victoria, and to cheer her up I said : ' Romilly is all right, I'll look after him.' But it turned out that both of them had a presentiment of coming disaster. When we got back we were very busy preparing for our part in the Loos offensive. We were using gas and the arrangements to be made were complicated. The day before we moved up to our positions for the attack, Romilly asked me for leave to go and see our good friends of a motor ambulance, some miles behind. I was surprised, but let him go. He came back in the evening, and I remember he was more silent and graver than usual. Our attack was not a success—it was more in the nature of a demonstration. I was standing up on the firing step of the trench looking at Weir's company's progress and Romilly was standing by my side at the bottom of the trench. Suddenly a machine gun let out at us, and the same bullet that went through my arm killed poor Romilly by hitting him in the head. He died at once without a word. One of the bravest men in the Army and a tremendous loss to the Regiment. When I got back to have my wound dressed, the first people I saw were Captain Carrol and John McKinlay of the motor ambulance, great friends of the Regiment. They told me about the visit of Romilly and how, in saying good-bye to them, he had said : ' Well, I am for it this time. I won't get out of this.' "

Of the services of the officers of the Battalion in this battle, the historian of the Indian Corps in France writes as follows : " Major Lewis showed conspicuous gallantry and ability during this action, in which he was second-in-command. Shortly after the attack was launched he was wounded in the neck by shrapnel, but remained at his post for three hours, and returned as soon as his wound had been dressed. When Colonel Gordon was wounded at about 3.30 p.m., Major Lewis took command of the Battalion. He had previously been brought to notice for gallant conduct and was now awarded the D.S.O.

" Captain Wilson, whose name had several times been brought to notice for gallantry and determination, was severely wounded while issuing final instructions to his men before the advance, but he refused to give in and went forward with the attack until he could see that the men were over the German parapet. He was then taken back in a state of collapse. For his conspicuous gallantry he received the D.S.O.

" Inseparably bound up with the record of the 2nd Leicesters in this war is the name of the Reverend Ronald Irwin, the regimental chaplain. Coming from

* Also missing.

India with the Corps, he was present at all the actions in which the Battalion was engaged, and, non-combatant though he was, showed on many occasions as high a degree of heroism as any soldier could attain. He accompanied the Indian troops to Mesopotamia, where he again displayed the greatest bravery and devotion to his duties, attended the wounded and dying under the heaviest fire, and was eventually severely wounded in carrying a man out of action. For his conspicuous gallantry he has received the D.S.O. and the Military Cross, with a bar."

Of the Medical Officer, General Willcocks wrote : " Here, too, fell a good soldier, of that brave but merciful band the Royal Army Medical Corps, Captain Deane, attached for duty. He had already earned the Military Cross, and died as he had lived—going about doing good. I hope I shall not be accused of aiding our next enemy when I give them my advice, viz., keep out of the way of the Leicesters " !

In the report on these operations furnished by Major-General Jacob, he wrote :—

" *The charge made by the 2/8th Gurkhas with the 2nd Leicesters of the Garhwal Brigade and by the 2nd Black Watch, 69th Punjabis and 1/4th Black Watch of the Bareilly Brigade could not have been finer.*"

General Sir Douglas Haig concluded his report on the battle with these words :—

" *The General Officer Commanding the First Army wishes to express his appreciation of the good work done by all ranks and his gratification at the good progress made by the I. and IV. Corps. Also, though the opposition north of the Canal prevented great progress of subsidiary attacks, the G.O.C. is very pleased with the manner in which the I., III. and Indian Corps carried out the rôle assigned to them of retaining the enemy in their front.*"

Finally, Sir John French, in his despatch of October 15th, 1915, wrote that :—

" *The Indian Corps attacked the Moulin de Plètre, while the III. Corps was directed against the trenches at Le Bridoux. These attacks started at daybreak and were at first successful all along the line. Later in the day the enemy brought up strong reserves, and after hard fighting and variable fortunes, the troops engaged in this part of the line occupied their original trenches at night-fall. They succeeded admirably, however, in fulfilling the rôle allotted to them, and in holding large numbers of the enemy away from the main attack.*"

This account of the action must not be allowed to close without mention of a very gallant act performed by Rifleman Kulbir Thapa, of the 2/3rd Gurkhas, for which he received the Victoria Cross, and which reflects as much credit on the man whose life he saved as upon the brave Gurkha himself.

" During this action a deed which could hardly be surpassed for sheer bravery and self-sacrifice was performed by Rifleman Kulbir Thapa. He entered the German wire and escaped alive. Kulbir succeeded, after being wounded, in getting through the wire in some extraordinary way and charged straight through the German trench. In rear of it he found a badly injured man of the 2nd Leicesters. *The wounded man begged Kulbir Thapa to leave him and save himself,* but the Gurkha refused to do so, and remained by his side throughout the day and the following night. Luckily there was a heavy mist on the morning of the 26th September, of which Kulbir took advantage to bring the man out through the German wire. He succeeded, after hairbreadth escapes, in doing this unobserved, and put the wounded man in a place of safety. Not content with this, he returned and rescued, one after the other, two wounded Gurkhas. He then went back again and brought in the British soldier in broad daylight, carrying him most of the way under fire of the enemy."*

On October 3rd the Battalion was moved from Paradis to billets in Locon, the Garhwal Brigade being now in Divisional Reserve; while during the rest of the month it was either up in the trenches on Givenchy Ridge or in Brigade Reserve at Albert Road. During this month considerable reinforcements, both in officers and other ranks, arrived to fill up the many gaps in the Battalion, and in all 19 officers and 496 non-commissioned officers and men joined the service companies; the officers were Major E. F. S. Henderson, Captains R. H. Ames, Lieutenants A. J. Boulter and A. H. Howell, Second-Lieutenants C. G. R. Swindells, G. L. Gwyther, J. R. Seal, O. H. Buckingham, H. Billings, H. D. Byers, H. E. L. Chudleigh, L. Dowding, T. C. D. Hassall, J. Redwood, H. D. Muggeridge, A. E. Sturdy, A. Belle and H. E. Martin; against these must be set certain losses which were incurred during this month, for in the course of it Captain C. C. Rolph and 2 men were killed, while Second-Lieutenants Seal, Hassall, Billings, Redwood and Muggeridge and 31 other ranks were wounded or gassed or shell-shocked.

On the last day of the month Lieutenant-Colonel Gordon rejoined on recovery from his wound, and resumed command of the Battalion, his return coinciding with an announcement which was now authoritatively made that the Indian Army Corps would shortly embark at Marseilles for an " unknown destination."

The question of reinforcements for the Indian units of the Indian Army Corps had from the first given cause for much anxiety, and in the late autumn of this year matters came to a head. The reserve organization had hopelessly broken down, the casualties in the Indian ranks could not be promptly and adequately replaced, while it was quite impossible to provide and maintain a satisfactory reinforcement of British officers. As time went on and wastage grew, Indian battalions became mere skeletons, and of the truth of this statement the following affords ample proof; by the beginning of November, 1915, the 47th Sikhs had only 28 *men* left—no British or Indian officers—of those who had originally landed with the regiment in France, while the 59th Rifles had no British officers and only 4 Indian officers and 75 other ranks of their original numbers !

* "The Indian Corps in France," pp. 410, 411.

" For some time past during the autumn of 1915, rumours had been current of the impending transfer of the Corps to other theatres of war less remote from its original base.   It was therefore without surprise that information was received on the 31st October that the Indian Corps would be required to embark at Marseilles in the near future," leaving behind the Territorial and other British units which had joined it in recent months.

The casualties in British units alone of the Corps amounted by November 19th, 1915, to the following numbers :—

	Killed.	Wounded.	Missing.	Total.
Officers	124	363	37	524
Other Ranks ...	1,806	8,388	2,089	12,283
Total	1,930	8,751	2,126	12,807

The 2nd Battalion The Leicestershire Regiment was relieved in the trenches on November 2nd, and marched to l'Epinette, where all rested and cleaned up as well as possible, marching again on the 4th eight and a half miles to Thiennes; here, on the 7th, the Battalion left for Marseilles in three trains; the first contained Captain R. H. Ames, Second-Lieutenant H. E. Martin and 100 other ranks; in the second were Second-Lieutenants J. P. Swain and O. H. Buckingham and 100 men; while in the third was the remainder of the Battalion, under Major F. Lewis, who had just assumed command of the Battalion *vice* Lieutenant-Colonel Gordon, posted to temporary command of the 70th Infantry Brigade.   In the first two trains were also the Garhwal Rifles and the 2/3rd Gurkhas.

Marseilles was reached at 11 a.m. on the 10th, when the Battalion was at once embarked in the following transports : in the *Clan MacGillivray* were Major F. Lewis, D.S.O., Major E. F. S. Henderson, Captains D. L. Weir and R. H. Ames, Lieutenants A. H. Howell, Second-Lieutenants A. E. Sturdy, A. C. L. Chudleigh, L. Dowding, J. Redwood, C. G. R. Swindells, C. B. Godfrey, G. L. Gwyther, H. D. Byers, H. Billings, J. P. Swain, T. C. D. Hassall, A. Belle and Lieutenant J. G. Waine, R.A.M.C., and 899 other ranks. In the *Urlana* was Second-Lieutenant D. W. Sutherland with 12 officers' chargers and 54 mules; while, there not being sufficient accommodation in the *Clan MacGillivray*, Second-Lieutenants H. E. Martin and O. H. Buckingham were embarked in the s.s. *Oranda*.   The whole sailed the same afternoon, speeded by valedictory messages from their Commander and their King.

The following was the message sent to the Garhwal Brigade from Field-Marshal Sir John French :—

" *As the Garhwal Brigade is now leaving my command to take part in operations elsewhere, I wish to send it my personal thanks for the services it has rendered to the King-Emperor since reaching France more than a year ago.*

" *The behaviour of the Brigade in action and its splendid discipline have been excellent throughout, and it has always maintained its fighting spirit in spite of heavy losses and under the most trying weather conditions.*

" I wish the Garhwal Brigade all good fortune wherever its duty may take it, and feel sure it will everywhere maintain the excellent reputation it has earned in France."

The message from the King-Emperor was conveyed to the Indian Corps by H.R.H. The Prince of Wales, at a parade held on November 25th at Château Mazinghem and attended by representatives of the Corps, and runs as follows : —

" Officers, Non-Commissioned Officers and Men of the Indian Army Corps.

" More than a year ago I summoned you from India to fight for the safety of My Empire and the honour of My pledged word on the battle-fields of Belgium and France. The confidence which I then expressed in your sense of duty, your courage and your chivalry you have since then nobly justified.

" I now require your services in another field of action, but before you leave France I send My dear and gallant son, the Prince of Wales, who has shared with My armies the dangers and hardships of the campaign, to thank you in My name for your services and to express to you My satisfaction.

" British and Indian comrades-in-arms, yours has been a fellowship in toils and hardships, in courage and endurance often against great odds, in deeds nobly done and days of memorable conflicts in a war waged under new conditions, and in particularly trying circumstances you have worthily upheld the honour of the Empire, and the great traditions of My Army in India.

" I have followed your fortunes with the greatest interest and watched your gallant actions with pride and satisfaction. I mourn with you the loss of many gallant officers and men. Let it be your consolation, as it was their pride, that they freely gave their lives in a just cause for the honour of their Sovereign and the safety of My Empire. They died as gallant soldiers, and I shall ever hold their sacrifice in grateful remembrance. You leave France with a just pride in honourable deeds already achieved and with My assured confidence that your proved valour and experience will contribute to further victories in the new fields of action to which you go.

" I pray God to bless and guard you, and to bring you back safely when the final Victory is won, each to his own home—there to be welcomed with honour among his own people."

When the 2nd Battalion left France, all those serving in it had probably seen the last of their brigadier, Brigadier-General C. G. Blackader, whose tenure of the command of the Garhwal Brigade expired on November 30th of this year. He was appointed extra A.D.C. to H.M. The King on January 1st, 1916, and from the 8th of this month to June 25th he held the command of the 177th Brigade. Home Forces, being on July 12th promoted to the command of the 38th Division in France. This command he resigned in June, 1918, having been obliged to undergo Pasteur treatment owing to the bite of a dog. On November 21st he was given command of the Southern District in Ireland.

A brother-officer writes : " A very keen soldier himself and well up in all the latest theories of tactics and administration, he soon made what is often a dull routine an affair of life and intense interest. His lectures kept us spell-bound, and the example he set and the high standard he demanded made of the 2nd Battalion the expert machine it showed itself in the war. I well remember in France his extraordinary gift for grasping the essentials of any situation. The Regiment loved ' old Black,' and he got this devotion not from any particular kindness in his make-up, but because all ranks realized what a splendid leader he was; he had the rare gift of inspiring confidence. Blackader had a forceful personality and in any company he was always noticeable, and without any apparent effort or seeking he made his influence felt.

" I went to see him at Millbank Hospital shortly after he was admitted, suffering from the hateful disease which eventually killed him; he was as cheery and interesting as ever, talking over old times and old friends; but in a few days he became worse and worse, and had to be given morphia continuously. The end was peaceful—he died on April 2nd, 1921—but in the death of General Blackader The Leicestershire Regiment lost one of its most gallant and distinguished commanding officers. He died for his country just as much as did those who gave their lives in action."

CHAPTER IV.

1916

THE ACTIONS AT SHAIKH SAAD, THE WADI AND HANNA, THE DUJAILA REDOUBT, FALLAHIYA AND SANNAIYAT.

SAILING in a south-easterly direction, the transports containing the 2nd Battalion The Leicestershire Regiment anchored off Alexandria on November 16th, and tied up alongside the quay on the following day, when the companies disembarked, then proceeding to Tel-el-Kebir in two parties. Here the Battalion occupied a camp on the north side of the Railway Station and about one mile from the little town. On the 22nd, however, orders were received for the Battalion to entrain next day for Suez, and, leaving early next morning in two trains, Suez was reached at 9.40 and 10.45 a.m. respectively, when embarkation was at once carried out and the Battalion sailed at 3 p.m. the same day.

In the *Clan MacGillivray* were Majors F. Lewis, D.S.O., and E. F. S. Henderson, Captains D. L. Weir, A. S. McIntyre and R. H. Ames, Lieutenant A. H. Howell, Second-Lieutenants A. E. Sturdy, A. C. L. Chudleigh, L. Dowding, J. Redwood, C. G. R. Swindells, C. B. Godfrey, O. H. Buckingham, H. Billings, J. P. Swain, D.C.M., A. Belle, D. C. Royce, Lieutenant and Quartermaster H. C. Brodie, Lieutenant J. G. Waine, R.A.M.C., 896 non-commissioned officers and men and the first line transport; Lieutenant H. N. H. Grimble, Second-Lieutenants G. L. Gwyther, H. D. Byers, H. E. Martin, T. C. D. Hassall and five other ranks, three native mule drivers and eight mules voyaged in the s.s. *Janus*.

About 10 a.m. on December 6th the two ships arrived off the mouth of the River Tigris, proceeding at once up-stream to Basra, which was reached at 4 the same afternoon, exactly a year since the Mesopotamian campaign had opened with the capture by Brigadier-General Delamaine of the Fao forts. Since then there had been almost continuous fighting—at Shaiba, on the Persian border, on the Euphrates and on the Tigris; and at the moment when the 2nd Battalion The Leicestershire Regiment arrived in the country military affairs were in a somewhat critical state. General Townshend's advance up country, commenced in May of the previous year, had met with a considerable measure of initial success, for he had captured Qurna and defeated the Turks in two actions; but the heavy losses sustained by his force at Ctesiphon in November had forced his retreat on Kut-el-Amara, where he was now very closely invested. In Mesopotamia one commander-in-chief had already resigned, a second was about to be relieved, while a third, General Sir Percy Lake, had only arrived in the theatre of war a very short time before the divisions of the Indian Army Corps had reached their new scene of operations from France. General Lake had brought with him from India General Sir F. Aylmer, who had up to recently occupied the post of Adjutant-General in that country, and who had been appointed to command what was to be known as " the Tigris Army Corps," and which, largely composed of the troops now arriving in Mesopotamia from France and Egypt, was to attempt the relief of Kut and the re-establishment of British prestige, which recent events had done something to impair.

The reinforcements now arriving or already arrived at Basra from France, Egypt and India consisted of the 3rd (Lahore) and 7th (Meerut) Divisions from France and Egypt, and a Field Artillery Brigade, an Indian Cavalry Regiment, a company of Sappers and two Infantry Brigades from India, whence two Heavy Batteries of Artillery were also later dispatched.

On December 8th the 2nd Leicestershire were trans-shipped into a river steamer, the *Medjidieh*, and Barge No. 30, when the voyage up the Tigris was commenced at four o'clock on the morning of the 9th, the whole of the first line vehicles, except four machine-gun limbers, being left behind at Basra. On reaching Ali Gharbi on the forenoon of the 13th the Battalion at once disembarked, and while " A " Company occupied a section of the defensible perimeter, the remainder of the Battalion went into general reserve, and here during the rest of the month war training was carried on, and tents, ammunition and field stores were drawn.

By this time the 7th Meerut Division had been completely reorganized and it was now composed as follows, the commander being Major-General Sir G. Younghusband :—

    19th Infantry Brigade, Lieutenant-Colonel Dennys.
    28th Infantry Brigade, Major-General G. V. Kemball.
    35th Infantry Brigade, Brigadier-General G. B. Rice.

The 2nd Battalion The Leicestershire Regiment was in the 28th Infantry Brigade, which also contained the 51st Sikhs, the 53rd Sikhs and the 56th Rifles.

As has already been stated, Major-General Aylmer was detailed to command the force intended for the relief of Kut, and in his instructions he was informed " that the main object of his operations was the defeat of the enemy on the Tigris line and the relief of General Townshend's force at Kut. For this purpose the force at his disposal would, as far as was then known, consist of the 7th Division (28th, 35th and 19th or 21st Brigades), the 3rd Division (7th, 8th and 9th Brigades), with divisional troops, Corps artillery and the cavalry and details at Ali Gharbi." General Aylmer was also told that General Townshend had been informed that the concentration of the relief force would be made on the line Shaikh Saad—Ali Gharbi, but, said General Aylmer's instructions, " the extent to which this could be accomplished would depend on the military situation from day to day."

" On the 12th December General Aylmer arrived at Amara to take up his command. At this time the information received showed that the force opposing General Townshend still consisted only of the four Turkish divisions which had fought at Ctesiphon; but a fresh division (52nd) was probably just arriving in the Baghdad area; and there was an unconfirmed report that a further division had reached Falluja (west of Baghdad on the Euphrates).

"On the 12th December the distribution of the British force in Mesopotamia, including the force in Kut, was as follows: at Ali Gharbi were thirteen squadrons of cavalry, four and three-quarter battalions of infantry and ten guns; at Amara four and a half battalions and six guns; on the line of communications between Amara and Basra one sapper company, one pioneer battalion and four companies of infantry; at Nasiriya and on the Euphrates line one squadron of cavalry, three and a half battalions of infantry and ten guns; in Arabistan three squadrons of cavalry and half a battalion of infantry; and at Basra, in addition to its garrison of three companies of infantry and two guns, there was a cavalry regiment and four guns under orders for Nasiriya, and a cavalry regiment, a sapper company and one and a half battalions of infantry under orders for Amara and beyond. In addition there were at Bushire a squadron of cavalry, seven guns and two infantry battalions."*

With General Townshend in Kut-el-Amara were 9,185 men, of whom 7,211 were infantry, while the enemy's total strength at the date when the advance of the Tigris Corps was timed to commence, was estimated at 22,000 men with 67 guns, in addition to a mixed brigade with two light guns or Maxims, assisted by at least 2,000 Arab irregulars; but this proved to be an exaggerated estimate.

On January 3rd, 1916, General Younghusband issued his orders for the advance of the Division on the 4th, and on receipt of these the following Operation Order was given out by Major Lewis to the Battalion under his command:—

"1. The Advance Guard of the enemy, strength about 2,500 Turks and Arabs with three or four guns, is reported to be entrenching astride the river about 34 miles south-east of Shaikh Saad. Small bodies of mounted men have been seen between this point and Ali Gharbi. From four miles west of Ali Gharbi the inhabitants of the country are to be considered hostile.

"2. The 6th Cavalry Brigade and 7th Division will advance to-morrow by both banks to the vicinity of a north and south line passing through the letter E of River Tigris [on the map]. The G.O.C. Division will move by river on board the *Julnar*. The following force will move on the right bank and bivouac near the bend of the river due north of the second A in Omaiyah: 6th Cavalry Brigade, which acts independently to the front and left flank; 28th Brigade and attached troops under the command of the G.O.C. 28th Brigade. The right flank column will direct: two gunboats will move approximately in line with main body of advance guard."

The 2nd Battalion The Leicestershire Regiment was to move in the centre of the main body.

* Moberly, "Mesopotamia Campaign," Vol. II, pp. 191, 192.

The following Order of the Day was published by Major-General Aylmer, addressed to " all in the Tigris Corps " :—

" *We have now to relieve our brother soldiers at Kut-al-Amara, who for a month have most gallantly repulsed every hostile assault, inflicting great losses on the enemy. Such a task must appeal very deeply to us all, and I feel the utmost confidence that, whatever the difficulties we may encounter, every man will do his utmost to ensure a glorious result.*"

The advance began, as projected, on the 4th, and on the following day, when the Battalion furnished the advance guard, bodies of enemy cavalry were seen on the left bank of the river; these were, however, dispersed by the fire of the guns with the advance guard and the march was continued uninterruptedly to the river bend near Musandaq, where the force bivouacked for the night, the Battalion finding the outposts, " B," " C " and " D " Companies forming a line of six picquets, while " A " Company was in reserve. That night the enemy sniped into the bivouac, without, however, doing any serious harm, the Cavalry Brigade only suffering a few casualties.

" The advance on the morning of the 6th, delayed by a dense mist, started at 9 a.m. and was carried out in the following order : preceded by an advance guard of one troop 16th Cavalry and the 37th Dogras and with the bulk of the 16th Cavalry as right flank guard, General Rice's column moved up the left bank, followed at one mile distance by the Reserve Column under Colonel Dennys. On the right bank the advance guard consisted of one troop 16th Cavalry, one section of the 9th Brigade, R.F.A., 56th Rifles and a company of the 128th Pioneers. General Kemball's main body moved in two parallel columns; the right one—moving along a track near the river bank—consisted of column headquarters, the 9th Field Artillery Brigade (less one section), 92nd Punjabis, one company 128th Pioneers, three field ambulance sections and all the wheeled first-line transport of the column; the left column consisted of half the 13th Sapper Company, the Brigade Machine Gun Company, 2nd Leicestershire, 51st Sikhs (less two companies, escort of the second-line transport) and 53rd Sikhs. The 6th Cavalry Brigade moved two miles from the left or outer flank of the two infantry and artillery columns; and one company 128th Pioneers remained behind in camp to prepare an aeroplane landing ground."*

On nearing Hibsh about 12 noon the enemy was reported as holding an entrenched position about two miles south-east of Shaikh Saad, extending outwards from the river bank for some 1,500 yards, and the 2nd Leicestershire were now deployed into a line of companies in fours at 50 paces interval and 200 yards in rear of the 56th Rifles, which, with the 128th Pioneer Company, advancing with its right on the river bank, was to engage the enemy, pushing in their attack when that by the main body developed.

The Battalion continued to move forward in this formation until later ordered to prolong the line to the left and in echelon of the 53rd Sikhs at 200 yards distance.

* " The Mesopotamia Campaign," Vol. II, p. 217.

L

At about 2 p.m. orders were issued to attack the Turkish position and advance to the bend of the river at Shaikh Saad, when the Brigade was formed as follows: the 56th Rifles on the right, 53rd Sikhs in echelon at 200 yards distance to the left, the 2nd Leicestershire in echelon again 200 yards to the left of the 53rd, and the 51st Sikhs in reserve. The advance of the Battalion was made in four lines; in the first or firing line were two platoons each from " B " and " A " Companies, on left and right respectively, the whole four platoons covering a front of 400 yards; then at 200 yards interval the remaining platoons of these two companies in support; the reserve, formed by " D " and " C " Companies, following in two lines at 400 and 200 yards distance respectively.

As the attack progressed it was met by very heavy rifle and machine-gun fire, and soon after three o'clock it was noticed and reported that enemy cavalry appeared to be working round the left flank of the Battalion; while shortly afterwards it was for the first time realized that the Turkish trenches extended very much further to the south than had been reported, so that instead of the main British attack outflanking the *Turkish* trenches, the left of the *British* attack was itself outflanked; while it now appeared that the enemy had reinforced his firing line, and the Battalion, having by this done the same, there remained only one company—" D "—in reserve. The advance, however, continued, and at 4.30 the O.C. " B " Company was ordered to move in echelon to the rest of the line, keeping his left slightly thrown back, while Major Henderson, commanding the reserve, drew " D " Company gradually closer to the front.

After suffering considerable losses the firing line reached a point within 500 yards of the Turkish trenches, and it had now become evident that, the enemy's line having been thrown forward, the left of the Battalion was becoming enveloped and was being subjected to enfilade fire; any further advance seemed impossible unless fresh troops could be brought up to engage the enemy's right. But General Younghusband had now come to the conclusion that the Turks intended to make a determined resistance, and that darkness would probably have set in before General Kemball's column could press its attack home—sunset here being at about 5.10 p.m. Orders were therefore given to stop the advance and take up battle outposts for the night, and the Battalion accordingly entrenched and established itself for the night in a strong position from which the attack could be resumed in the morning.

During the night rain fell, while an incessant and heavy fire was kept up by the enemy, so that the bringing up of reserve ammunition and supplies presented many difficulties and caused more casualties, in the 2nd Leicestershire ten officers alone having this day been killed or wounded. But the Battalion stretcher bearers, under Lance-Corporal Queenan, did excellent work throughout and brought in the killed and wounded of the Battalion and other units.

At 11.12 a.m. on the 7th orders were received that the attack would shortly be renewed on both banks. That on the left bank, though gallantly pressed, was finally brought to a standstill within 300 or 400 yards of the Turkish trenches, but that on the right bank met with more success. Here the advance began at 2 p.m., the Battalion being again on the extreme left wing and moving forward as soon as the 53rd Sikhs were seen to leave their trenches. " According to the orders issued to the 28th Brigade a general assault was to be made as soon as the 92nd Punjabis came up from the reserve on the left of the line. About 3 p.m. the 92nd commenced their advance, and, pushing forward in rushes, reached the left of the line. But the hostile fire still prevented an assault and General Kemball brought up his last reserves, a company of the 51st Sikhs and half the 13th Sapper Company.

" He was on the point of pushing them in to give the firing line the necessary impetus, *when at about 4 p.m. the Leicestershire, and then the 51st, 53rd and 92nd rose and, with a fine assault over the last 300 yards, carried the Turkish front line of trenches.* A second line of trenches not far behind was quickly occupied, practically without opposition, and, 400 yards beyond this, two mountain guns abandoned by the Turks were captured and brought in. Over 300 Turkish dead were found, and three machine guns with much ammunition and equipment, as well as some 600 prisoners, were captured. But further advance was for the time being found to be impossible owing to the stout resistance from hostile trenches to the front and flank. . . . . General Kemball's infantry consolidated the position gained and the guns were brought up in close support. Here they remained for the night."*

In this final rush two of the Battalion machine guns, pushing forward along a nullah, greatly assisted the advance, first by enfilading a Turkish trench marked " P " on the map, and later by distributing their fire along Trench " Q "; while the Battalion was throughout splendidly supported by two guns of the 28th Field Battery, the observing officer of which advanced with his field telephone immediately in rear of the 2nd Leicestershire. About 80 prisoners were taken by the Battalion and also a large quantity of rifles, ammunition and equipment, etc., and many dead and wounded Turks were found in the captured trenches, 62 of the former being buried in the Battalion section of the front alone.

The casualties in the two days' fighting had again been very serious : Major E. F. S. Henderson, Captain R. H. Ames, Lieutenant A. H. Hassall, Second-Lieutenants L. Dowding, D. C. Royce, G. L. Gwyther and A. B. Privett were killed or died of wounds, and Captains A. S. McIntyre and D. W. Sutherland, Second-Lieutenants C. G. R. Swindells, J. Redwood, C. B. Godfrey, C. G. Fraser, O. H. Buckingham, H. Billings and A. Belle were wounded, while the casualties among the other ranks numbered 303.

An " Eyewitness "† writes of this day's attack : " The Leicesters on the left sustained the reputation of dash and fearlessness earned in France. Sixteen officers of the Regiment fell in the attack—seven killed and nine wounded, and 298 of the rank and file. The 51st Sikhs on the right of the Leicesters were the first to secure a footing in the enemy's lines, and it fell to them to capture the two mountain guns and three maxims which were opposite their position. The 53rd Sikhs and 56th Rifles on the right advanced with the same resolute *élan*.

---

* " The Mesopotamia Campaign," Vol. II, p. 232.
† Candler, " The Long Road to Baghdad," Vol. I, p. 46.

These three regiments, part of the old Punjab Frontier Force, with the Leicesters, made up the 28th Brigade. They, with the 92nd Punjabis, made the great haul on January 7th. . . . But the cost of the victory was heavy. The casualties in the 28th Brigade alone, apart from the 92nd Punjabis, were 1,106.''

During these days of fighting, and those which immediately followed, the sufferings of the sick and wounded were almost beyond belief. In the Official History of the Mesopotamia Campaign* we are told that '' on the 7th January there was insufficient accommodation for the wounded either in the *Julnar* or in tents which had been pitched for the purpose. In consequence, a very large proportion of the wounded had to lie out all night in the rain on the bare ground without shelter and without sufficient clothing and food. The medical personnel were too few to attend to all of them without delay, and the supply personnel were also too few to arrange for food for them. The removal of the wounded from the front line was mainly carried out after dark on the 7th, and it was not until daylight on the 8th that the very bad state of affairs became apparent. Efforts were then made with some success by officers and personnel of the corps to assist and get some shelter and food for the wounded. Even then, however, and for some days after, the medical arrangements were unable to cope with all the work, and as a result the wounded and sick endured very great suffering. The total British casualties amounted to 4,007, of whom 417 were killed.''

'' Of this number,'' it is stated in '' The Medical History of the War,''† '' 90 British officers, 900 British other ranks and 2,500 Indian other ranks were admitted to the medical units during the 6th, 7th and 8th January. The wounded after the action on the 6th were put on board the *Julnar* and a paddle-steamer; those of the 7th and 8th January were admitted into No. 20 Combined Field Ambulance and the improvised British sections. On the 8th January another paddle-steamer was placed at the disposal of the medical service and 41 British officers, 182 British other ranks and 313 Indian other ranks, sick and wounded, were placed on board. . . . . By 8 p.m. on January 7th the supply of dressings and blankets was completely exhausted. A few of the wounded were lucky and had been covered by one blanket. Very many were uncovered and became delirious during the night from fatigue, exposure and hunger. Two thousand wounded were transferred to the post hospital at Shaikh Saad, and three medical officers with a few subordinate personnel were left to look after them. Rations were dumped both for British and Indians, but there was no Supply and Transport personnel to issue them, and this had to be done by the medical officers, the senior of whom had to spend his time issuing rations instead of dressing wounded. . . . . At Musandaq . . . . there were three medical officers and three subordinates to look after 1,200 wounded. . . . . The evacuation of the wounded was not completed until 24th January.''

* Vol. II, pp. 241, 242.
† Vol. IV, pp. 205, 206.

The Regimental Officer is more outspoken. "After the battle, even more than during it, the results of the confused haste with which the units from France had been brought up became apparent. . . . . The Meerut Division went into action on the 6th; the Divisional Ambulances began to arrive on the 18th. The casualties at Shaikh Saad numbered over 4,000; the beds available were 250. One ambulance on the left bank which received 1,900 patients consisted of two tents, three doctors and a supply of stretchers so limited that only one was available for each fifty cases. Dressings ran out; there were no arrangements for feeding the patients and only one overcrowded boat to take them downstream. The only land transport available was the springless, jolting, mule transport cart."*

Finally, an officer of the 2nd Battalion The Leicestershire Regiment writes as follows of the sufferings of his wounded comrades : " It rained heavily and was freezingly cold and the mud was awful. Medical arrangements had completely failed and the sufferings of the wounded were horrible. At times men lay out all night in pitiless, icy rain, dying from exposure. Many were found dead without a mark on them; others were picked up and slowly jolted, petrified and sodden with freezing mud, in springless carts to the dressing station. Later, a man arrived at Amara with wounds which for eight days had remained unattended—wounds which were putrifying, gangrenous and full of maggots."

The care of the wounded of the Battalion was mainly undertaken by Lieutenant and Quartermaster Brodie, who did most admirable work .

Excellent work was done throughout the action by the Battalion signallers, machine gunners, and especially by the ammunition carriers, and the casualty list seems to show that their losses were disproportionately heavy. The ammunition supply was so well maintained by the Battalion carriers that on the night of January 7th these were able, by request of the G.O.C. Brigade, to furnish ammunition to refill the pouches of the Indian battalion on the left, the 92nd Punjabis.

The Battalion remained throughout the whole of the 8th in occupation of the Turkish trenches captured on the previous day, while the Corps and Divisional commanders consulted as to whether a further attack should or should not be made, reports being very conflicting as to whether the enemy was still holding his ground and as to whether he had or had not been reinforced, and if so to what extent. But at 10 a.m. on the 9th the cavalry reports showed that the Turks had evacuated many of their trenches on the left bank, which were then occupied; at 2 p.m. the 28th Brigade advanced and occupied Shaikh Saad; and some two hours later it was found that the enemy had fallen back to or beyond Ora, where he occupied an entrenched position on and to the west of a nullah opposite Ora, known as the Wadi.

At Shaikh Saad the Battalion remained several days in bivouac, cleaning up and reorganizing, and filling up the many gaps in the ranks with a draft of 211 non-commissioned officers and men which arrived on the 11th under Lieutenant

* Wauchope, " A History of the Black Watch in the Great War," Vol. I, p. 214.

A. E. Dakin and Second-Lieutenant R. W. G. Card. On this day, too, the following congratulatory Orders were received :—

1. From the Commander of the Tigris Army Corps.

" *Though deploring the heavy losses which have taken place, the Corps Commander wishes heartily to congratulate all ranks under his command on the great gallantry they have shown during the recent operations and on the success which they have gained.*"

2. From the Commander of the Right Bank Column.

" *Before the Right Bank Column breaks up, Major-General G. V. Kemball wishes it to be known that he received the congratulations of the Corps Commander on the successful results achieved by the gallant troops under his command.*

" *He would add on his own behalf that the dash and fearlessness of the 2nd Leicesters were the admiration of the whole Column, and that the Indian regiments of the 28th Brigade well sustained the reputation of the Frontier Force. He feels sure that the Frontier Force Brigade will join with him in thanking the 9th Brigade, R.F.A., and the 23rd Mountain Battery F.F., and the 92nd Punjabis for the very efficient support which they gave to the frontal attack.*

" *Although the losses of the Right Bank Column in the attack were unfortunately heavy, those of the strongly entrenched enemy were undoubtedly heavier —a very rare occurrence in such circumstances. Over 350 Turkish dead were buried by us on the field, 2 guns, 3 maxims and 600 prisoners were taken, together with a large amount of ammunition, and finally the Turkish commander was compelled to withdraw his force on both banks.*"

The new position now taken up by the Turks and occupied by some 11,000 men, was about three and a half miles eastward of and astride the long and narrow Hanna defile formed by the Suwaikiya marsh and the Tigris River; and it was decided that while the 28th Brigade should make a frontal attack on the enemy's position on the 13th, the 19th, 21st and 35th Brigades should cross the Wadi by a ford to the north, the cavalry moving on the outer flank, and attack the enemy's left flank and rear. To this end the 2nd Leicestershire moved, on the afternoon of the 12th, to the left bank of the Tigris, together with the remaining units of the 28th Brigade, and an hour later marched on some four miles and took over a line of trenches which had been dug by the 19th Brigade.

Patrols sent out at daybreak on the 13th reported the presence of small parties of the enemy in the direction of the Wadi, and orders were now given that the 2nd Leicestershire and the 56th Rifles should drive the enemy from his forward position and take up a line 800 yards beyond it, under cover of which the British guns could shell the main position on the Wadi. The two battalions advanced, of the 2nd Leicestershire " C " and " D " Companies being in the firing line and " A " and " B " in reserve, and the position indicated was occupied without serious opposition and both battalions dug themselves in. At 4 p.m. the 28th Brigade was ordered to move against the enemy's position, supported by the Corps artillery, and to direct its attack against the left centre of the Turkish line along the Wadi—the 56th Rifles forming the firing line and supports, the 53rd Sikhs in the second line, the 2nd Leicestershire echeloned on the left flank level with the 53rd, the 51st in rear of the 53rd in reserve. In the 2nd Leicestershire " C " and " D " were in front and " A " and " B " in the second line.

" The attack was pushed forward with speed and determination. Hostile fire was encountered at about 1,100 yards from the Wadi, and when they got within about 600 yards the infantry began to suffer heavy casualties. But they had been instructed to attack with great vigour, and, in spite of these heavy losses, the 28th Brigade responded grandly. The ground, which was dotted with low bushes, had been cleared within 500 yards of the Wadi, the Turks having marked the range on it by sticks at every hundred metres; and, with the exception of the bushes, it was practically destitute of cover except for a shallow irrigation cut some 50 yards short of the Wadi. . . . . Eventually, after heavy losses, the 56th Rifles, 53rd Sikhs and Leicestershire were merged in an irregular firing line at a standstill 200 to 300 yards from the Wadi. . . . . The fight remained thus stationary under a heavy cross-fire of machine guns. . . . . As darkness fell, there being no longer any hope of success, the remnants of the 28th Brigade were withdrawn, having suffered a total of 648 casualties. Of these, which included three out of the four battalion commanders, the Leicestershire contributed 210, the 53rd Sikhs 194, the 56th Rifles 172 and the 51st about 60. Though the attack failed, its conduct affords a fine testimony to the gallantry and soldierlike behaviour of the Brigade, already much weakened by their heavy losses at Shaikh Saad a week before."*

The actual loss in the 2nd Battalion The Leicestershire Regiment amounted to 4 officers wounded—Major F. Lewis, D.S.O., Lieutenant A. E. Dakin, Second-Lieutenants R. W. G. Card and T. C. D. Hassall—while 197 other ranks were killed and wounded.

On the morning of the 14th patrols sent out established the fact that the enemy had evacuated his position, and some of the troops now moved forward, the Battalion remaining during some days of very windy weather here in bivouac, burying their dead and filling in the Turkish trenches.

The enemy had by this fallen back to a very strong position, only a mile in extent, but consisting of five lines of trenches each 200 yards in rear of one another, and with one flank resting on the Tigris and the other on the Suwaikiya Marsh—a position known as the Umm-el-Hanna Defile. This position was attacked on January 21st, but the 28th Brigade was this day in Corps Reserve and was not seriously engaged, though the Battalion came under enemy fire and had some twelve men wounded. This attack, like its predecessors, failed of complete success and the casualties were very heavy, numbering 2,741, and the wounded again suffered terribly; while, though the Turkish losses had been relatively great, the enemy had at last succeeded in bringing the relieving force to a temporary halt, and the troops under command of General Aylmer

* " The Mesopotamia Campaign," Vol. II, pp. 251, 252.

settled down to await reinforcements before further efforts should be made for the relief of Kut, whence had come a message from General Townshend that he could hold out for a further period of 84 days; twenty-five miles of difficult and stoutly-defended country still separated the garrison of Kut from the relieving force.

During January and part of February there was very heavy rain, the Tigris rose and much of the adjacent country was flooded, but the force remained stationary in front of the Hanna position, and the Battalion suffered a few casualties from enemy fire, among which was Lieutenant K. H. Pegg, who was killed on February 21st. During this month the 28th Brigade was strengthened by the inclusion of a Provisional Battalion of the Oxford and Bucks Light Infantry.

In General Sir Percy Lake's despatch of August 12th, 1916, he gives the following appreciation of the military situation at this time:—

" The situation at the end of February was briefly as follows : on the left bank the enemy, having been reinforced, still held the Hanna position in force; further in rear were other defensive lines at Fallahiya, Sannaiyat, Nakhailat and along the northern part of the Es Sinn position. All except the last-named had been constructed since the battle of Hanna on 21st January. They were all protected on both banks by the Tigris and the Suwaikiya marsh respectively. On the right bank the Es Sinn position constituted the Turkish main line of defence with an advanced position near Beit Aiessa. The right flank of the Es Sinn position rested on the Dujaila Redoubt, which lay some five miles south of the river and fourteen south-west of the British lines on the right bank. It was decided to attack the Turkish right flank and Dujaila Redoubt as the first step towards the relief of Kut, before the arrival of the flood season about the middle of March.

" The central point of support in the Turkish defences between the Tigris and the Shatt-el-Hai was a considerable work called the Dujaila Redoubt. At this point the line of the Turkish defences was crossed by the bed of an ancient tributary of the main river, dry in the summer season but a sinuous swamp during the wet months, and the Dujaila Redoubt was situated at the point of one of the bends and on the further side, so that it was partly surrounded by a sort of natural ditch. Both the apparent security of the position, and the difficulty of obtaining upon the spot a supply of drinking water, had led the enemy so far to hold the Redoubt lightly. If he could be surprised, and the bend or peninsula on which the Redoubt was built seized, his line west of the Tigris would be effectively broken and the siege of Kut would have to be raised."

When on the afternoon of March 7th General Aylmer issued his final orders to his subordinate commanders, he laid great stress on the fact that the attack was to be a surprise one and that the assault on the Dujaila Redoubt was to be pushed through with the utmost vigour.

His dispositions were as follows : the 7th Division and attached troops under General Younghusband were to contain the enemy in the Hanna position and protect the Wadi Camps and the bridge over the Tigris, while the remaining troops, formed in three columns—Columns " A " and " B " under Major-General Kemball and Column " C " under Major-General Keary—were to attack the Redoubt from the south and east respectively; the 28th Brigade was in Column " B."

General Kemball's orders were to the following effect : " the 36th Infantry Brigade, supported by the 8th Battery, was to attack the Turkish trenches lying about two miles south-west of the Redoubt, the right of the attack being directed on Imam-al-Mansur. After clearing these trenches, the 36th Brigade, which was to keep in touch with, and cover the left flank of, the brigades attacking the Redoubt, was to swing northwards in readiness for a further advance. The 9th Infantry Brigade was to deploy on a front of 600 yards, and with its right on the western bank of the depression, which it was warned not to enter or cross, was to advance against the Redoubt. The 28th Brigade was to follow in echelon on the left of the 9th Brigade on a frontage of 400 yards, so as to support but not join in its assault, which was to be supported by the whole of General Kemball's artillery except the 8th Battery, R.F.A."

We may now quote from the War Diary of the 2nd Leicestershire Regiment.

" 7th March. At 5.30 p.m. Brigade formed up and marched south-west to a point about one mile south of the Dujaila Redoubt, arriving there at about 7.30 a.m. 8th.

" 8th. Shortly after this the Brigade deployed, 53rd Sikhs and 56th Rifles being in the front line on a frontage of 400 yards, Leicestershire Regiment and 51st Sikhs in reserve, the battalions moving forward in two lines of platoon columns. The objective allotted to the Brigade was a line extending from the Dujaila Redoubt westwards for 400 yards. The objective of the 9th Brigade on our right was the Dujaila Redoubt, while the 36th Brigade on our left worked westward on a special mission. The two leading battalions of the 28th Brigade were met by a very heavy rifle and machine-gun fire, but succeeded in getting well forward, while the two reserve battalions were kept a considerable distance in rear to meet any counter-attack which it was believed would almost certainly be delivered against the left of the Brigade."

The Official History, as regards the opposition initially experienced, hardly seems to bear out the foregoing, for it states (Vol. 2, p. 330) that " the advance of the 28th Brigade at first met with little opposition, and at 10.40 a.m. Colonel Elsmie,* its commander, in giving his position, reported to General Kemball that he had no report from the front line, but the enemy appeared to be retiring. But shortly afterwards a body of Turks, occupying trenches about 1,400 yards to the front, opened a heavy rifle and machine-gun fire on the Brigade. Colonel Elsmie's infantry continued, however, to advance steadily, forcing the Turks to retire from two or three positions, until about 11.45 a.m. The Brigade firing line was then about level with that of the 9th Brigade, their casualties had been heavy, and the Turkish opposition had so strengthened that the firing line was checked at about 500 yards distance from the Turkish position."

---

* Lieut.-Colonel A. M. S. Elsmie, C.M.G., 56th Rifles.

To continue to quote from the Battalion War Diary :—

" The two leading battalions, owing to heavy casualties, were compelled to entrench some 400 yards short of the enemy's position. About 10 a.m. Major D. L. Weir, D.S.O., was wounded and Captain R. J. McIntyre assumed command. At 10.50 the Battalion faced north-west to meet an expected counter-attack, the formation being two lines of half-battalions—" B " and " A " in the front line with the machine guns and " C " and " D " in the second line; the counter-attack, however, did not take place.

" The 36th Brigade met with considerable opposition and did not make much headway, and at 1 p.m. the Battalion received orders to join in the attack and reinforce the right of the 1/6th Devons who were on the right of the 36th Brigade. The Battalion extended and advanced in four lines, " B " Company, directing, on the right and " A " Company on the left, each company having two platoons in the front line and two in the second. On advancing it was found that the Devons were mixed up with the Highland Light Infantry and 1/9th Gurkhas, and, there being no room, the Battalion made a right incline and prolonged the right. The front line then advanced to within 350 yards of the enemy's trenches and arrangements were being made for reinforcements to come up when the order was received to halt. The attack had now stopped at 2.40 p.m.

" At 4.30 p.m. orders were received that another attempt was to be made to capture the enemy's position and that all troops were to co-operate and assault at 5 p.m. The attack took place and the front line reached a ridge about 200 to 250 yards from the enemy when orders were received to dig in on the ground gained."

As to this final attack the Official History states that " in response to their orders the 9th, 28th and 36th Brigades had made in the meantime another gallant attempt to carry the trenches immediately to their front; but they were now under Turkish gun fire as well as heavy machine-gun and rifle fire, *the whole of the British artillery fire was concentrated on the Redoubt,* and they were definitely checked after a further short advance." (As to these words here italicised it is repeatedly stated in the Official History that the British gunners had been definitely ordered to direct their fire exclusively on the Redoubt and *not* on the enemy trenches, the fire from which was hindering the infantry advance.)

The action was now broken off and the Battalion was withdrawn, finally crossing the Tigris Bridge and reaching camp about 1.30 a.m. on the 10th, having during these operations " dug in " on three occasions and marched 48 miles in 53 hours; it had also incurred the following casualties : killed, 13 non-commissioned officers and men; wounded, 4 officers—Major D. L. Weir, D.S.O., Captain J. P. Swain, D.C.M., Lieutenant A. E. Sturdy, Second-Lieutenants H. E. Martin and F. W. Woodfield (also missing) and 136 other ranks, while 14 men were missing.

In General Sir Percy Lake's despatch of August 12th, the following reasons are given for breaking off the action : "the troops, who had been under arms for some thirty hours, including a long night march, were now much exhausted, and General Aylmer considered that a renewal of the assault during the night of the 8th-9th March could not be made with any prospects of success. Next morning the enemy's position was found to be unchanged, and General Aylmer, finding himself faced with the deficiency of water already referred to, decided upon the immediate withdrawal of his force to Wadi, which was reached the same night."

During the remainder of the month of March no military events of any great importance took place, Major Weir rejoined on recovery from his wound, and the Battalion was chiefly employed in taking steps to check the encroachments of the rapidly rising river. On March 11th, Lieutenant-General Gorringe relieved General Aylmer in the command of the Tigris Army Corps, while reinforcements began to come up the river from Basra, among these being the 13th Division, under General Maude; and it was determined to resume active operations as soon as possible, making a fresh attack upon the Hanna position and advancing by the left bank of the river.

On April 3rd a draft of 296 non-commissioned officers and men arrived from England, while the following officers joined on appointment or on recovery from wounds : Major R. N. Knatchbull, D.S.O., who took over command of the Battalion from Major Weir, Major A. E. R. Colquhoun, Captains C. A. Bamford, A. C. L. Powell and A. S. McIntyre, Second-Lieutenants M. R. Barron, A. H. Webb, J. Harbottle and H. S. Ellis. On the same day the Battalion made ready for an early move forward against the Hanna position.

Quoting again from the Battalion War Diary, we read that on April 4th "the Battalion marched out of camp at about 9 p.m. to occupy trenches, Captain R. J. McIntyre being wounded *en route*. The front line of trenches throughout the position was occupied by the 13th Division, which was supported by the 7th Division, the 28th Brigade being in the centre.

"5th and 6th April. Heavy bombardment of the enemy's position from both banks of the Tigris was carried out, and first-line trenches were captured at 5 a.m. by the 13th Division, the capture of other lines following; about 50 wounded and unwounded prisoners were taken. Enemy retired to Fallahiya position, about two miles in rear; this was attacked and carried about 7.30 p.m. by the 13th Division. Enemy now retired to Sannaiyat position. The 19th and 28th Brigades, supported by the 21st Brigade, were ordered to carry out a night march with the intention of attacking at dawn. The march was commenced shortly after midnight [on the 6th], in massed formation, the 28th Brigade on the right, the 19th on the left and the 21st in Reserve.

"Formation of 28th Brigade—front line, 51st Sikhs and Provisional Battalion Oxford and Bucks L.I.; second line, 2nd Leicestershire Regiment, 53rd Sikhs and 56th Rifles. Owing to considerable delay during the march*

---

* Due, so the Official History states, to the road being congested by bodies of the 13th Division marching back or bivouacked across the line of advance, and to loss of time caused in the passage of the trenches.

the attacking brigades were 1,000 yards short of the enemy's position at day-light, when the Turks opened a withering fire. The first two lines of the Brigade pushed forward to within 800 yards until compelled to halt through very heavy casualties (our own artillery on the right bank of the Tigris being responsible for a considerable number), when they entrenched. Some 400 yards in rear of these another line was established and consolidated by 200 men of The Leicestershire Regiment and Highland Battalion (Seaforths and Black Watch of the 19th Brigade), the remaining units of both Brigades entrenching in rear."

Of this advance the Official History gives the following account (Vol. 2, pp. 381, 382) : " At 5.30 a.m. both Brigades, 19th and 28th, were advancing and although it was light enough to distinguish objects within about half a mile, the enemy's trenches could not be discerned. It was seen, however, that the north-west wind, which had begun that morning, was driving the waters of the Suwaikiya Marsh southward, and this had already contracted the front between the marsh and the communication trench to about 350 or 400 yards. The Turks were evidently fully prepared for the attack, for five minutes later a storm of machine-gun and rifle fire, followed immediately by gun fire from both banks of the river, fell on the 28th Brigade, who were still leading, and then on the 19th Brigade. The enemy trenches could still not be discerned, but the gallant 28th Brigade dashed forward in a desperate attempt to carry out their orders."

" Eyewitness "* tells us of the action of April 6th that " the gallant, broken and patched-up battalions of the 7th Division, the remnants of Shaikh Saad, the Wadi and El Hannah, were called upon once more to illustrate the impossible, to advance in broad daylight on an entrenched position without gun preparation over a perfectly open plain. Even their machine guns were wanting. One had fondly hoped that their thin ranks would not be thinned again. But the Sinn garrison had come out and held Sannaiyat in force, the rising marsh gave them a stronger natural position than the one they had prepared behind. It would have been better if the attack had been postponed till dark, or if a halt had been made until the guns could be brought up. But the General Commanding acted strictly upon orders, and the brigade was committed to the advance at all costs. . . . . Eleven hundred in the 28th Brigade alone fell in the first few minutes, and 700 in the 19th Brigade on the left. When they came under the enemy's fire, part of the line had not even deployed. The Oxfords lost 13 officers, the Leicesters 11, the 51st Sikhs 8, the Highland Battalion 11. It was a torrent of death. . . . . A Staff Officer handed me his glasses.

" ' Do you see that line of khaki,' he asked, ' about 500 yards from the enemy ?'

" ' Yes. Why haven't they dug themselves in ?'

" He explained that they were our dead."

The enemy maintained a very heavy fire while daylight lasted, but at dusk some of the less severely wounded of the two brigades managed to crawl back from where they had fallen, while stretcher parties were organized and sent out.

* " The Long Road to Baghdad," Vol. I, p. 180.

The following casualties had been incurred by the Battalion, most of them early in the operations : killed, Second-Lieutenant H. Billings and 45 other ranks ; wounded, Majors R. N. Knatchbull, D.S.O., and A. F. R. Colquhoun, Captains C. A. Bamford and H. N. H. Grimble, Lieutenant H. Stockley, Second-Lieutenants T. Monaghan, J. Harbottle, H. S. Ellis and B. Brake and 257 non-commissioned officers and men, while 19 men were missing. Major Weir now reassumed command of the Battalion.

No. 4850446 Private—now Sergeant—S. Garner, D.C.M., who on this day was Commanding Officer's orderly, states that on Major Knatchbull being wounded, he was told to inform Major Colquhoun that he was now in command. Finding this officer also wounded, Private Garner then sought for Captain Grimble, the next senior, and met him being taken to the rear on a stretcher. No other officers being then to be seen among companies at hand, Private Garner then went to Company Sergeant-Major William Bale, M.C., D.C.M., and suggested he should take command, which he did, exercising it until relieved later in the day by Major Weir, and rising splendidly to the occasion. Company Sergeant-Major Bale, M.C., D.C.M., was gazetted Second-Lieutenant in the *London Gazette* of August 21st, 1917, under date of June 21st; he survived the campaign, but died in England in 1922 of dysentery contracted on service in Mesopotamia.

The casualties in the 19th and 28th Brigades numbered 1,168.

In the early morning of the 7th it was surmised that the enemy had evacuated the Sannaiyat position during the night, and the 19th and 28th Brigades were sent forward at 9.15 in attack formation to clear up the situation. The enemy, who had not retired, allowed the advance to come within 900 yards and then opened fire, the 28th Brigade again suffering many casualties. The general line of trenches was advanced some 300 yards after dark, the Battalion holding the extreme right.

On the 9th the 13th Division again attacked, but unsuccessfully, and on the 10th a fresh difficulty arose, seriously impeding the operations of the Relief Force. A very strong wind drove across the Suwaikiya Marsh, banking up the water, until waves actually swept over the extreme right flank of the Battalion trenches and water poured rapidly in. All attempts to block the trenches proved futile, for no filled sandbags were at hand and the loose sand was at once washed away. All hands were busily engaged in clearing the trenches of ammunition and kits, and although by great exertions the whole trench-system was saved from being flooded, certain portions on the flanks had to be evacuated. But in rear the bursting of *bunds* and the washing away of causeways made the matter of supply one of no little difficulty and anxiety.

On April 21st orders were issued that the 7th Division, supported by the 35th and 36th Brigades, would attack the Sannaiyat position early next morning, the 19th and 21st Brigades in front, the 28th in support, with the two attached brigades in reserve, and covered by a bombardment from both banks of the Tigris. The 28th Brigade was to advance in close support in four lines, 300 yards in rear of the leading brigades, and each line at 300 yards interval; the

Battalion was on the right of the first and second lines. Just before the attack opened on the 22nd it was found that the floods had so narrowed the front that the attack could only be delivered on a one-brigade frontage, and the 19th was now to attack supported by the 28th Brigade. When the attack was launched certain units reached the first line of Turkish trenches; the battalions of the 19th Brigade were, however, very weak in numbers, the going was very heavy, many of the men being in mud and water up to their knees; and when the Turks counter-attacked the 19th Brigade was driven in, so that by 8.20 a.m. all the assaulting troops were back in the British line and the proposed attack by the 28th Brigade was countermanded.

Of the situation at this period General Lake wrote as follows in his despatch of August 12th : " General Gorringe's troops were nearly worn out. The same troops had advanced time and again to assault positions strong by art and held by a determined enemy. For eighteen consecutive days they had done all that man could do to overcome, not only the enemy, but also exceptional climatic and physical obstacles—and this on a scale of rations which was far from being sufficient in view of the exertions they had undergone, but which the shortage of river transport had made it impossible to augment. The need for rest was imperative."

But by this the garrison of Kut was at the end of its straightened resources. One final effort was made to reprovision the besieged, when the *Julnar,* laden with a cargo of supplies, attempted to run the blockade. But in the passage up stream the vessel was heavily fired upon by the guns of Fort Magasis, the vessel was sunk and her crew were killed or captured; and so at long last, on April 29th, after a siege of five months, the British flag at Kut was hauled down and the garrison surrendered and passed into a hideous captivity, and thus for a time offensive operations came perforce to a standstill.

In the course of nearly four months' fighting the losses of the Tigris Army Corps amounted to over 23,000 officers and men; those of the 7th Division, which had been with the Corps from the commencement of the relief operations and had been out of contact with the enemy for *three days only* during that time, had been especially heavy, those of the 28th Brigade numbering 3,731.

To the Commander of the Tigris Corps His Majesty the King sent the following message :—

" *Although your brave troops have not had the satisfaction of relieving their beleaguered comrades in Kut, they have under the able leadership of yourself and subordinate commanders fought with great gallantry and determination under most trying conditions. The achievement of relief was denied you by floods and bad weather and not by the enemy whom you have resolutely pressed back. I have watched your efforts with admiration and am satisfied that you have done all that was humanly possible and will continue to do so in future encounters with the enemy.*"

In the Official History of the Mesopotamia Campaign, Vol. 2, p. 232, dealing with the events of January 6th and 7th, it is stated that " three

Company Sergeants-Major of The Leicestershire Regiment were granted posthumous commissions (they were killed a week later) for their conspicuous gallantry in this assault." These three were Company Sergeants-Major William Wells, Percy Reuben Foister, D.C.M., and Horace Patrick, who, with Sergeant Bert Brake, D.C.M., of the Regiment, were all promoted Second-Lieutenants under date of January 20th, 1916 (subsequently ante-dated to January 10th) in the *London Gazette* of February 8th, 1916. In the action of January 6th and 7th Wells and Patrick were fighting as officers, by order of General Kemball, consequent on the shortage of officers. All these three Company Sergeants-Major were killed in action on January 13th, 1916, while Sergeant Brake died in the rank of Lieutenant on January 5th, 1918, attached to the Machine Gun Company, 210th Brigade.

CHAPTER V.

1916, 1917

TIGRIS, 1916—KUT-AL-AMARA, 1917—BAGHDAD.

" AFTER the surrender of Kut, the British and Turkish forces on the Tigris settled into a state of comparative inactivity, which endured till near the end of 1916. Both sides were exhausted by their efforts, hardships and losses; and both had suffered from long and imperfectly organised lines of communication, from the atrocious weather and from the local physical conditions. The British were no longer under the necessity of persisting in hazardous attacks which neither their condition nor their circumstances now justified; while the Turks, having achieved their immediate object, but being inferior in numerical strength, were in no condition to press their advantage by assuming the offensive. Moreover, the Russian threat to Baghdad, then materialising, would probably require the diversion of most, if not all, available Turkish reinforcements. . . . .

" The effective strength of the Tigris Corps (6th Cavalry Brigade, 3rd, 7th and 13th Divisions, and 35th, 36th and 37th Brigades) amounted to about 2,000 sabres, 23,450 rifles and 143 guns. The 41st Infantry Brigade, which had been reconstituted of four weak battalions from the trenches, was being sent back from Shaikh Saad to form a reserve at Basra in place of the 42nd Brigade (only three battalions strong) under orders to reinforce Nasiriya, in which area trouble seemed possible. . . . .

" The Tigris Corps still maintained close contact with the Turks at Sannaiyat and Beit Isa, the British line on the right bank of the Tigris extending southwards for about four miles with its left flank refused. The opposing Turkish force was believed to consist of a cavalry brigade, the 35th, 45th, 51st, 52nd and part of the 2nd Divisions, its strength being estimated at 1,700 sabres, 21,600 rifles and 96 guns. Between Kut and Baghdad there were thought to be some 4,600 Turkish troops, with another 1,700 scattered in many detachments on the Euphrates line below Baghdad; and on the Persian frontier the Turkish force was estimated at from 3,000 to 4,000."*

On May 19th it became apparent that the Turks, under the pressure of the Russian advance towards Baghdad, had withdrawn from their advanced positions about Es Sinn on the right bank, though the lines of Sannaiyat were still strongly held. At this time the greater part of the British 7th Division

---

* " The Mesopotamia Campaign," Vol. III, pp. 1, 2 and 4.

was on the left bank between Sannaiyat and Fallahiya, the front-line trenches being held by an infantry brigade supported by eighteen guns.

In consequence of this retirement the 7th and 8th Brigades of the 3rd Division moved forward, covered by a cavalry brigade, from Shaikh Saad, early on the morning of the 20th, and while the cavalry advanced as far as the Hai, the river which joins the Tigris near Kut, the infantry, under great suffering from the heat, occupied the Dujaila Redoubt. Orders were now issued that the 7th Division should attack the enemy's rearguard at 3.30 a.m. on the 21st and turn it out of the Sannaiyat position, the 28th Brigade assaulting the northern flank; but these orders were subsequently cancelled, as General Gorringe's instructions to avoid heavy losses prohibited attempts to evict the Turks from their fortified positions. But as matters stood at this time, and for many subsequent weeks, the British were in no condition to make any serious advance. " The Tigris Corps would not be an effective force for some time to come. It had suffered over 22,000 casualties in action and from disease during April and May; and it had been impossible to give formations the period of rest required for reorganisation and recuperation. Until the recently commenced light railway from Shaikh Saad reached Sinn, General Gorringe would have insufficient transport for an advance beyond the Hai; and even if his troops were fit and the transport adequate, any idea of an extended offensive was precluded by the very low state of the supplies' reserve at Shaikh Saad. So many river steamers were out of action that it was only possible to deliver at the front the quite inadequate daily average of 330 tons on all accounts; but it was anticipated that the situation would improve soon when local supplies became available after the harvest at and above Amara.

" The heat was now becoming very great, the thermometer rising daily, and in June the heat became intense and sickness and disease levied a very heavy toll on the Tigris Corps. The day temperature averaged 110° to 120° and the air was muggy and oppressive. The men in Mesopotamia received for many weeks none of the 'comforts' which had so freely reached them in France from well-wishers at home, while the ration from January to May, 1916, was normally two biscuits per man per day, a tin of ' bully ' beef and plenty of tea, but sugar and milk were rare issues. Occasionally potatoes and onions were issued and at rare intervals bread, baked at the Base and hard, mouldy and uneatable when it arrived belatedly at the front."

There was much sickness, and, even in the hospitals, ice, soda water and fresh vegetables were unknown during the long summer of 1916.

An officer states : "when I joined the Battalion in June, I believe I am right in saying the number of effective officers was five and other ranks about 150 to 200; the latter were mostly full of fever or ill with mild dysentery, but carrying on as best they could. The flies were terrible and you had literally to fight your way to your mouth with each bite of food. The men's backs were usually black with flies."

In orders dated June 3rd it was announced that Company Sergeant-Major W. Bale had been awarded the Military Cross, the first warrant officer in the

M

Regiment to gain this award; and in this month Captains P. H. Creagh, D.S.O., and C. A. Bamford, Lieutenants H. Stockley, V. Buxton, G. S. Rodger, F. F. S. Passmore and W. N. Sanders joined the Headquarters of the Battalion, the first-named of these bringing out a greatly-needed draft of 98 non-commissioned officers and men and taking over the command of the Battalion a few days after arrival.

Towards the end of July seven men who had served continuously since the outbreak of the war were granted furlough to India; on the 25th Second-Lieutenant H. S. Symington was wounded by the premature explosion of a Mills hand-grenade, and on the 30th Major A. W. S. Brock arrived and took over the command from Major Creagh. In the higher commands, too, certain changes took place during July, General Maude relieving General Gorringe in the command of the Tigris Corps, while Major-General A. S. Cobbe, V.C., took the place of Major-General Younghusband at the head of the 7th Division.

During August, Captain R. J. McIntyre, Second-Lieutenants J. H. Raine, T. J. R. Warren and J. Y. Copeman joined, as did also some 90 other ranks from Basra; and on August 28th a change took place in the high command, destined to exert a great influence upon the successful conduct of the Mesopotamian Campaign, when Lieutenant-General Sir Stanley Maude relieved Sir Percy Lake in the chief command in that country.

The months of September, October and November went by, the temperature gradually becoming lower and the health of the force improving under the better conditions of life which now prevailed at the Mesopotamia front. The cessation of the extreme heat of the summer permitted a certain amount of sport being indulged in, in which all ranks of the 2nd Leicestershire more than held their own; but the presence and general activity of the Turks in the opposing trenches allowed of no relaxation of vigilance, and sniping and bombing were kept up on both sides.

Since the appointment of General Maude to command, certain changes had been made in the distribution of the force and in the command of certain of its units; the force was now contained in a I. and a III. Army Corps, the I., commanded by Lieutenant-General A. S. Cobbe, V.C., containing the 3rd and 7th Divisions, the latter of which was now commanded by Major-General V. B. Fane, while the III. Corps was commanded by Major-General W. R. Marshall and was composed of the 13th and 14th Divisions.

In General Sir Stanley Maude's despatch of April 30th, 1917, he gives the following appreciation of the military situation at the moment when he considered that the time had arrived to resume the offensive: " At the beginning of December the enemy still occupied the same positions on the Tigris front which he had occupied during the summer. On the left bank of the Tigris he held the Sannaiyat position, flanked on one side by the Suwaikeh Marsh and on the other by the river. In this position he had withstood our attacks on three occasions during the previous April. Since then he had strengthened and elaborated this trench system, and a series of successive positions extended back as far as Kut, fifteen miles in the rear. The river bank from Sannaiyat to

Kut was also entrenched. On the right bank of the Tigris the enemy held the line to which he had withdrawn in May when he evacuated the Es Sinn position. This line extended from a point on the Tigris three miles north-east of Kut in a south-westerly direction across the Khaidari Bend to the River Hai, two miles below its exit from the Tigris, and thence across the Hai to the north-west. . . . . The enemy occupied the line of the Hai for several miles below the bridge-head position with posts and mounted Arab auxiliaries. On the left bank of the Tigris our trenches were within 120 yards of the Turkish front line at Sannaiyat. On the right bank our troops were established some eleven miles from his position on the Hai.''

General Maude estimated the Turkish strength on the Tigris at about 20,000 rifles and 70 guns, of which some 2,500 rifles and 15 guns were on the right bank, but according to the Turkish General Staff their total strength here was actually no more than 10,500 rifles and 50 guns. The striking force at General Maude's disposal—the 6th and 7th Cavalry Brigades and the I. and III. Army Corps—was approximately 3,500 sabres, 45,000 rifles and 174 guns.

The following was the order in which offensive operations were now to be carried out :—

    1. To secure possession of the Hai.
    2. To clear the Turkish trench system on the right bank of the Tigris.
    3. To sap the enemy's strength by constant attacks.
    4. To endeavour to compel his withdrawal from the Sannaiyat position.
    5. To cross the Tigris and sever his communications.

During the month of December several drafts joined the 2nd Leicestershire Regiment and also the following officers: Captain H. Stockley, Lieutenants J. Redwood and F. J. Thorpe, Second-Lieutenants R. D. Otter, G. S. Hebden, L. A. Fowke, G. W. Palfreyman and O. M. Mansfield, so that by the end of this month it was quite a strong battalion which was ready again to take the field.

At midnight on December 13th-14th the I. Corps was thus disposed : the three brigades of the 7th Division were on the left bank of the Tigris, the 21st being in the front line opposite Sannaiyat, with the 19th in rear and the 28th near Arab Village. The 3rd Division was on the right bank, the 7th Brigade holding the river bank from opposite Sannaiyat to the mouth of the Nasifiya Canal, the 9th was north of the Twin Canals, while the 8th was about to move from near the Triangle to Sinn Abtar to form an Army Reserve. On this night, while the I. Corps was to bombard the enemy positions on the right bank so as to give the impression that an assault on Sannaiyat was imminent, the III. Corps was to secure the line of the Hai and bridge that river.

General Marshall's Corps was concentrated before Es Sinn on the night of the 13th, crossed the Hai at 6 on the next morning, and, moving north, drove in the enemy's advanced posts. By December 18th the III. Corps Commander had extended his grip on the Turkish defences and had cut in opposite Kut between the outer Turkish defences and west of the Hai.

During the whole of this time the troops of the I. Corps had been busy bombarding the Sannaiyat position, bridging the water-way and making new roads, under the very heavy rain which fell almost unceasingly. But it was the end of the first week in January, 1917, before anything further could be attempted, and the operations which then followed "took the form of a prolonged attack by portions of the I. Corps upon the elaborately constructed series of defence works stretching across the Khaidari Bend, which secured to the Turks a footing on the right bank of the Tigris below Kut," a position which formed a menace to the British communications with the Hai, as from it the Turks could inundate portions of our line whenever the river rose sufficiently.

Between January 5th and 7th, General Cobbe's troops dug some 25,000 yards of saps and trenches and advanced to within 200 yards of the enemy position to be assaulted; but in the active operations which now commenced and which were carried on until after the middle of February, involving the capture of the Khaidari Bend and of the Hai Salient, the units of the I. Corps were not concerned, remaining in the trenches opposite Sannaiyat, harassing the Turks as much as possible, bombarding his trenches and systematically cutting his wire.

Of the activity of the 2nd Leicestershire the following account of a raid may suffice as an example. On the early morning of January 9th a raid on the enemy saps had been planned for the units of the 28th Brigade in the front line, the Battalion providing a raiding party of 2 officers—Second-Lieutenants C. G. R. Swindells and G. S. Rodger—and 30 men—grenadiers, bayonet men and covering party for the Sappers and Miners taking part. This party was to demolish enemy Sap F. Punctually at 5 a.m. the British artillery put down a heavy barrage on the Turkish first and second lines, to which the enemy vigorously replied. After ten minutes the barrage lifted from the points to be raided, and the raiding party, having crept forward during the barrage, rushed on and cleared the Sap.

Unfortunately the trench on either side of the Sap was found to be strongly wired close up to the fire trench, and only a few of the party, including Second-Lieutenant Swindells, were able to get into the latter.

The enemy kept up a very heavy rifle fire and sent over many hand-grenades, and the Sappers and Miners suffered especially heavily. When the time allotted for the duration of the raid had expired, Second-Lieutenant Swindells, who was then in the trench in command of the party, ordered the retirement before the barrage should again descend, and this officer was not seen again, while the losses incurred in the raid were both the officers and six men missing and three men wounded, one of the missing men returning, dangerously wounded, on the following night.

The majority of those officers and men who served in Mesopotamia and Palestine bear witness to the *clean* methods of fighting employed by the Turk—very different to those of his ally on the Western Front. In this raid, however, the Turk behaved in a manner very unusual to him—stripping two of the Battalion dead and hanging their dead bodies naked on the wire—an act very greatly resented by all who witnessed it. The bodies were left out all day and removed by the enemy during the night.

" The action at Sannaiyat was a singularly bloody and desperate affair. Three of the raiding parties were drawn from the 28th Brigade—the Leicesters, the 53rd Sikhs and the 56th Rifles; each battalion supplied two officers and thirty men. The fourth party was drawn from the Sappers—one officer and ten men. All the officers were lost, killed or missing, and a large proportion of the rank and file. Whether the loss was made good in the diversion I will not presume to judge; but the sacrifice demanded of the raiders was one of that devoted kind in which the men who give their lives see nothing of the reward, which is reaped elsewhere."[*]

" For some time past the I. Corps Commander had been making out his plans for attacking Sannaiyat; and during the last few days General Maude had been discussing these in detail with General Cobbe. Consequently by the 16th February preliminary arrangements were ready. The 9th Brigade and two battalions of the 8th Brigade were still attached to the III. Corps, but the remainder of the 3rd Division infantry held the Tigris right bank from opposite Sannaiyat to the mouth of the Hai; while the 7th Division was on the left bank facing the Sannaiyat trenches—the 28th and 21st Brigades, in this order from the right, being in front line, with the 19th Brigade in rear."[†] The attack by the 21st Brigade failed, but as General Maude says in his report, " though this attack failed, considerable loss had been inflicted on the enemy, and the operation had served its purpose in attracting the enemy to the Sannaiyat front."

General Maude now issued orders for the renewal of the attack on the 22nd, the I. Corps being directed to attack and capture a portion of the Sannaiyat position and so to act as to draw as many Turks as possible from the Kut and Shumran peninsulas, while the III. Corps was to commence the passage of the river in the Shumran Bend early on the 23rd.

General Cobbe's orders for the assault on Sannaiyat directed that 350 yards of the first two enemy lines immediately adjoining the Tigris were to be captured and consolidated by the 19th Brigade; the 28th Brigade, on the right of the 19th, was to contain the enemy in its front by fire; while the 21st was to be in Divisional Reserve.

The 19th Brigade, after some hard fighting, occupied the trenches pointed out, and was so securely established that General Cobbe now ordered General Fane to attack the enemy's first and second line trenches, immediately to the north of the portions occupied by the 19th Brigade. To quote now the official account :—[‡]

" The assault started at 3.15 p.m. under cover of an intense bombardment, being carried out by the 53rd Sikhs (on the right) and the 51st Sikhs of the 28th Brigade. It was entirely successful, and the captured frontage was thus extended northwards for a further 550 yards. The leading waves of the 51st, finding no trace left of a second line, advanced nearly to the enemy's third line before they discovered their mistake and retraced their steps to dig themselves

* Candler, " The Long Road to Baghdad," Vol. II. p. 18.
† " Mesopotamia Campaign," Vol. III, pp. 151, 152.
‡ Ibid., Vol. III, p. 160.

in where the second line should have been. For this reason, and owing to the lack of cover in the other captured trenches, which had been much damaged by our artillery fire, these two battalions suffered considerable losses from the hostile gun, machine-gun and rifle fire; and soon after 4 p.m. they began to give way before a determined counter-attack against their right. But companies from the 2nd Leicestershire and 56th Rifles were at once sent forward to support them, and, steadied also by the resolute attitude of the Seaforths on their left, the 51st and 53rd quickly rallied and the position was made good.

"By 5 p.m. the 19th and 28th Brigades were securely established all along the captured 900 yards frontage, and although the Turks made further counter-attacks, especially against our right, these were all repulsed before dark without great difficulty."

Of this action the Battalion account says that "at 3.15 p.m. the 51st and 53rd Sikhs attacked the enemy left under a heavy bombardment. The 53rd Sikhs were on the right and 'C' Company of The Leicestershire Regiment were in support to them. The 53rd entered the enemy first line, but on the Turks counter-attacking, many of them retired.* About 4 p.m. 'C' Company supported and passed through 53rd Sikhs, rallying many, and soon passed into the Turkish second line. 'B' Company supported 'C' very shortly after, 'D' Company going into Prince's Fire Trench. Splendid reports came from 'C' and 'B' Companies and the Turkish second line was soon consolidated. During the attack there was heavy rifle fire from the enemy, but luckily it was pretty high and we had very few casualties—Second-Lieut. Vincent and 31 men were wounded during the day and seven killed. The Turkish shelling during this attack was not heavy. At night things were quiet except for sniping, and the consolidation of the enemy trenches was completed.

"23rd February. During this day we pushed bombing patrols into the Turks' third and fourth lines and during the afternoon occupied their fourth line with 'C' and 'D' Companies and third line with 'A' Company. Five men wounded during the day. Turks sniped a little during the day. Very many Turkish dead were found in the captured trenches. The following message was received from the Divisional Commander :—

"' Divisional Commander congratulates Leicestershires on the excellent progress made and initiative shown.' "

This attack cost the 7th Division 1,332 casualties, practically all among the battalions of the 19th and 28th Brigades.

By nightfall on February 23rd the 19th and 28th Brigades, pushing forward, had occupied the enemy's fourth line, the latter brigade meeting with little opposition, and early next morning the Turkish fifth line was securely held. The I. Corps was now ordered to press forward vigorously, by 8 a.m. the enemy's sixth line was in our position, and by 9 p.m. on this day the infantry brigades of the I. Corps were disposed generally as under :—

* It should be stated in explanation of this temporary disorganization that practically every British officer of the 53rd became a casualty.

28th Brigade and 8th Brigade, the Ataba—Suwada line.

21st Brigade, the Suwada position, with patrols at Saddleback Hill.

19th Brigade, Nakhailat position.

7th Brigade, concentrated near the pentagon in the Dujaila depression.

During this day the I. Corps had only 29 casualties, all in the 7th Division, and captured 62 prisoners, three *minenwerfer* and one machine gun.

While these operations were in progress the gunboat flotilla had moved up the Tigris, and about 9.30 p.m. it anchored off Kut, which was found to be deserted and in ruins, and here next morning the Union Jack was hoisted. Telegraphing on the night of the 24th General Maude reported that " As a result of these operations we now have the whole of the enemy's positions from Sannaiyat to Kut; and Kut itself, to which no interest but a sentimental one attaches, passes automatically into our hands. . . . . We have also secured navigation of the river up to Shumran."

On the 25th news of the occupation of Kut reached the Battalion as it moved forward; on the night of the 26th-27th it advanced in heavy rain to a point north of the Dahra Bend; and the following night, the 7th Division having been ordered to move to Shaikh Jaad and picquet the road between that place and Shumran to keep off any marauding Arabs, the Battalion marched to Shaikh Jaad and there bivouacked at 1 a.m. on the 28th.

" So rapid had been the enemy's flight that on the evening of February 27th his troops reached Azizieh, 50 miles from Kut. They had covered that distance in two days. Nevertheless, all through the 27th the British gunboats had hung on to and shelled them from the river, while the British cavalry harried their outer flank, and when the retreating army reached Azizieh and streamed through that place it was as a broken, demoralised and, in part, unarmed mob."* To this the Official History† adds that " the road and adjacent areas were littered with dead and wounded men and animals, guns, arms of all sorts, ammunition, wagons and stores; while in the rear of the Turkish army toiled numbers of men in small groups, exhausted, starving and supplicating our aeroplanes for rescue from the marauding Arabs. No sign remained that this was the fine army which had held us in check for over a year."

At Shaikh Jaad the 7th Division remained until March 4th, clearing the neighbouring battlefield and awaiting any further movement on Baghdad until the supply arrangements could be organized and perfected.

On March 4th, then, the Battalion made a short march to Shargy, reached by the 28th Brigade at 10 a.m., and here the 7th Division concentrated, preparatory to an 18-mile march to Azizieh the following day. In this march the Battalion provided the advanced guard, " A " and " B " Companies being in front and " C " and " D " Companies leading the main column, and Azizieh, where the Division bivouacked, was reached at 2.45 p.m. Marching on again by Renie and Ctesiphon, Bawi was reached on the morning of the 8th, and here orders were received during the course of the day that the 28th Brigade was to

* Dane, " British Campaigns in the Near East," p. 272.
† Vol. III, p. 195.

cross over to the right bank of the river at dark, moving during the night on Baghdad in support of the cavalry, now 24 hours ahead, and pushing into Baghdad if possible.

The Brigade marched off accordingly at 8 p.m., " A " and " B " Companies of the Battalion supplying the advanced guard, and, moving forward throughout the night, a halt was made at 6 a.m. on the 9th at Shawa Ruins, where touch was established with the cavalry. An hour later the enemy began to shell the cavalry and infantry, and the 2nd Leicestershire were ordered to send forward one company, with another in support, to locate the enemy position, discover where its flanks rested, and, if possible, the approximate strength of the Turkish force; " C " Company therefore advanced with " D " in support, " A " and " B " Companies remaining in reserve in artillery formation.

The account in the Battalion War Diary states that, " during the day the enemy shelled occasionally, but our guns, when they got into action, kept the enemy artillery well in hand; enemy rifle and machine-gun fire was heavy. During the day we pushed slowly forward, 'A' and 'B' Companies later taking part. We had no connection on our right or left flanks. The 51st Sikhs and 56th Rifles had gone round some way on the left to turn the enemy's right flank, but we did not get in touch with them during the day. In the afternoon the 53rd Sikhs came up to support our right, and at night continued our right towards the 35th Brigade, with which they made connection. At dusk we straightened our forward line and consolidated the connection on the left. The whole Battalion was in the front line, the order from the left being 'A,' 'C,' 'D' and 'B' Companies. In support one Company of the 125th Punjabis. One section from the Machine Gun Company was sent up about midnight and the Turkish sniping continued until about 2 a.m.

" Casualties during the day—14 killed, Second-Lieuts. W. Hilton and G. W. Palfreyman and 86 non-commissioned officers and men wounded.

" 10th March. At 1.25 a.m. an order was received to be prepared to carry on the attack at 7 a.m. At 2.40 a.m. a message was received that attack would not be carried out until definite orders were received from the Division, but all preparations were to be made and patrols pushed out to ascertain if the enemy's position were still held. About 7.30 a.m. we began pushing out 'A,' 'B' and 'D' Companies in front and 'C' Company in support and for some 500 yards there was no opposition. Then we came under very heavy shell fire, our guns not replying. We pushed on, however, with our left Company—'D'—directing. At 9.30 a.m. a message was received from 'D' Company—'Enemy strongly entrenched 700 yards north of me, cannot get forward without supporting fire.' Our leading line was now under heavy shell fire—no support from our guns. At 9.48 a.m. a message was received—'35th Brigade on right report you are blocking their way, please move straight to your left and clear their front. You will probably be withdrawn shortly.' About 11.30 a.m. we got an order to withdraw to 1,000 yards north of Shawa Ruins, where the Brigade would concentrate. Withdrawal and relief by 35th Brigade completed at about 1 p.m.

" During the 9th and 10th March we had pushed the enemy back over two miles and obtained all the information required.

" The following message was received from the G.O.C. 28th Brigade :

' *Corps and Divisional Commanders have asked me to convey their thanks to all ranks for their excellent work last night and to-day.*'

" The Brigade bivouacked 1,000 yards north of the ruins and awaited further orders. A heavy wind rose during the afternoon and continued all night, the dust storm being terrific. Brigade in Divisional Reserve. Casualties during the day—3 non-commissioned officers and men killed, 35 wounded."

In the account of this action in the Official History we read that " throughout the day the British and Indian troops, fighting with dash and spirit and encountering unexpectedly stubborn resistance, had incurred 768 casualties."

On March 11th the 28th Brigade entered Baghdad, the Battalion bivouacking near the Railway Station.

On entering Baghdad Railway Station, the station bell—a very fine brass one with " Baghdad " engraved upon it, was taken possession of by the Battalion. It is now with 2nd Battalion Headquarters and the sentry on the main guard always sounds the hours on it.

" With the near approach of the flood season it was now necessary to obtain control of the river *bunds* upstream of the city, and Yahudie and Kisirin on the left bank of the Tigris, 20 and 28 miles respectively above Baghdad, were consequently occupied on March 13th and 14th. On the right bank of the Tigris the retreating enemy had entrenched a strong position south of Mushaidie Railway Station some 20 miles north of Baghdad. Lieut.-General Cobbe was entrusted with the mission of securing the *bunds* on this bank, and on the night of the 13th-14th a column marched from Baghdad and reached Tadjiye Station by daybreak on the 14th. The Turkish position was some seven miles in extent, extending from the river in a north-easterly direction towards the railway which runs due north and south. The western flank rested on successive lines of sand hills, which lie on both sides of the railway line, whilst east of the railway the defensive system centred in two dominant heights, linked to each other and to the river by a series of trenches, *nalas* and irrigation cuts. In front lay a bare flat plain, whilst undulating ground behind gave the enemy concealment for manœuvre and cover for reserves. It was decided to attack the Turkish right flank with the whole force, as such a movement, aimed directly at the enemy's railhead and general reserve, would turn the main position east of the railway."*

For the operations outlined above General Cobbe had at his disposal two squadrons of the 32nd Lancers, the 7th Division and 46 guns, and his advanced guard, composed of the 28th Brigade, one company of Sappers and one of Pioneers, was to leave camp at 1.30 p.m. on March 13th, take up a covering position at Bait Nawab, some nine miles distant, sending out patrols at daybreak to reconnoitre and locate the Turkish position; at 6 a.m. the advance was to be

* General Maude's Despatch of April 10th, 1917.

renewed. The main body, starting an hour later from camp, was to form up on arrival at Bait Nawab with two infantry brigades west of the railway.

Starting at the appointed hour—the 2nd Leicestershire Regiment at the head of the main guard, at daylight on the 14th the Battalion opened into artillery formation—four lines of platoons at 50 paces interval and 50 paces distance, " B " and " D " Companies being in front, and the 53rd Sikhs in the same formation 100 yards in front again. The left flank of the Brigade was on the railway line.

The enemy gave the first sign of his presence by opening fire at 9 a.m., after which the shelling became heavy, and both leading battalions—53rd Sikhs and 2nd Leicestershire—extended and awaited orders, which soon arrived and were worded—" Stand fast for the present," succeeded shortly after by a message from the Division—" Confine yourself to holding and obtaining information of the enemy; do not commit your troops to serious attack without definite orders from the Division." Then about 2 p.m. information was received that the 21st Brigade, *plus* two battalions of the 19th Brigade, would move with the right flank on the railway, the 28th Brigade to co-operate when the 21st should draw level. The Battalion was to move in echelon on the right of the 53rd Sikhs, the 56th Rifles being on the left of the 53rd with their left flank on the railway connecting with the 21st Brigade. The 51st Sikhs to be in reserve.

The advance, which commenced at 4.55 p.m., was continued, under very heavy shell and some rifle fire, until dark, when all dug in about 600 yards from the enemy's position, and remained here all night. During the night the 21st Brigade captured Mushaidie Railway Station, when the Turks fled. By March 17th the force had returned to Baghdad, leaving behind the 21st Brigade to guard the river embankments.

The Turks, whose force was estimated at not less than 5,000 rifles and 24 guns, had suffered 800 to 1,000 casualties, including over 50 prisoners remaining in our hands, while the losses among General Cobbe's troops totalled 518, to which the 2nd Leicestershire contributed Second-Lieutenant O. M. Mansfield and 2 men killed, 25 non-commissioned officers and men wounded.

In his report on these operations General Cobbe described the " endurance and determination of his officers and men, who had marched and fought practically continuously for over twenty-four hours, as being above praise."

On March 16th the following gracious message from His Majesty the King on the fall of Baghdad was communicated to all ranks of the Army in Mesopotamia :—

" *March 11th. It is with the greatest satisfaction that I have received the good news that you have occupied Baghdad. I heartily congratulate you and your troops on this success achieved under so many difficulties.*"

The Battalion remained in Baghdad until March 25th, when, having some few days previously been detailed to form part of the 28th Brigade Mobile Column under orders to be held ready to move out at four hours' notice, the 2nd Leicestershire marched on that day to Babi, 21 miles distant, and there relieved the Black

Watch, the rest of the Brigade remaining some five miles lower down stream. Babi, being the most advanced post on the right bank of the Tigris, was a place of some importance and was garrisoned by the Battalion, two guns of a field battery, a section of Sappers and Miners, a section of the 135th Machine Gun Company and a non-commissioned officer and six sowars of the 32nd Cavalry. Picquets, strength one platoon per company, were furnished each night, and daily a half company was sent out at dawn to a fort two miles distant, whence patrols were dispatched to Mushaidie Station, another three miles further out. This fort was more than once advanced upon and fired into by bands of mounted Arabs during occupation by the Battalion, of which Lieutenant-Colonel R. N. Knatchbull, D.S.O., had now assumed command.

On the 28th the remaining units of the Brigade closed up to Babi, and on April 4th the whole of the Mobile Column moved out by Kermeah and Syndia to Sumaika, with orders to occupy Balad Station, six and a half miles up the railway and known to be garrisoned by Turkish advanced troops, and secure the line Balad—Sidigharib.

At 5 a.m. on the 8th the column marched from Sumaika, the 53rd Sikhs finding the advanced guard and the Battalion forming a left flank guard, and the advance came under hostile gun fire when about 5,000 yards from Balad Railway Station, immediately south of which the Turks were holding an extended line of interrupted trenches astride the railway, their right being covered by the Dujail Canal, running roughly parallel to the line of railway and at an average distance from it of three-quarters of a mile. On each side of the railway the country was flat and open with a few small irrigation cuts : but half a mile east of the railway, and roughly parallel to it, lay a strip of broken and undulating ground. The Battalion account of the action which followed states that " A " and " D " Companies supported the 53rd Sikhs, " A " on the right of the railway and " D " on the left, while " C " and " B " Companies went round to the left to try to turn the enemy's right flank. These two last-named companies reached a line of sand-hills on the left, where a good many Turks were met, but the companies pushed forward with their left on the Dujail Canal and speedily cleared up the situation. In the meantime " A " and " D " Companies, in conjunction with the 51st and 53rd Sikhs, advanced on Balad Station and this was in British hands by 3 p.m., the column capturing 200 prisoners, including nine officers, and three machine guns.

Picquets were put out for the night, during which the Arab snipers were active, while a party of twenty of the enemy attacked one of the posts, but was driven off without loss.

During the action, a model of a successful little battle, the Battalion had Lieutenant G. L. S. Marner and 2 men killed, Second-Lieutenant R. D. Otter and 16 men wounded. " Marner's loss was greatly felt. ' I hear you have lost a good officer,' said the Brigadier, and the Brigade Major replied, ' He was the Brigade's great stand-by for maps and drawings, I don't know how we can replace him.' "*

* Thompson, " Beyond Baghdad with the Leicestershires," p. 38.

Next morning the column occupied Harba without opposition, the remnants of the Turkish 51st Division—200 sabres, 3,000 rifles and 16 guns—falling back on an entrenched position at Istabulat, about seven miles north-west of Harba.

During the last few weeks the following officers had joined or rejoined the 2nd Leicestershire Regiment: in February, Second-Lieutenants C. N. C. Copeman and J. C. G. Plant, the latter attached from the Norfolk Regiment; in March, Second-Lieutenant J. Y. Copeman; and on April 14th, Lieutenant U. H. E. Sowter, an officer who had seen much fighting in France and Flanders with the 2nd Battalion The Sherwood Foresters and had been badly wounded at Armentières; and Second-Lieutenant T. C. S. Keely, attached from the King's Liverpool Regiment.

The 7th Division took no part in the operations carried on early in April against the Turks in the Jebel Hamrin, and, the enemy's opposition on the left bank having been completely overcome, a further advance was now ordered on the right bank, where the Turks were holding the Istabulat position, their left on the river and extending over some two and a half miles of frontage across the Dujail Canal to the Baghdad—Samarah Railway. This position was held by 6,700 rifles, 200 sabres and 31 guns, while the reserves about Samarah consisted of some 4,500 men and 15 guns.

General Cobbe was ordered to assault this position, and he proposed in the first place to attack north of, and along, the Dujail Canal, endeavouring to capture the enemy's bridges over the canal; while, as a preliminary to this attack on the morning of April 21st, it was intended on the night of the 19th-20th to gain an advanced line astride the canal, about one mile north-west of Al Khubn, with its left refused along Low Bank, in order to cover the occupation of artillery positions.

" The two actions which it is customary to call the two battles of Istabulat were fought in positions some miles apart. The title of Istabulat, or of Dujail River, may fitly be reserved for the first action. The actions of the 22nd April may then be known as that of Istabulat Mounds. The Istabulat fight was one in which my own brigade were spectators, except for isolated and piece-meal actions. We were in reserve; and the 8th Brigade, of the 3rd Division, were in support in line with us and behind the Median Wall."*

On April 20th the orders for the attack next day were issued to the 7th Division—21st Brigade to attack on right, 19th Brigade on left and the 28th Brigade in Divisional Reserve, and at 5 a.m. next morning the artillery bombardment opened and the 21st Brigade moved out to the attack, the 125th Punjabis of the 19th Brigade going forward to capture Istabulat Station. At the same time " B " Company of the Battalion was sent well out on the left flank to attract the enemy's attention. This manœuvre succeeded, as the Turks at once reinforced their right and " B " Company came in again about 8 a.m.

During the whole day the Battalion remained in rear of the Median Wall, and lost one man killed and three wounded from enemy shells.

By noon the fight had become stationary, for our troops were held though

* " Beyond Baghdad with the Leicestershires," p. 62.

the whole enemy front line was in our hands, and orders were now given to keep the Turkish position under a systematic bombardment during the evening and capture it under cover of an intense bombardment on the 22nd.

At midnight of the 21st the following orders were received : " 28th Brigade less 53rd Sikhs [who were with the 21st Brigade and rejoined later], and 56th Rifles [still at station and also rejoined later], will move forward to the left bank of the Dujail Canal, starting at 4 a.m." The Brigade accordingly marched off and reached the position about 5.30 and remained halted till about 7.45, when it was reported that the Turks had wholly evacuated their trenches and that a pursuit was to be entered upon. The 28th Brigade then passed through the 19th and 21st, the Battalion leading with its right on the Tigris, the 56th on the left with their left on the railway, and the 51st and 53rd Sikhs in support. The Battalion formation was " B," " A " and " D " Companies in front from left to right in two lines of platoons at 50 paces interval and 150 paces distance, and " C " Company in two lines of platoons 300 paces in rear of the three leading companies.

The enemy maintained a heavy shell fire, but the elevation was too high. The line kept advancing, covered by patrols ; but soon after midday there was a halt until at 3.20 p.m. the following order was received from Brigade Head-quarters, which had closed up to the Median Wall in rear : " At 4.20 the 2nd Leicestershires, supported by the 51st Sikhs, will assault and capture the enemy's position. The assault will be preceded by a bombardment of 20 minutes. The 56th Rifles will not advance nearer to enemy's line than 500 yards till the assault takes place, when they will press forward and capture the line opposite to them under a howitzer bombardment. The Machine Gun Company will co-operate from the Wall."

Of the attack which now followed the Rev. E. J. Thompson, M.C., gives the following account :* " At 4 p.m. we put down a concentrated bombardment of twenty minutes. The Leicestershires, a forlorn and depleted hope, moved swiftly up to within assaulting distance, ' C ' Company in reserve behind the right. The 51st Sikhs supported the attack. The 56th Rifles put down the heaviest fire they could of rifles and all the efficient machine guns with the Brigade. At 4.20 the guns lifted one hundred yards and the Leicestershires rushed in.† Hasted, watchful behind with ' C ' Company, pushed up rapidly to assist the front line. A long line of Turks rose from the ground. All these, and the enemy's second line also, were taken prisoners. Dug-outs were cleared, and many officers were taken, where lofty cliffs over-hang the Tigris. These prisoners were sent back with ridiculously weak escorts. They were dazed, their spirit broken. Grant-Anderson, wounded and falling back in search of the aid-post, came on a large body, wandering sheep without a shepherd. These he annexed and his orderly led them ; he himself coaxed them forward. Prisoners came, ten and twenty in charge of one man. . . . . Altogether the ' Tigers '—

* " Beyond Baghdad with the Leicestershires," p. 84 *et seq.*

† No limit had been put on the objective, and the orders were to " pursue the enemy vigorously."

hardly two hundred strong by now, took over 800 prisoners. Many of these escaped by reason of the poverty of the escort.

" Whilst our scanty stock of ammunition was being fired at the Turks, retiring rapidly, the Leicestershires were pushing far out of reach of telephone communication. . . . . To Captain Diggins fell an amazing success. Suddenly there were flashes almost in his face. ' Guns !' he shouted, and rushed forward. On and on he rushed till he reached the enemy's guns, he and three of the men of ' A ' Company which he commanded. These guns were in nullas by the river-bank. Their crews were sitting round them. Diggins beckoned them to surrender, which they did. He was so blown with running that he felt sick and faint. . . . . In all, from several positions, Diggins took seven 14-pounders and two 5.9's. They were badly hit, some of them. . . . . Diggins sent his prisoners back, battery commander and all, in charge of Corporal Williamson and one private.

" Very soon on Diggins' arrival his subalterns, Thorpe and McInerney, joined him. He sent them racing back across the perilous mile which now lay between them and the wall. Thorpe went to Lieut.-Colonel Knatchbull and McInerney to Creagh, the second-in-command* this day. All did their best to get reinforcements. . . . . The handful at the guns waited. . . . . now came the counter-attack. The Turks began to shell the captured gun-position. Then, from the railway embankment, nearly a mile to the Leicestershires' left front, several lines of Turks emerged, in extended formation, a distance of 50 yards between each line. At least 2,000 were heading for the 50 Leicestershires holding the guns—' it was like a crowd at a football match,' a spectator told me. Diggins sent word to Lowther, commanding ' B ' Company, a little to his left rear, ' the Turks are counter-attacking.' Lowther replied that he was falling back and Diggins and Hasted fell back in conformity. . . . . The Leicestershires damaged the guns as they might for half a dozen fevered, not to say crowded, minutes of glorious life. Then they fell back. One of the Sergeants was hit in the chest; he was put on one of the Turkish garrons and led along. ' From the attention he received from the enemy's guns, they must have thought him a Field-Marshal.' The Turks, for all their force, crept up timidly, and after securing the guns they raced to Tekrit, 30 miles away. But they sent a large body in pursuit of the retreating ' Tigers.'

" The Leicestershire fell back rapidly, the enemy pressing hard. The 51st Sikhs were found, hidden by the hollows of the ground; they had been a buttress to the left flank of that handful of adventurous infantry in their forward sweep into the heart of the Turkish position. It was now that the 56th Rifles checked the counter-attack which threatened to drive a wedge between the Leicestershires and the river. The whole front was now connected up, and, in face of an attacking army, British and Indians dug themselves in. The 51st sent along some ammunition. The sun was setting and in the falling light the last scene of this hard-fought day took place. The enemy came rushing and halting, and now our men were down to their last rounds of ammunition. Our

---

* This is incorrect. Major Creagh was in command of " D " Company till wounded.

guns opened again, but too late and did not find their target.   But the Leicester-shires' bombers, 60 men in number, were thrown forward, bringing ammunition which saved the day.   Thirty of the sixty fell in that rush.   The Turks were now within 250 yards, but here they wavered.   For half an hour they kept up a heavy fire, but then, at 6 o'clock, the 19th Brigade poured in and the thin lines filled up with Gurkhas, Punjabis and Seaforths. . . . . Darkness fell and our line pushed forward.   For over two hours we could hear the Turks man-handling their guns away, but there were strong covering parties and our own patrols were driven back with loss.   Our guns put down a spasmodic and ineffectual fire.   Then all became quiet.   All along the enemy's line of retreat and far up the river were flares and bonfires ; away in Samarah buildings were in flames and down the Tigris floated two burning barges.''

A Company Commander of the Battalion this day contributes the following account of Istabulat : " At 4 p.m. our artillery put down a heavy and concen-trated fire on the Turkish trenches.   Particular tribute should be paid to the guns of General Thomson's brigade operating on the left bank of the Tigris. Being unopposed, they were able to come within close range and get direct observation, and their very accurate flanking fire paved the way for us.   The Battalion, now very weak in numbers, attacked the Turkish left, which was resting on the Tigris, and was drawn up as follows from left to right—' B,' Captain Lowther, ' A,' Captain Diggins, ' D,' Major Creagh, with ' C ' Company, Captain Hasted, in reserve.   The 51st Sikhs supported and the 56th Rifles were on our left.   At 4.30 the guns lifted and we went forward.

" We soon captured the Turkish trenches, where numerous dead and wounded were found ; the remainder surrendered and were marched back under ridiculously small escorts, owing to the fact that the leading companies were very weak and more men could not be spared ; further, our orders were to pursue the enemy vigorously.   This the leading companies did, and, after going about 1,000 yards, a nullah was reached in which nine Turkish guns were found with their detachments complete.   As Turkish gunners were not armed with rifles the whole battery surrendered to Captain Diggins—the guns could not fire at us as we advanced, they being in a deep depression.

" It was now realised how very much these leading companies were in the air.   The 51st had formed to the left and so prevented any counter-attack against our left rear.   Urgent messages were sent back asking for reinforcements.

" In the meantime 'B' Company, seeing a party of about thirty Turks falling back along the railway line, wheeled to the right and opened fire on them, whereupon these put up their hands, marched some 500 yards towards us and surrendered.   Suddenly all the battery horses were seen galloping towards us, and it was evident they had not realised that we had taken their guns and were intent on limbering up and getting the guns out of action !   A few shots, how-ever, turned them, and away they went towards Samarah Station, and no doubt informed the Turkish general of the loss of his guns !

" Now the Turk is a pastmaster in the art of local counter-attack, and it was not long before a body of troops, about 2,000 strong, could be seen marching across the open some two miles away.

" In the meantime more urgent messages were sent, saying that unless reinforcements were sent immediately, the guns could not be retained. The leading company commanders then conferred together and realised that unless reinforcements came at once the companies would have to withdraw and leave the guns—for 150 men could not hope to stem the onrush of 2,000. Further, the O.C. ' B ' Company had received a message from the 51st Sikhs on his left rear—' For God's sake withdraw or you will be cut off from the rear.'

" As no reinforcements came up, and as the Turks in front were now only about 500 yards off, all the leading companies fell back about 300 yards behind the guns, having first damaged them by firing into the mechanism and putting Mills bombs down them. The sun had now set and we knew that darkness would soon be on us. Happily the Turks contented themselves with recapturing the guns and holding the near face of the nullah in which they were, withdrawing after dark. Just before dark reinforcements began to arrive, but unfortunately half an hour too late.

" During this action Padre Thompson did particularly good work attending to the wounded, and for this he was subsequently awarded the Military Cross."

" It was afternoon when the 28th Brigade began their advance," so the Official Eyewitness tells us.* " The Leicesters led the attack. They had not gone far when they came in for the heavy enfilade fire from the left. . . . . By 1.30 they [The Leicestershire Regiment] had advanced 1,200 yards and were near the ridge held by the Turks. At four o'clock our guns opened a tremendous fire on the trenches, and the weight of metal poured in on the Turks was augmented by the artillery of General Thomson's column. . . . . As soon as the guns lifted the Leicesters swept forward up the slope. An officer on the spot told me it was the most inspiring, whole-hearted charge he had ever seen, and apparently the Turk thought so too, for he did not wait for the bayonet. The leading company reached the first summit tired and winded, but still game. The Turkish trenches were crossed without a check. . . . . Exhausted, breathless, scorched by the sun and thirsty to the point of desperation, the first wave of pursuing infantry raced on and did not halt till they burst over a battery of astonished gunners in a depression a full 1,500 yards beyond the trench. . . . . This was about 5 o'clock. The three advanced companies of the Leicesters began to consolidate their position, but they had been carried on beyond the immediate reach of their supports, who had, in fact, been diverted to deal with the enfilading fire from the left."

" The assault," wrote General Maude in his despatch of October 15th, 1917, " was delivered in dashing style by the Leicesters, supported by the 51st Sikhs and 56th Rifles "; while in the Official History we read that " the Leicestershire advanced with great dash and by 4.30 p.m. were in possession of their objective." It was indeed, as the Battalion War Diary states, " a great day in the annals of the Battalion," but the losses had been heavy, three officers and 18

* " The Long Road to Baghdad," Vol. II, pp. 172, 173.

other ranks were killed or died of wounds, while four officers and 101 non-commissioned officers and men were wounded.* The officers who were killed were Second-Lieutenants E. L. Hall, M.C., and G. S. Hebden, Lieutenant U. H. E. Sowter, who had only joined a week previously, died next day of his wounds, and the officers wounded were Captain P. H. Creagh, D.S.O., Second-Lieutenants T. J. R. Warren, H. T. Grant-Anderson and H. W. G. Westlake, M.C.

Of some of those who died " Padre " Thompson writes : " By that fatal wall, and on the bullet-swept face before it, died many of our bravest. Hall, M.C., aged nineteen, who looked like Kipling's Afridi :

" ' He trod the ling like a buck in spring and he looked like a lance in rest.' Hall fell, facing the finish of our journey and those bright domes of Samarah, already gilded from the sloping sun. His death was merciful, a bullet through the heart, and sorrow came, not to him, but to those who loved him. . . . . I wandered back some miles and found hospital tents. I saw Sowter, who was dying. ' It's been a great fight, Padre,' said Sowter, ' a great fight. I'm getting better.'

" No loss was felt more severely than that of this quiet, able man. He had seen much fighting in France, and in this, his first action with us, he impressed every one with his coolness and efficiency. He had walked across to Lowther, his company commander, to draw his attention to a new and threatening movement of the enemy. Then, as he stopped to bandage a wounded sergeant, a bullet pierced his stomach. . . . . Sowter had been with us one week; I never knew anyone whose influence went so deep in so brief a time. . . . .

" In those exalted moments of victory, glorious almost beyond belief, Sergeant-Major Whatsize fell, twenty yards from the enemy's line. In his last minutes he was happy as a child is happy."

" It had been a trying campaign for the British troops. The distance to be covered, the heat, the dust storms, the scarcity on occasion of water, called for physical exertion of no ordinary kind. Nevertheless, as their gallant General recorded, ' the spirit of the troops seemed to rise as conditions became more trying, and to the end of this period they maintained the same high standard of discipline, gallantry in action and endurance.'

" There were now before them five months of hot weather during which active campaigning was impracticable. While no necessary precautions were neglected, most were withdrawn into reserve, and distributed along the river in camps where a liberal supply of water for drinking, bathing and washing was obtainable. In camp manly sports were encouraged, training carried on in the early mornings and late evenings when the weather was cool enough, and periods of leave granted to India."

The Battalion spent the greater part of the summer in and about Samarah, a " dirty, sand-coloured town," so the Rev. E. J. Thompson states, " with no touch of brightness but what its famous dome gives it. The town is walled and sits above steep bluffs. The Tigris, swift and clear like a mountain stream,

* The Official History, Vol. III, p. 344, notes, gives the total Battalion loss as 129.

N

races by, dividing round an island.   Summer dragged by, in Samarah the desert throbbed and shimmered in the growing and great heats."

During the month of May a parade was held at which the Army Commander decorated officers and men of the 7th Division for service in recent operations; the following non-commissioned officers and men of the Battalion received awards : Sergeant Batten, Corporals Buncher, Jacques and Coleman and Lance-Corporal Beard.   Company Sergeant-Major Woodcock (on leave) and Sergeant Brown and Private Underwood (in hospital) had also received immediate awards. A hundred men under Captain J. O. C. Hasted attended this ceremony, which took place near the 7th Division camp.

Men and officers continued to join the Battalion in parties of varying strength during the months from May to October—some of these being new arrivals, others, men rejoining on recovery from wounds or sickness.   In May 273 men arrived, of whom rather more than half were from England; in June Second-Lieutenant F. C. Mason, 3rd D.C.L.I., joined, as did Second-Lieutenant G. W. C. Burrows, of the same corps, and Second-Lieutenant A. Reeves and 132 other ranks, while Lieutenant B. Haigh relieved Captain D. McD. Wilson as Medical Officer; in July the reinforcements totalled 133 other ranks, with three officers—Second-Lieutenants H. G. B. Fergusson, D. J. W. T. Wallace, Cameronians, and T. B. Jones; 129 was the total of reinforcements for August, and in September these numbered 102; so that on October 1st, when active operations might be expected shortly to recommence, the strength of the Battalion was 20 officers and 968 other ranks.

The death-rate had been remarkably low, all things considered, but in July the Battalion suffered a very great loss in the death of Lieutenant-Colonel R. N. Knatchbull, D.S.O., who was admitted to hospital on the 12th and died of fever in Baghdad on the 24th.   "By Colonel Knatchbull's death the Battalion lost its commander and the Division a very fine soldier.   Wounded at Shaikh Saad in January, 1916, he had returned in time for the three railhead battles.   He struggled on with sickness, refusing to contemplate a second leave to India, and died at midsummer," so writes one who knew him.

In General Marshall's despatch of April 15th, 1918, he states that in October of the previous year the XVIII. Turkish Army Corps had advanced as far as El Huweslat, eight miles north of Samarah, where they entrenched themselves, and that General Maude had decided to attack this force before it had had time to consolidate its position to any great extent.   It was accordingly arranged that this body of the enemy should be attacked on the morning of October 24th by the 7th Division, reinforced by the 32nd Lancers, the 8th Infantry and the 4th Field Artillery Brigades.   During the night of the 23rd-24th, however, the Turks hastily retired northward and El Huweslat was found to be evacuated. " Part of the Division pushed on for a further three miles northward without encountering opposition; and Eski Baghdad on the Tigris left bank was also found to be clear of the enemy by our cavalry patrols.   In the afternoon our troops, most of whom had covered many miles in the previous twenty-four hours, returned to Samarah."*

* " Mesopotamia Campaign," Vol. IV, p. 72.

The result, so far as the Battalion was concerned, was an eventless and wearying night march, described as follows by the Rev. E. J. Thompson* :ᵢ " We moved off just before dark, raising a white dust. . . . . About midnight a stranger was seen talking to some *drabis*. A Leicestershire sergeant, coming up, said, ' Hallo, it's a bloody Turk.' Hearing himself identified, Johnny turned round and saluted. He was led to the proper authorities and proved to be a Turkish cadet. He was armed with a penknife and a pair of gloves ! The night was bitterly cold. At 3.30 a.m. we rested, having reached what in Mesopotamia would be considered well-wooded country, an upland studded with bushes. Just on dawn we rose, with teeth chattering and limbs numbed with contact with the cold ground, and moved on. Our planes appeared scouring the sky ; and a few odd bursts of rifle fire were heard about 7 a.m. We had now reached the edge of the dead ground against the river and looked down to the Tigris. . . . . A report came in from our air-folk that 5,000 Turks were on Juber Island, opposite Huweslat. We moved steadily forward to the attack, steadily but unbelievingly. . . . . Nevertheless the airmen insisted that the Turks were there, so we dug ourselves in, in a semi-circle facing the island, preliminary to attacking it. It was noon, hot and maddening with flies. The Leicestershires sent scouts out, who pushed up to Juber Island, and found that there were indeed 5,000 there—5,000 sheep and several Arab shepherds. . . . . So we abandoned the battle, had breakfast at 2.30 p.m. and returned. The day was wearying beyond conception, yet the men were singing as they passed Al Ajik."

During the operations the Battalion had three mule-drivers and one mule wounded by distant fire.

Considering that a good opportunity now offered of attacking the Turkish force at Daur, General Maude ordered General Cobbe to move against it with the I. Corps, which expected to be opposed by some 4,000 rifles and 20 guns ; and on the night of October 31st-November 1st the 28th Brigade moved up to the trenches about Al Ajik preparatory to an attack on the Daur position on the 2nd, it being directed that the attack would be made by the 28th Brigade with the 19th in support, and with the 8th Brigade of the 3rd Division in Divisional Reserve. The cavalry division was to operate on the left flank and cut off the Turkish retreat.

At 4.30 a.m. on the 2nd the 28th Brigade moved out, the 56th Rifles leading, then the Leicestershire and 51st Sikhs on right and left respectively in artillery formation, followed by the 53rd 800 yards in rear in Brigade Reserve. Soon after six o'clock the enemy's advanced picquets were driven in, the advance was pressed with the utmost vigour, and by 11 a.m. all objectives had been gained and the Turks were in full flight. Though the hostile gun fire had been heavy the Battalion casualties were happily low, only Captain F. J. Diggins and eleven other ranks being wounded. That night the 28th Brigade took up an outpost position, the Battalion being on the right. " The night," says the Rev. E. J. Thompson, " was maddening with cold, and the rum ration came as

---

* " Beyond Baghdad with the Leicestershires," pp. 121 *et seq.*

a sheer necessity. All through this brief Tekrit campaign the British troops were without coats or blankets. . . . . The night was one of insane wretchedness.''

Early next day Auja was occupied by the 19th Brigade, and it had at first been intended that the force should now return to Samarah; but early on the 4th orders were issued to stand fast, and later General Cobbe was directed to move forward and attack Tekrit, whither the Turks had withdrawn. This had been their river-head on the Tigris since March, and here they had an elaborate trench system, seven miles in circumference, with both flanks on the river, and with strong rear-guard positions thrown back several miles to the north.

The attack upon Tekrit was delivered on November 5th by the 8th supported by the 19th Brigade, the 28th Brigade being in Divisional Reserve; Tekrit was captured and the Turks again retreated many miles to the north.

On the 10th the 7th Division started back via Daur and Huweslat to Samarah, where on the 16th the Battalion was established in camp, remaining here during the rest of its stay in northern Mesopotamia.

On November 16th Sir Stanley Maude—the commander who had repaired all the early mistakes of the campaign and under whom British prestige had been revived—was taken ill. The same evening the malady was pronounced to be a very virulent form of cholera, and on the evening of Sunday, November 18th, the General passed peacefully away. His successor in command of the troops in Mesopotamia was Lieutenant-General W. R. Marshall.

At the end of November eight officers joined or rejoined the Battalion and some 20 non-commissioned officers and men; the officers were Captain H. W. Sharp and G. A. Quayle, Second-Lieutenants H. S. Littlewood (Northampton-shire Regiment), W. B. Beale (The Buffs), R. Chamberlin, C. H. Greenhalgh and E. N. Penfold.

"On the 4th December, His Majesty's Government decided that, in view of the greatly improved situation in Mesopotamia and of the fact that the number of rifles in our force there was more than treble that of the enemy, one of the Indian divisions should be removed from Mesopotamia to Egypt. General Marshall . . . . selected the 7th Division, which left for Egypt before the end of the month, its place in the I. Corps being taken by the 17th Division."*

The orders for the move to a new theatre of the World War reached the Battalion at Samarah on December 7th, and, on relief next day by the 11th Battalion The Manchester Regiment, the Battalion marched with the 28th Brigade via Istabulat, Balad, Sumaikcha, Kermeah, Husaiwa and Baghdad to Hinaidi—13 miles down-stream and on the left bank of the Tigris, remaining here until the 18th. On this day the Battalion embarked on river steamers, strength 33 officers, 853 other ranks, 34 Indian followers and 15 horses, and reached Maqil on the evening of the 23rd, remaining there until January 1st, 1918.

The numbers present this day with the Battalion were 35 officers, 1,036 non-commissioned officers and men and 35 Indian followers. The officers were:

* " Mesopotamia Campaign," Vol. IV, p. 97.

Lieutenant-Colonel A. W. S. Brock, D.S.O.; Major P. H. Creagh, D.S.O.; Captains A. S. McIntyre, M.C., H. Stockley, M.C., R. A. N. Lowther, J. F. Ferguson (Durham L.I.), G. A. Quayle and F. J. Diggins; Lieutenants W. N. Sanders, F. F. S. Passmore and C. N. C. Copeman; Second-Lieutenants V. J. Jones, A. J. Reeves (King's Liverpool Regiment), H. S. Littlewood (Northamptonshire Regiment), H. T. Grant-Anderson, T. J. R. Warren, G. W. C. Burrows (D.C.L.I.), W. B. Beale (Buffs), J. Y. Copeman, H. K. Barron, T. C. S. Keely (King's Liverpool Regiment), D. J. W. T. Wallace (Cameronians), F. S. Goddard (Bedfordshire Regiment), R. Chamberlin, E. N. Penfold, E. R. Cook, T. B. Jones, H. G. B. Fergusson, F. C. Mason (D.C.L.I.), F. E. McInerney, C. Matthews, C. H. Greenhalgh and J. Lyons; Lieutenant and Quartermaster H. Cox; and Captain B. Haigh, R.A.M.C., Medical Officer.

On January 1st, 33 officers, 952 other ranks and 35 Indian followers embarked in the hired transport *Bandra;* 1 officer and 11 other ranks with 28 Lewis gun mules in the *Rossetti;* and 7 men and 12 horses in the *Hyperia;* the surplus personnel—2 officers and 91 other ranks—remaining at No. 1 British Base Depot, Maqil. The transports sailed in company on the 2nd.

CHAPTER VI.

1918

EGYPT AND PALESTINE.

THE voyage commenced in the transports *Bandra, Rossetti* and *Hyperia* was not to be completed in these vessels, for on January 3rd, 1918, the three ships came to an anchor, somewhere off the mouth of the Tigris, and there awaited for some three days the arrival of other vessels into which it was proposed that the Battalion should be transshipped. In due course these made their appearance, whereupon 24 officers, 267 other ranks, 25 Indian followers and all the heavy baggage were transferred to the *Minnetonka*, while the remainder of the 2nd Leicestershire—9 officers, 699 non-commissioned officers and men and 10 Indian followers transshipped to the *Mutlah*, when, on the 8th, the westward voyage was resumed.

The vessels reached Suez at 7 a.m. on January 22nd and all disembarked at 1.15 p.m., entraining at once and arriving at a camp at Ismailia, on the Canal, the same evening. Next day, 7 officers and 566 other ranks joined from the Depot in India, and from these two Depot Companies were formed of 6 officers and 431 other ranks, the remainder being distributed among the other companies; on January 26th 7 officers and 1 man joined from Mesopotamia, so that by the end of this month the Battalion probably stood at a greater strength than at any other period in its existence, viz., 46 officers and 1,650 non-commissioned officers and men. This exceptionally large corps of officers was composed as follows : Lieutenant-Colonel A. W. S. Brock, D.S.O.; Major P. H. Creagh, D.S.O.; Captains C. A. Bamford, A. S. McIntyre, M.C., H. W. Sharp, H. Pickbourne, H. Stockley, M.C., R. A. N. Lowther, J. F. Ferguson (D.L.I.), G. A. Quayle and F. J. Diggins; Lieutenants J. Lingham, M.C. (Northamptonshire Regiment), W. N. Sanders, F. F. S. Passmore, C. N. C. Copeman and H. S. Littlewood (Northamptonshire Regiment); Second-Lieutenants M. L. Hardyman, H. A. Symington, V. J. Jones, P. J. Shaw, A. J. Rowland (Northamptonshire Regiment), A. J. Reeves (King's Liverpool), H. T. Grant-Anderson, T. J. R. Warren, W. Hilton, W. B. Beale (The Buffs), J. Y. Copeman, H. K. Barron, T. C. S. Keely (King's Liverpool Regiment), E. R. B. Apton (Northamptonshire Regiment), D. J. W. T. Wallace (Cameronians), F. S. Goddard (Bedfordshire Regiment), R. Chamberlin, E. N. Penfold, E. R. Cook, T. B. Jones, G. W. Palfreyman, M.C., R. D. Otter, H. G. B. Fergusson, F. C. Mason (D.C.L.I.), F. E. McInerney, C. Matthews,

C. C. Clover and J. Lyons; Lieutenant and Quartermaster H. Cox; and Captain B. Haig, R.A.M.C., Medical Officer.

The Battalion remained in the neighbourhood of Ismailia until nearly the end of March, engaged in training of all kinds, while officers and men were granted leave to visit Cairo and Alexandria, and—to a limited extent—England, sport of every kind was encouraged, and in the many competitions which took place the 2nd Leicestershire more than held their own.

On March 12th there was a grand parade at which H.R.H. The Duke of Connaught presented decorations to those to whom these had been awarded, expressing the great pleasure he felt at having been " able to present decorations which had been so well earned during the hard fighting in France and Mesopotamia, and also his great satisfaction at the smart turn-out of the troops." On the following day the Battalion furnished a Guard of Honour at Ismailia Pier on the occasion of the Duke's departure.

As a result of the major operations which had been carried out by the Expeditionary Force under the command of General Allenby during the latter part of the preceding year, and of the minor offensives which had been undertaken during the first three months of 1918, the Expeditionary Force was now in occupation of a general line covering Jericho, Jerusalem and Jaffa, and this was held by three Army Corps, the Desert Mounted Corps on the right, the XX. Corps in the centre, and the XXI. Corps on the left, this having its left flank on the sea. After describing in his despatch of September 18th, 1918, the operations culminating in those of the early part of this year, General Allenby wrote as follows :—

" The dispatch of troops to France and the reorganization of the force, has prevented further operations of any size being undertaken, and has rendered the adoption of a policy of active defence necessary. During the first week in April the 52nd Division embarked for France, its place being taken by the 7th (Meerut) Division which had arrived from Mesopotamia.

" The departure of the 52nd Division was followed by that of the 74th Division, which left Palestine during the second week in April. The 3rd (Lahore) Division was sent from Mesopotamia to replace the 74th Division, but it was not till the middle of June that the last units disembarked. In addition to the 52nd and 74th Divisions, nine Yeomanry regiments, five and a half siege batteries, ten British battalions, and five machine-gun companies were withdrawn from the line, preparatory to embarkation for France. By the end of April the Yeomanry regiments had been replaced by Indian cavalry regiments, which had arrived from France, and the British battalions by Indian battalions dispatched from India. These Indian battalions had not, however, seen service during the present war; and, naturally, had not the experience of the battalions they replaced. Thus in April the strength of the force had been reduced by one division, five and a half siege batteries, and five machine-gun companies; while one mounted division was in process of being reorganized, and was not available for operations.

" In May a further fourteen battalions of British infantry were withdrawn and dispatched to France; only two Indian battalions were available to replace them. Thus at the end of May the force had been further reduced by twelve battalions, while the loss of the 74th Division had not yet been fully made good. On the other hand, the reorganization of the mounted division had been completed.

" In June the places of the British battalions which had been dispatched to France were filled by Indian battalions. Six of the Indian battalions had, however, been formed by withdrawing a company from twenty-four of the Indian battalions already in the Force. As few reinforcements were available for the battalions thus depleted, the Force had been completed in name only.

" During July and the first week in August a further ten British battalions were replaced by ten Indian battalions, the personnel of the British battalions being used as reinforcements."

The reason for the initial weakening of the force under General Allenby's command was the great success of the German offensive in March, and the urgent call for more troops to stem the enemy advance consequent on the very great wastage caused by this offensive; and the 7th Meerut Division, with the 2nd Leicestershire Regiment, was now required to move from Egypt to Palestine and relieve the 52nd Division in the XXI. Corps, which was commanded by Lieutenant-General Sir E. Bulfin, K.C.B., C.V.O., and which contained the 3rd (Lahore), 7th (Meerut), 54th and 75th Divisions.

Leaving Ismailia soon after midday on March 28th, the Battalion reached Kantara some twenty-four hours later, and departed next day in two trains for Ludd, " A " and " D " Companies being in the first train and " B " and " C " in the second. The Battalion arrived at Ludd at a strength of 32 officers and 1,034 other ranks, Lieutenants J. Lingham, M.C., and H. S. Littlewood, Second-Lieutenants G. W. C. Burrows, W. B. Beale, D. J. W. T. Wallace and T. B. Jones having been left behind at the Yeomanry Base Depot, Kantara, while Second-Lieutenant F. E. McInerney had been sent as Instructor to the Imperial School of Instruction at Zeitoun, near Cairo.

On April 3rd the 7th Division moved forward, and during the next few days relieved the 52nd Division in the coastal sector of the front line from near Tel-el-Mukhmar to Arsuf, the 28th Brigade being for the time being accommodated in a camp some short distance beyond Sarona, facing the Turkish XXII. Corps; but on the 16th the Battalion relieved the 28th Punjabis of the 19th Brigade in the front line, and at once came in contact with the enemy. Very early on the morning of the 17th, Captain J. F. Ferguson went out with forty men of his company to post a day picquet on a piece of rising ground, known as Bedouin Knoll, but encountered very heavy machine-gun and rifle fire, and the party on return reported Captain Ferguson and five men missing. Later in the day a search party was sent out towards the Knoll, but their search was fruitless and the party withdrew, having seen nothing of the missing officer or men. At dawn on the 18th, however, a patrol came upon No. 23775 Lance-Corporal G. T. Gray, some 200 yards north of the observation post, who was crawling in towards the British lines, and he reported that Captain Ferguson had been wounded and taken prisoner, while the following men who had accompanied his party were missing: 23444 Private F. Corbridge, 40574 Private A. Booth, 32603 Private B. W. Haywood and 23292 Private G. York.

During the rest of this day there was considerable enemy activity and four more men were wounded by the explosion in the trench of a 4.2 high explosive shell—Lance-Corporals Hollingsworth and Eyre, Privates Davis and Sneath; and during the ten days or more that the Battalion held the front line here the Turks were unusually aggressive, one of them one night attacking a sentry of the Leicestershire inside the wire; the sentry, however, shot the man dead.

The Battalion now went back for some days to Brigade Reserve.

During the early part of April the *right* of the line held by the XXI. Corps had been advanced on a front of twelve miles to a maximum depth of three miles, and it was now—during the latter part of May—decided to attempt a similar forward movement on the *left,* near the coast; the brief official account reads as follows : *" May 28th–29th. Advanced the line one and a half miles on a seven-mile front; 2nd Leicesters and 53rd Sikhs (28th Brigade) were prominent in this fighting and took over a hundred prisoners."

The story of what happened is given as under in the Battalion War Diary :—

" 28th May. Battalion Headquarters established at Arsuf. Objectives of Battalion—Brown Ridge (' C ' Company supported by ' D ' Company), Dud Post (' A ' Company supported by ' B ' Company). These posts to be captured by surprise. At 8.45 p.m. assaulting companies in position. At 8.55 companies advance and assault position. Advance commenced on time. Dud Post was occupied without opposition, but considerable opposition was encountered at Brown Ridge. Several counter-attacks were suitably dealt with. Owing to the activity and proximity of the enemy Brown Ridge could not be wired, but the trench line about V.10.c.2/2 was occupied and consolidated.

" 29th. At dawn the enemy was still holding strongly a line of rifle pits about V.10.c.2/4, but our snipers accounted for several, and forced the remainder to withdraw into Wadi. Enemy casualties estimated about 350. The advance came as a surprise to the enemy, who took about half an hour to open his artillery fire. There was heavy enemy gun fire at frequent intervals, mostly about Bedouin Knoll and Arsuf, but fortunately it came too late to do us much damage. Soon after dark ' C ' Company captured the remainder of Brown Ridge under a very effective bombardment. The rest of the night was spent by ' C ' and ' D ' Companies in wiring, consolidating the new position. All quiet at Dud Post.

" 30th. Quiet day at Brown Ridge and Arsuf. Enemy snipers active on Brown Ridge at times. During night consolidation and wiring carried on. A patrol of ' B ' Company reported Little Mary occupied. Enemy machine guns active against our position on Brown Ridge during night.

" 31st. Quiet day at both positions. A little enemy sniping on Brown Ridge. Our casualties during operations—Second-Lieutenant E. N. Penfold

---

* " The Advance of the Egyptian Expeditionary Force," p. 58.

killed, Lieut. J. Redwood and Lieut. T. C. S. Keely wounded. Other ranks, killed three, missing two and wounded 28."

During the first three weeks of June the 28th Brigade was out of the line " at rest," and consequently was not engaged in the operations whereby the 19th Brigade captured from the enemy, after hard fighting, an important observation post known as " the Sisters "; but on the 23rd the Battalion took over from the 92nd Punjabis of the 19th Brigade the Centre Sub-Section of the Right Section of the 7th Division. Here Battalion Headquarters was at Boche Spur, and the 56th Rifles and 53rd Sikhs were on right and left of the Battalion respectively, with the 51st Sikhs in Brigade Reserve.

In this manner the summer months went by, considerable activity being displayed on either side, but the wastage from wounds and sickness was nothing like that which had been experienced in other theatres of war, and the Battalion strength was well maintained, though the drafts that reached it were few in number and arrived at long intervals.

During these months the following new officers joined: Lieutenant A. B. Gibaud, Second-Lieutenants G. C. Hodgson, F. L. Pentelow, W. Batten, E. F. J. Bulfin and H. M. Bygott.

By the beginning of September, General Allenby judged that while it would have been well to afford his newly-organized formations more time to accustom themselves to the conditions prevailing on this front, operations such as he contemplated could not be postponed beyond the middle of the month, since the rainy season usually commenced at the end of October, when the plains of Palestine would become practically impassable. He had now at his disposal some 12,000 sabres, 57,000 rifles and 540 guns, while he estimated the total enemy strength at 4,000 sabres, 32,000 rifles and 400 guns south of the line Rayak— Beirut; General Allenby had thus a considerable superiority in numbers over the enemy, especially in mounted troops.

His plan was to strike at and defeat the Turkish force west of the Jordan, engaging the Seventh and Eighth Turkish Armies, the one holding a front of some twenty miles astride the Jerusalem—Nablus road, while the front of the latter extended from Furkhah to the sea.

In his despatch of October 31st, 1918, General Allenby thus describes his plan of campaign: " I entrusted the attack on the enemy's defences in the coastal plain to Lieut.-General Sir Edward Bulfin, K.C.B., C.V.O., commanding the XXI. Corps. In addition to the 3rd (Lahore), 7th (Meerut), 54th and 75th Divisions, which already formed part of the XXI. Corps, I placed at his disposal the 60th Division, the French detachment, the 5th Australian Light Horse Brigade, two brigades of mountain artillery, and eighteen batteries of heavy and siege artillery. I ordered him to break through the enemy's defences between the railway and the sea, to open a way for the cavalry, and, at the same time, to seize the foot-hills south-east of Jiljulieh. The XXI. Corps was then to swing to the right, on the line Hableh—Tul Keram, and then advance in a north-easterly direction through the hills, converging on Samaria and Attara, so as to drive the enemy up the Messudie—Jenin road into the arms of the Cavalry at El Afule.

"I ordered Lieut.-General Sir Harry Chauvel, K.C.B., K.C.M.G., commanding the Desert Mounted Corps, less the Australian and New Zealand Mounted Division, to advance along the coast, directly the infantry had broken through and had secured the crossings over the Nahr Falik. On reaching the line Jelameh—Hudeira, he was to turn north-east, cross the hills of Samaria, and enter the Plain of Esdraelon at El Lejjun and Abu Shusheh. Riding along the plain, the Desert Mounted Corps was to seize El Afule, sending a detachment to Nazareth, the site of the Yilderim Headquarters. Sufficient troops were to be left at El Afule to intercept the Turkish retreat there. The remainder of the Corps was to ride down the Valley of Jezreel and seize Beisan.

"I ordered Lieut.-General Sir Philip Chetwode, K.C.B., K.C.M.G., D.S.O., commanding the XX. Corps, to advance his line east of the Bireh—Nablus road, on the night preceding the main attack, so as to place the 53rd Division on his right flank, which was somewhat drawn back, in a more favourable position to advance and block the exits to the lower valley of the Jordan. I ordered him to be prepared to carry out a further advance with both the 53rd and 10th Divisions, on the evening of the day on which the attack in the coastal plain took place, or later as circumstances demanded."

"The Turkish line on the plain consisted of two defensive positions, well constructed and heavily wired. The first, 14,000 yards in length and 3,000 in depth, ran along a sandy ridge in a north-westerly direction from Bir Adas to the sea. It consisted of a series of works connected by a continuous network of fire trenches. The second, or El Tira system, 3,000 yards in the rear, ran from the village of that name to the mouth of the Nahr-el-Falik. On the enemy's extreme right the ground, except for a narrow strip along the coast, was marshy, and could only be crossed in a few places. The defence of the second system did not, therefore, require a large force."*

Before the operations began the XX. Corps took over the extreme right of the XXI. Corps line from Berukin to Rafat, reducing the front of the XXI. Corps from 25¼ to 21¼ miles. The formations taking part in the attack and the frontages allotted to them were :—

"French Detachment—5,900 yards.
"54th Division—9,500 yards.
"3rd Lahore Division—11,300 yards.
"75th Division—1,900 yards.
"7th Meerut Division—5,500 yards.
"60th Division—3,300 yards.
"5th Australian Light Horse Brigade."†

During the days immediately preceding the attack rehearsals had been carried out on ground similar to that occupied by the Turks, while the concentration had been carefully concealed from the observation of the enemy airmen by

---

* Preston, " The Desert Mounted Corps," pp. 198, 199.
† Massey, " Allenby's Final Triumph," pp. 126, 127.

making use of the many orange groves in the vicinity of Jaffa, and by so distributing the reserves that no increase in the size or number of the camps was apparent.

On September 18th a large force of bombing aeroplanes was sent over Nablus, where it was well known that the enemy had his main telephone and telegraph exchanges. These were completely destroyed, a fact which played an important part in enabling the British cavalry to reach the Plain of Esdraelon on the 19th before the enemy G.H.Q. was aware that our mounted troops had broken through.

At 4.30 a.m. on the 19th the four hundred British guns concentrated on the front of attack opened an intense fire on the Turkish positions, and the five infantry divisions dashed forward to the assault, the objectives of the 7th Division being, in the first place, the Turkish defences west of Tabsor, and then, swinging to the right, the Division was to make for Et-Taiyibeh, leaving Et Tireh on its right.

" On the 60th Division's right was the 7th Meerut Division, which had some nasty ground to cover. The division had been in this area several months, and the British and Indian troops composing it had had many opportunities of looking over the country about to be conquered. In it were numerous trenches and cleverly fashioned posts for machine gunners and gun emplacements, and though there were other difficult places on the front there was none prepared so strongly. Between the lines the land was broken by many watercourses running usually from east to west, but apart from these there was little cover, and the enemy trenches were so placed that troops advancing against them could be caught by enfilade fire. Once through the trench system the 7th Division were instructed to advance along the wadi Hurab-el-Miskeh, which flows from north to south, to the western edge of the marsh called Birket Ramadan, a big swamp separated by a narrow neck of more or less firm ground from the impassable marsh of Zerkiyeh. When past the soft ground the division was to face eastward to capture the Et Tireh defences, which were some 800 yards from the spot where the swamps were crossed. . . . . As soon as the path had been cleared through the defences by the 7th Division, General Shea was to issue orders to the 5th Light Horse Brigade to move on to Tul Keram, and, when the Turkish defences had been carried, the 7th Division was to close to their right so as to leave the long road from Zerkiyeh to Hudeira entirely to the troops of the Desert Mounted Corps."*

The attack was carried out by the 19th and 21st Brigades of the 7th Division, the 28th Brigade being in reserve, and the front-line objectives were quickly taken by the leading waves of the attacking battalions, when the supporting battalion passed through and seized the second and third lines, many guns and prisoners being captured. The 28th Brigade had moved on steadily in rear, and about midday was directed to advance upon and assault the Taiyibeh-El-Medzel position, the 21st Brigade moving on the right rear in echelon, and the 19th Brigade being now in Divisional reserve.

* Massey, " Allenby's Final Triumph," pp. 127, 128.

The following was the order of the advance : advanced guard, 56th Rifles; main body, 264th Brigade Royal Field Artillery on the road, 2nd Battalion The Leicestershire Regiment on the right in artillery formation—four lines of platoons at 50 paces interval and 50 paces distance, " A " and " B " Companies in front; 53rd Sikhs on the left; the 51st Sikhs, the Machine Gun Company and Stokes Battery were in rear.

The advance was now for some distance in a northerly direction and then to the west upon Taiyibeh, on nearing which the advanced guard was checked by small parties of the enemy occupying strong positions; the British guns came into action and about 3.35 p.m. " B " Company of the Battalion was ordered forward to reinforce the advanced guard and moved up in two lines in extended order. Some little time later the O.C. " B " Company reported that the Turks, to the number of some 300, were holding a hill running from El Medzel towards the north, and the remaining three companies of the 2nd Leicestershire pushed on vigorously and Taiyibeh was in our hands by six o'clock in the evening, the enemy having evidently vacated the place in considerable haste. The Battalion bivouacked to the south of the village, throwing out two picquets to the front.

The casualties in the companies actually with the Battalion were very light— only two men being wounded, one of whom died of his wounds; but the loss was mainly confined to " B " Company, which had fought with the 51st Sikhs, and this party had nine men wounded, including Lieutenant G. W. Palfreyman, M.C., and Second-Lieutenant F. C. Mason, M.C., while one man was missing.

It had been a very long and trying day and all ranks were greatly exhausted when night came.

Early on the 20th the advance was resumed into the hills, via Zisa, Kefr Sur, Beit Lid and Messudieh, the Battalion moving at the head of the main body of the Brigade, while the road followed was no more than a track along which movement was possible only in single file. About 3.30 p.m. a halt was called at Ras-el-Burj, during which the 19th Brigade attacked and carried the village of Beit Lid after a most determined resistance. The 28th Brigade now passed through the 19th and occupied Messudieh Railway Station, and the town and Samaria Hill were then captured, with 200 prisoners and four machine guns, after a sharp fight. In the hospital at Messudieh were found many wounded, sick and dead German and Turkish soldiers.

That night " D " Company furnished picquets to command the Nablus Road and also supplied a guard at Samaria Station, the Battalion moving to Deir Sheref village and " B " Company to Samaria Station.

" The Division had fought and marched for 48 hours, and had covered 34 miles over difficult and rocky country, but all objectives had been reached, with the capture of over 2,000 prisoners and twenty guns."*

" The 7th Division had the worst of the country and marched over tracks which nowhere deserved the description of roads. The 21st Brigade took what was called on the map the Felamieh—Kefr Zebad road. The 19th and 28th

* " The Advance of the Egyptian Expeditionary Force," p. 58.

Brigades went along the Kefr Sur road, but these roads were found to converge at a spot near Kur, and from this place forward the whole Division was on one bad narrow track, with the 19th Brigade leading.

" All wheels were left behind—a general service waggon would have been held up in a hundred places along the track—and only mountain guns could be moved with the infantry, but so physically fit were the men of the Division that the leading troops were within 1,000 yards of Beit Lid by 11 o'clock, having crossed some ten miles of broken mountainous country in six hours with all sorts of obstacles in their path, to say nothing of an active enemy. Beit Lid is a village on the side of a hill which dominates Messudieh and the railway junction at that place. . . . .

" The 28th Brigade of the 7th Division after making a hard march during the day did a fine night march. They moved past Beit Lid and over the wadi Esh Shair, and got on to the Tul Keram—Nablus road at Ramin by half-past one. They then turned eastwards and advanced on Messudieh station, which they occupied at three in the morning, capturing an engine, sixteen railway waggons and a complete Turkish hospital train in the station, containing 400 sick Turks. . . . . . Leaving a detachment in the station, the 28th Brigade passed on further to the east, and . . . . took Samaria with slight loss."*

" When the knowledge that there had been not only a defeat but that the army was trapped spread through the enemy ranks with the proverbial rapidity of bad tidings, confusion shaded into panic. In the course of September 21 the resistance lost all semblance of being organised. The rearguard no longer stood. It had become a mere business of sweeping up the fragments. Guns, transport, stores, small arms were left abandoned or littered along every road, and thrown into every gorge and gully. On one five-mile stretch of road there were found abandoned 897 motor lorries and other vehicles, and 87 guns. Seventy-five thousand prisoners were taken, among them 3,500 Germans and Austrians, and 360 pieces of artillery. The captures of transport, baggage, animals, locomotives and railway carriages and trucks were on a corresponding scale. As always in the operations against the Turks, this loss of guns and equipment was fatal and final. It took until September 23 to collect the parties of stragglers. The most serious attempts to break out were across the Jordan Valley between Jisr-ed-Damieh and Jisr Mejamieh. One column of 3,000 men, which had got partly across at the latter point, was intercepted by the 11th Cavalry Brigade. Part of the Brigade attacked on the west bank, part, after swimming the river on horse back, on the east bank. All the column were captured, together with twenty-five machine guns. The last belated enemy body was rounded up on September 24 in the El Maleh defile. Lock, stock and barrel, the Seventh and Eighth Turkish Armies had ceased to be."†

General Allenby had now decided upon the occupation of Beirut, the port of Damascus, and on September 24th the Battalion, then at Kakon, was ordered to proceed to Haifa by motor lorries. Fifty motor lorries were provided for the

---

* Massey, " Allenby's Final Triumph," pp. 171, 172, 173.
† Dane, " British Campaigns in the Nearer East," pp. 150, 151.

accommodation of the Battalion, and, starting at 6 on the evening of the 24th, Haifa was reached at 6.30 on the following morning, horses and mule transport remaining behind to follow on with the Brigade. The day was spent in bivouac near the sea, " C " and " D " Companies taking over the outpost line from the 5th Cavalry Division, while " A " Company was made responsible for the town guards and picquets.

On the 26th Major Creagh marched to Acre with " B " and " C " Companies, and the garrison of this place was now two companies of the 2nd Leicestershire Regiment and one squadron of the Gloucestershire Hussars; while that of Haifa was " A " and " D " Companies of the Battalion and the Sherwood Rangers. Next day—the 27th—the 21st Brigade closed up to Haifa, and Battalion Headquarters with " A " and " D " Companies moved to Acre.

On September 29th " orders were received to continue the march to Beirut along the coast road. A section of this road, upwards of half a mile in length, known as ' the Ladder of Tyre,' consisted of a narrow rocky track on the side of the cliff with a deep drop to the sea, and at one point became a flight of steps roughly hewn out of the rock. The Sappers and Miners and 121st Pioneers, assisted by Infantry, made the road fit for armoured cars, motors and 60-pounder guns.

" The Division marched in three columns as follows :—

" Column A. XXI. Corps Cavalry and Infantry Detachment.

" Column B. 28th Brigade, 8th Mountain Artillery Brigade, one and a half companies Sappers and Miners, 121st Pioneers, one Machine Gun Company and one Field Ambulance.

" Column C. Divisional Headquarters, 19th and 21st Brigades, Composite Brigade R.F.A., 15th Heavy Battery R.G.A., 522nd Field Company R.E., two sections Sappers and Miners, Machine Gun Battalion (less one Company), Divisional Ammunition Column and two Field Ambulances."

Column B, with which the Battalion marched, made halts as under : on October 4th at Ras Nakura, on the 5th at Ras-el-Ain, on the 6th at Nahr-el-Kasmiye, on the 7th at El Khidr and on the 8th at Ed Damur, marching on October 9th into Beirut, where the Battalion had a great reception from the inhabitants, and going on to Minas, north of Beirut, where it bivouacked. " The Battalion," we read in the War Diary, " after several days' hard marching, had marched about 18 miles since 6 a.m., but the way the men marched through Beirut was magnificent and a great credit to the Regiment."

To the 7th Division, the inhabitants of Beirut handed over 660 Turks, including 60 officers, who had surrendered to them some days previously.

The XXI. Corps was now ordered to continue its march along the coast to Tripoli, and the 19th Brigade started for that place on the 14th, the remainder of the 7th Division just a week later, and, marching by Junie, Jebeile, Kuba and Shaikh Jedid, Tripoli was reached on the 26th, the Battalion marching

through the town and bivouacking at Shaikh Bedawi.   Here, on the 31st, news
was received that the Turks, despairing of victory for the Central Powers, had
sued for peace, and that an Armistice had been concluded, to come into effect
at noon on that day, followed on November 11th by the conclusion of an
Armistice with Germany.

" The advance up the coast [to Beirut and Tripoli] was work entrusted to
General Fane's Indian Division.   It is not possible to exaggerate the arduous
nature of that advance.   The Scottish and English regular battalions and the
magnificent soldiers of India composing the Division did not have much fighting
to do after they left Messudieh, but they had heavy marches and had to make
roads and fight nature for many miles. . . . . One battalion of infantry was
sent from the neighbourhood of Tul Keram to Haifa in motor lorries, and arrived,
after a moderately good journey, on the night of the 25th.   The remainder of
the Division proceeded on foot and arrived on September 29th.   A battalion of
the 28th Infantry Brigade was sent on to Acre, but no further advance was
possible until the Royal Navy delivered stores by sea, and had made arrangements to cope with any submarine effort to prevent a continuous supply by
ships.   The hard sandy beach on the shore of the beautiful bay which holds
Haifa and Acre at its two ends was good going for wheels, but north of Acre
there was nothing worthy of being designated a road.   Between Nakura and
Abiad, was a track six feet wide but impassable for wheeled transport, and the
Division had to send men ahead to make a road.

" Further on was the Ladder of Tyre, a series of steps cut into a rocky cliff.
That bold promontory had been an impediment to movement up the coast-line
for countless centuries.   Armies had avoided it and made a detour many miles
inland.   It was negotiable by men on foot by means of the rock steps hacked
into its face, and natives had been accustomed to take lightly-laden camels and
donkeys over the height, but their progress had been slow, and nothing on
wheels had ever moved across the hill.   In a few moments the 7th Division's
mind was made up.   To make a road over the hill would mean a long and
difficult undertaking.   Time pressed, and there was no opportunity to construct
a zig-zag highway with easy gradients, miles long.   The quickest and shortest
route that could be made ready for heavy traffic was to cut a shelf out of the
face of the cliff where it reared its rough forbidding head above the Mediterranean.
The shortest distance round the face of the Ladder of Tyre was 1,000 yards, and
there were other bluffs still presenting a barrier to the passage of guns.   But
the Ladder of Tyre was the biggest obstacle.   An infantry battalion and the
7th Division's pioneers set to work with all sorts of tools and explosives.   It
was not enough to blast an enormous amount of rock in the cutting itself, but
huge boulders overhead, which threatened to fall and crush anything passing
beneath, had to be loosened. . . . . In two days, when the 7th Division moved
forward, they were able to take with them a field artillery brigade and a
60-pounder battery.   The surface was still very rough and the bends in the
road were sharp, but the field guns were hauled by their own teams and the
heavies were man-handled round the bluff in four hours.   The work had been

PALESTINE

MEDITERRANEAN SEA

HOMS
Kabline
Kuseir
Hüttle
Netek
El'Ymm
Tripoli
Ras Baalbek
Baalbek
BEIRUT
DAMASCUS
Jisr Banat Yakub
Nawa Sta.
Hasanye
Bosra eski Sham
Mafrak Sta.
Leban Sta.
Deraa
Amman
Deban Sta.
El Kutrane
El Kerak
El Yarkic
El Hesa
El Busaira
Sh. Miskin
Es Salt
Jericho
Jerusalem
Bethlehem
Hebron
Beersheba
Gaza
El Mejdel
Rafa
El Arish
Bir Hassana
Port Said
KANTARA
ISMAILIA

INSET MAP:
ADVANCE INTO SAMARIA
Scale
Jenin
Abu Shushah
El Lejjun
Afule
Kakon
Tul Keram
Samaria
Nablus
Kaisarie
Hudeira
Nahr-el-Falik
Arsuf
Jaffa
Sarona

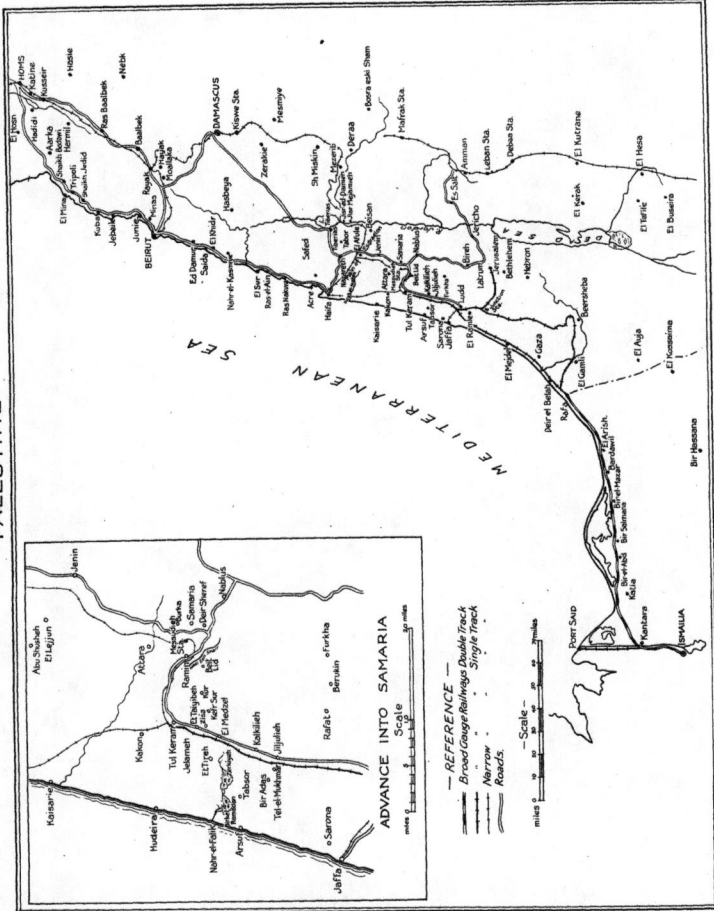

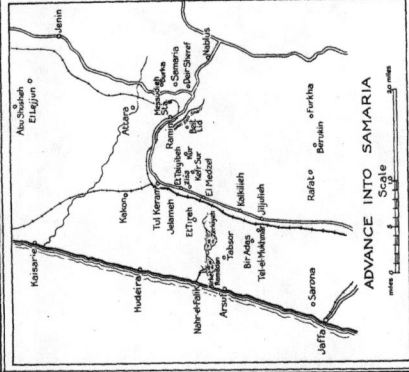

— REFERENCE —
Broad Gauge Railways Double Track
Single Track
Narrow
Roads

— Scale —
miles

extremely hard and continuous night and day, and, in General Bulfin's words, it was accomplished ' in an incredibly short time '."*

On Armistice Day the strength of the 2nd Battalion The Leicestershire Regiment was 31 officers and 521 non-commissioned officers and men, the names of the officers then present being as follows :—

Lieutenant-Colonel A. W. S. Brock, D.S.O.; Majors P. H. Creagh, D.S.O., and A. S. McIntyre, M.C.; Captains H. W. Sharp, H. Pickbourne, H. Stockley, M.C., and R. A. N. Lowther, M.C.; Lieutenants F. F. S. Passmore, M. L. Hardyman, P. J. Shaw, H. S. Littlewood, H. T. Grant-Anderson, T. C. S. Keely, E. R. B. Upton, F. S. Goddard, R. Chamberlin, E. R. Cook, L. de V. Ponthein, and E. F. J. Bulfin; Second-Lieutenants D. Woods, A. R. Rackham, C. Matthews, C. C. Clover, F. A. Simmons, C. H. Greenhalgh, H. M. Bygott, W. Batten, M. M. F. C. Copeland and H. L. Judge; Lieutenant and Quartermaster H. Cox, D.C.M.; and Captain E. R. Gilmore, R.A.M.C., Medical Officer.

On November 7th the following gracious message was published which General Sir Edmund Allenby had received from His Majesty the King :—

" I wish to express My admiration for the spirit and endurance of the troops under your command, who, regardless of fatigue and hardships, have so pressed the retreating Turkish Columns as to overcome all resistance. Their efforts have been deservedly rewarded by the complete surrender of the Turkish forces. This is a glorious and memorable achievement, and on behalf of your grateful fellow countrymen I thank you and all ranks of the Egyptian Expeditionary Force."

Though the war was to all intents and purposes over, drafts continued to arrive, no fewer than 3 officers and 406 other ranks joining during the month of November, at the end of which the strength of the 2nd Leicestershire stood at 37 officers and 940 non-commissioned officers and men; but in December demobilization began, 8 men leaving for England on the 24th, followed by 71 on the 31st. In January, 1919, men began to leave more frequently and in parties of greater strength—27 on the 7th, 79 on the 14th, and 3 officers and 20 other ranks on the 21st; but on the 22nd the Battalion moved as part of the 28th Brigade group to Homs, where it was accommodated in billets in the American Mission School, until lately occupied by the 14th Australian Light Horse; from here detachments were furnished to Hama and Rayak.

While at Homs demobilization recommenced with increased vigour, 131 non-commissioned officers and men being sent during March to the Demobilization Camp at Kantara, while 28 officers and 235 other ranks were transferred to the 2nd Battalion 19th London Regiment to form the Composite Battalion of the 28th Infantry Brigade. By the end of March the Battalion had been reduced to a Cadre strength of 5 officers and 46 non-commissioned officers and men, and these, accompanied by 87 men remaining to be demobilized, entrained on March 30th for Port Said.

O   * Massey, " Allenby's Final Triumph," pp. 276-279.

CHAPTER VII.

1919-1927.

The Years of Peace.

It had been intended that the Cadre of the 2nd Battalion should have proceeded direct to Port Said, but for some reason it was detrained at Kantara and did not resume its journey for nearly two months, spending only a few weeks of the remainder of its stay in Egypt at Port Said, and sailing thence for England in June; the officers then serving with the Cadre were Lieutenant-Colonel A. W. S. Brock, C.M.G., D.S.O., Captain F. J. Diggins, M.C., and Lieutenant and Quartermaster H. Cox, D.C.M.

On arrival in England the Cadre was dispatched to Brocton Camp, in Staffordshire, where, since the previous April, the Battalion had been reforming under the command of Lieutenant-Colonel B. C. Dent, C.M.G., D.S.O., and, by reason of the difficulty then experienced in obtaining sufficient recruits for the Regular Army, serving soldiers were permitted to extend their Army service for from one to four years with the Colours.

When in November, 1918, the Great War came to an end, there were rather less than a dozen Regular infantry battalions serving in India, the establishment of British troops being made up by some 35 battalions of the Territorial Force; it was imperative to evacuate these latter and send them back to England for demobilization as early as possible, and it consequently became necessary to replace them in India by battalions of the Regular Army, even before these had been brought up to their pre-war strength; and among those selected to proceed to India was the 2nd Battalion The Leicestershire Regiment, which sailed in July from Tilbury in the *Moora*, a German prize and a very small and uncomfortable ship.

Almost immediately after leaving England it was discovered that the *Moora* was infested with rats, and, on reaching the Mediterranean, Lance-Corporals Reader and Deer of the Battalion were found to have contracted plague. As a result the ship was ordered to proceed to Malta, where she was to be disinfected and the troops disembarked. Throughout the process of disinfection the Battalion was isolated in barracks in the Lazaretto, and during this time two more cases of plague occurred in the Battalion and several others among the ship's crew, while the two lance-corporals first attacked died of the disease.

Early in September the Battalion again embarked in the *Moora* and sailed from Malta, reaching Bombay towards the end of September, and being sent thence by train to Secunderabad, Deccan, where six weeks were spent. While here the heavy baggage of the Battalion arrived from Bombay; this had remained in the hold of the *Moora* during the process of disinfection, and it was found that the poisonous gases used to destroy the plague-rats had had the most disastrous results on the heavy baggage, which included 500 rifles and many spare sets of web equipment, all of which were found to be useless and had to be condemned and replaced.

At the expiration of six weeks the Battalion moved by rail to Delhi, where it arrived early in December, and here three years were passed, one company garrisoning the Fort, while the remainder of the Battalion was quartered during the hot weather months in the new cantonments some ten miles out of Delhi, the winter being usually spent at Kingsway in camp.

In 1920 H.R.H. Field-Marshal the Duke of Connaught visited India and came to Delhi during the winter to inaugurate the new Legislative Assembly and perform several other ceremonies, and in connection with these the Battalion was more than once called upon to find Guards of Honour, while on other occasions it assisted with other troops in lining the streets. Again in 1921, when H.R.H. the Prince of Wales visited Delhi, the 2nd Leicestershire Regiment performed similar duties.

In May, 1920, Lieutenant-Colonel B. C. Dent had been appointed to the command of a brigade in Mesopotamia, and Major and Brevet Lieutenant-Colonel W. T. Bromfield assumed temporary command of the Battalion pending the arrival from England of Lieutenant-Colonel C. H. Haig, D.S.O., who arrived in Delhi early in 1921.

During the three-years' stay of the Battalion at Delhi several minor disturbances took place in the city and in some of the surrounding villages, mainly due to the activities and propaganda of a firebrand of the name of Gandhi; on several occasions parties from the 2nd Leicestershire were sent to the scene of these disturbances, but were fortunately not called upon to take any really decisive or drastic action, and in March, 1922, Mr. Gandhi was arrested, and, on trial, was sentenced to six years' simple imprisonment.

In November, 1922, the Battalion left Delhi for Jhansi, and while stationed here it won the All-India Boxing Competition, open to all British units; it had provided the runners-up in the previous year.

Less than a year was spent at Jhansi, for in October, 1923, the Battalion left Bombay *en route* for Khartoum in the Sudan, and, disembarking at Port Sudan, it was sent from there by rail and reached Khartoum early in November, and very shortly after its arrival the political situation, both in the Sudan and Egypt, assumed a serious and in some respects a dangerous aspect.

" The relations between the British and the Egyptian Governments, or rather the efforts of the latter to escape from the last threads of the bonds that had tied Egypt to the British Empire, overshadowed all else in the history of Egypt during the year (1923). The elections were completed in the first month, and as a consequence Zagloul Pasha found himself practically dictator with a party overwhelmingly devoted to him. . . . . Almost simultaneously a Labour

P

Government came into power in England, and as the two Prime Ministers had had friendly relations in the past, Zagloul's expectations of an entirely sympathetic attitude on the part of the British Government were not unjustified. . . . . The principal topic of discussion between the two Governments was expected to be the status of the Sudan. The Egyptians claimed the unquestioned incorporation of this region in an Egyptian Empire, and Zagloul more than once declared that only on this basis would he enter into a discussion. The declaration of the British Prime Minister in the House of Commons, therefore, that no arrangement would be accepted whereby the administration and development of the Sudan would be jeopardised aroused surprise and some consternation in Egypt. . . . . In the meantime slight anti-British disturbances, undoubtedly influenced by propaganda from Egypt, had broken out in Khartoum. At first they were of small consequence."*

Fortunately for the Battalion, and for the general peace of the Sudan, there was no concerted action by the revolutionary party on any one day throughout the country, but such disturbance as occurred was spasmodic and could therefore be more easily and effectively dealt with. The first serious act took place on August 10th, 1924, when the cadets of the Military College at Khartoum proceeded in a body to the jail, demanding the release of one Abdul Latif, who had been arrested for his seditious speeches. On the return of the cadets to their quarters they discovered that their ammunition had been removed, and they were now called upon to surrender their arms and such ammunition as was contained in their pouches. On their refusing to comply with this order, " C " Company of the Battalion was ordered out, with machine guns and signallers attached, the whole under Captain Lowther, and was directed to surround the body of cadets, who, finding any resistance was useless, surrendered without it being necessary to fire upon them, and they were subsequently removed and placed on gunboats on the Nile.

Simultaneously soldiers of the Egyptian Railway Battalion at Atbara and Port Sudan mutinied and did considerable damage before they were got under control. Lieutenant Copeman of the Battalion was sent with two platoons to Atbara, and here the Arab troops fired on the strikers, but Lieutenant Copeman's party was not engaged. Again in the following month a detachment under Captain Lowther was sent by steamer to Malakal—500 miles south of Khartoum—where the 13th Sudanese† had refused to obey their British officers; on arrival there, however, it was found that the ringleaders had been arrested and quiet restored. The detachment returned to Khartoum after an absence of some six weeks.

These events led to a protest by the Egyptian Government and a demand for the appointment of an Egyptian-Sudanese Commission to investigate them. Simultaneously the British Government protested against the incomplete information that was being distributed by the Egyptian Government, and declared

---

* *Annual Register for* 1923, p. 284.

† Originally raised in the early days of the British occupation by Captain (now General) Sir H. L. Smith-Dorrien, G.C.B., G.C.M.G., D.S.O.

that the Governor-General alone was responsible for the maintenance of order in the Sudan. The rioting was considered a direct result of incitements in the Egyptian Parliament and Press, and it was intended to remove from the Sudan the Egyptian troops that had mutinied and other disaffected bodies, and to replace them by such British troops as might be considered necessary. The tone of this note had a salutary effect in Government circles in Egypt. What Zagloul Pasha demanded was the withdrawal of all British forces from Egyptian territory and the recall of the financial and judicial advisers; the disappearance of all British control over the Egyptian Government, notably in foreign relations; and the abandonment of the British claim to protect foreigners and minorities in Egypt and to share in protecting the Suez Canal. To these demands the British Government gave a categorical refusal.

On November 19th, Sir Lee Stack, the Sirdar and Governor-General of the Sudan, was murdered in the streets of Cairo, and Lord Allenby, the High Commissioner, then presented certain demands to the Egyptian authorities in the name of the British Government, one of which was that all Egyptian troops should be withdrawn from the Sudan within twenty-four hours and returned to Egypt. The 2nd Battalion The Leicestershire Regiment and the 1st Battalion The Argyll and Sutherland Highlanders, which had recently arrived at Khartoum, were told off to assist in the carrying out of this duty. The majority of the Egyptian troops were evacuated without incident, but certain artillery and other units refused to leave the Sudan without written orders signed by King Fuad. As this meant a delay of two or three days they were confined to barracks, and guards were furnished to enforce this by both British battalions. In spite of these precautions, however, the Egyptian soldiers managed to get a letter through to a platoon of soldiers of the 11th Sudanese, then on guard at the War Office, in which it was stated that if these would only attack the British, they could rely on the close support of the remaining Egyptian troops, and especially of the co-operation of the batteries of Egyptian artillery. This platoon was soon joined by another of the same regiment, and these, foolishly taking the Egyptians at their word, went on the afternoon of November 27th to the Musketry School, broke into the place and possessed themselves of the arms, machine guns and ammunition they found there, being at once joined by men of other Sudanese battalions who were there going through a course of musketry. They then marched towards the bridge over the Blue Nile, meeting *en route* Major-General H. J. Huddleston, C.M.G., D.S.O., M.C., then commanding in the Sudan, who did all he could to persuade them to return quietly to barracks. On being met by a refusal the 1st Battalion The Argyll and Sutherland Highlanders, who were then blocking the road against their advance, was ordered to open fire on the Sudanese; this was done and the fire was returned.

It was about 5.30 p.m., and the " Alarm " was sounded.

Both the British infantry battalions on the spot were at this time very greatly under strength, for many parties had been sent away on escort duty to Egypt, and detachments were absent in other districts of the Sudan where disturbance had threatened; while so far as the 2nd Leicestershire were concerned they were now busy furnishing guards on all important points—as, for instance, over the bridge over the Blue Nile.

Darkness had now set in, and Captain Lowther was sent with one platoon of " C " Company to reinforce the Highlanders on their left, while Captain Tunks, with a composite platoon, made up largely of bandsmen, was directed to move to the Egyptian Hospital on the right of the Argyll and Sutherland, but on arrival at the hospital he found that the mutineers had already murdered Major Carlyle, R.A.M.C., a sergeant of the same corps and two Syrian doctors. Isolated shots could be heard all over Khartoum, and the General Officer Commanding now decided that since unnecessary casualties would be risked by any attempt to discover and follow up the mutinous troops in the dark, no further action should be taken until dawn on November 28th.

The British troops accordingly moved out that morning as soon as it was light, when the Sudanese soldiers were found to be in occupation of some outhouses in the *compound* or enclosure of the Hospital which Captain Tunks had entered the previous afternoon. This latter officer, as he was now advancing to the enclosure, was shot in the throat and killed, Lieutenant Sykes being ordered up to take his place. The Hospital buildings were surrounded when a heavy fire was opened by the mutineers, and fighting began and went on all day until 4 p.m. A 4.5-inch howitzer was then brought up, and, opening fire at seventy-five yards' range, blew up the house, the enclosure was charged and all the mutinous soldiers were killed or wounded, except a few who had made their escape during the night. Four of these were later captured, tried by court-martial and sentenced to death, three of them being shot, while the fourth, who turned King's evidence, was sentenced to penal servitude for life.

For good work during these disturbances the following awards were made :—
Colonel C. H. Haig, D.S.O., received the C.B.E., while Lieutenant C. Sykes was awarded the Military Cross, and No. 4850397 Lance-Corporal Percival and No. 4850700 Private Jones received the Military Medal; these awards were announced as follows in the *London Gazette* of October 20th, 1925 :—

" *The King has been graciously pleased to approve of the undermentioned rewards in recognition of valuable and distinguished services in connection with operations at Khartoum, in 1924 :—*

" *Awarded the Military Cross.*

*   *   *   *

" *Lieut. Carlton Sykes, 2nd Battalion The Leicestershire Regiment.*

" *The King has been graciously pleased to approve of the award of the Military Medal to the undermentioned for bravery in connection with operations at Khartoum, in 1924 :—*

" *2nd Battalion The Leicestershire Regiment.*"

" *4850397 Private (Lance-Corporal) Thomas Baden Percival.*
" *4850700 Private Joseph Jones.*"

*   *   *   *

It was at the same time notified that approval had been given to the insertion of a note in the Record of Services of the undermentioned officers and men of the Battalion of the valuable services rendered by them in connection with these disturbances :—

Lieutenant-Colonel C. S. Davies, C.M.G., D.S.O.
Captain R. A. N. Lowther, M.C.
No. 4848762 Bandsman G. Hurley.
No. 4850060 Bandsman S. J. Nunn.

In these operations the 1st Battalion Argyll and Sutherland Highlanders had some ten casualties, including an officer killed, while in the 2nd Leicestershire, Captain G. P. d'A. G. Tunks, No. 4849580 Lance-Corporal A. Wright died of wounds received and No. 8489482 Private G. H. Bogg and No. 4849516 Private L. Brown were wounded.

The Egyptian soldiers took no offensive action during these disturbances, and by the end of November they had all been evacuated to Lower Egypt and everything was again quiet in the Sudan.

In March, 1925, the Battalion left the Sudan for England, sailing from Port Sudan in the *Neuralia,* and being speeded on its way by the following valedictory letters :—

Major-General H. L. Huddleston, C.M.G., D.S.O., M.C., Commanding Troops in the Sudan, wrote as under to the Officer Commanding the Battalion :—

" *On the departure of the Battalion under your command from the Sudan, I wish to place on record my very great appreciation of their service, and to express my admiration of such a really fine Battalion. Their smartness and bearing on and off the parade ground and the way in which all ranks joined in every kind of sport that the Station provided, have earned them a reputation here of which any Regiment might well be proud. That troops imbued with such a fine spirit in their ordinary daily life will carry the same spirit into the field is the recognised principle of our system of training. This principle was amply borne out by your Battalion here, and their gallantry in action upheld the finest traditions of the British Army, while reflecting the utmost credit on you as their Commanding Officer. I wish, therefore, to thank and congratulate you, your officers and your men, to express to you all my very real regret and sympathy for the casualties you suffered here, and to wish you good-bye and good luck in the future. How much Khartoum will miss you will only be fully realised when you have gone, but for myself I ask nothing better than that I should some time have the honour to include such a Battalion in my command again.*"

In forwarding the above letter to Colonel Haig, Colonel R. R. Headlam, C.M.G., D.S.O., Colonel Commandant, British Troops, Sudan, wrote as follows :—

" *In forwarding the attached letter from Major-General H. L. Huddleston,*

C.M.G., D.S.O., M.C., I would like to add that I heartily congratulate you and your Battalion on the splendid reputation for efficiency, smartness, good conduct and good fellowship which you have established in both military and civil circles in the Sudan. I would also like to add my great personal regret at the departure of the Battalion, and to say how much I hope that at some future time I may have the pleasure of again serving at the same station with it.

" I wish all ranks a pleasant voyage home and the best of luck and success at their new station."

In recognition of the good work done by the Battalion while stationed in Khartoum, all the civilian inhabitants—including Greeks, Jews, Armenians and Syrians—as well as members of the European population, joined in raising a subscription and presented very fine mementoes to both the Officers' and the Sergeants' Messes.

On disembarking at Southampton on March 25th, 1925, the 2nd Battalion The Leicestershire Regiment completed a tour of foreign service which had commenced in 1906, and during which the Battalion had taken a very distinguished part in the World War and had served in India, France and Flanders, Mesopotamia, Egypt, Palestine and the Sudan.

On disembarkation the Battalion proceeded by train to Colchester, where it occupied Sobraon Barracks, and here, on July 25th of this year, Lieutenant-Colonel W. T. Bromfeld assumed command.

While stationed at Colchester new Colours were presented to the Battalion by Field-Marshal Sir Claud Jacob, G.C.B., G.C.S.I., G.C.M.G., on March 25th, 1927, but unfortunately the ceremony, which had been assiduously practised for weeks past, had to be curtailed and held at the eleventh hour in the Garrison Gymnasium, owing to the very heavy rain which fell that morning.

After the Field-Marshal had inspected No. 1 Guard, which was drawn up in the Gymnasium under Captain and Brevet Major H. S. Pinder, M.C., with the old King's Colour carried by Second-Lieutenant D. F. Coburn, the drums were piled and the new Colours were brought to the front by Company Sergeants-Major Langton and Gill, being then uncased and placed against the drums by Major and Brevet Lieutenant-Colonel A. W. S. Brock, C.M.G., D.S.O., and Major A. T. Le M. Utterson, D.S.O. The Consecration Service was conducted by the Chaplain-General, the Rev. A. C. E. Jarvis, C.M.G., M.C., D.D., assisted by the Rev. F. F. S. Smethwick, B.A., the Rev. J. Thorn, M.C., M.A., Canon J. Bloomfield and the Rev. J. W. Almond, and the Chaplain-General then dedicated the Colours.

The Consecration Service over, Sir Claud Jacob received the King's Colour from Major and Brevet Lieutenant-Colonel Brock and handed it to Lieutenant C. Sykes, M.C., who received it kneeling, while the Regimental Colour was received from Major Utterson, who presented it to Lieutenant L. G. Mackinstry in similar manner. The Field-Marshal then addressed the Battalion as follows :—

" Lieutenant-Colonel Bromfield, Officers, Non-Commissioned Officers and Men of the 2nd Leicestershire Regiment.

" It gives me very great pleasure to be here to-day, not only for the ceremony of presenting you with new Colours, but also for the opportunity it gives me of renewing my acquaintance with your Battalion, an acquaintance which dates from before the war.

" The Leicestershire Regiment was raised by Colonel Solomon Richard on September 27th, 1688, in the troublous days that marked the closing period of the reign of King James II. Of the seven regiments raised in that year, the 16th Bedfordshire and Hertfordshire Regiment and the 17th Foot, The Leicestershire Regiment, alone remain. The 2nd Battalion was formed in 1799 for service with the Duke of York in North Holland against the French Revolutionary Army, and afterwards went to Minorca. After the Peace of Amiens in 1802 the Battalion came home and was disbanded. In 1825 King George IV was graciously pleased to approve of the Regiment bearing on its Colours and appointments the figure of the Royal Tiger, superscribed ' Hindoostan,' as a testimony of its exemplary conduct during its service in India. Owing to the Indian Mutiny the Army was increased, and twenty-five new battalions were added to the first twenty-five regiments of infantry, and the 2nd Battalion was reformed under the command of Lieutenant-Colonel Crofton.

" On the 3rd February, 1859, the Battalion received its Colours from Lady Vivian on Mount Wise parade ground at Plymouth.

" In 1861, during the American Civil War, the 2nd Battalion was sent to Nova Scotia. The Battalion returned home in 1868 and remained there till 1878. It then had a very strenuous period of service in India and Burma until 1890. On the 4th December, 1885, new Colours were presented to the Battalion at Lucknow by the Countess of Dufferin, the wife of the Viceroy.

" In 1900 the Battalion was ordered to Egypt, where it remained until 1902, when it returned home. In 1906 the Battalion was ordered to India in relief of the 1st Battalion, where it remained until the outbreak of the Great War in 1914.

" On the outbreak of war the Battalion was stationed at Ranikhet, in India, and was under the command of Lieutenant-Colonel C. G. Blackader, D.S.O. The Battalion mobilized on August 9th, 1914, and was under orders to proceed to France with the Indian Corps, forming part of the Garhwal Brigade (General Keary) of the 7th Meerut Division (General Anderson). The Battalion eventually arrived in the firing line on the night of the 28th-29th October, 1914, and remained in France until November, 1915. During this period it took part in the Battle of Festubert (November, 1914), a night raid on the German lines on December 19th, when two German machine guns, now outside the Officers' Mess, were captured; the Battle of Neuve Chapelle (March 11th, 1915), where Private Buckingham of the Battalion gained his Victoria Cross, and the Battle of Loos. From France the Battalion proceeded to Mesopotamia, arriving there in December, 1915, and was now in the 29th Indian Infantry Brigade of the 7th Division of the I. Corps; the object of this Corps being the relief of General Townshend, besieged in Kut. The Battalion took part in the actions at Shaikh Saad, Dujaila Redoubt, Falahiya and Sannaiyat.

" After the fall of Kut a period of trench warfare ensued from April, 1916, to February, 1917, when the Battalion took part in the final Battle of Sannaiyat. In the advance on Baghdad and beyond, again the Battalion had two hard days' fighting on the right bank of the Tigris just east of Baghdad, which helped in the capture of Baghdad. In March, 1917, the Battalion entered Baghdad Station, where they took the bell which is now outside the guard-room. In the advance north of Baghdad, the Battalion fought in the engagements at Belad, Mushaidie and Istabulat, at the latter place capturing nine guns and 250 prisoners.

" The Battalion remained in Mesopotamia until January, 1918, when it proceeded to Palestine, and was soon in the firing line on the sea-coast just north of Jaffa, where it remained until September, 1918, when it took part in General Allenby's advance. The Battalion marched to Samaria, Haifa, Acre, Tyre, Sidon, Beirout, Tripoli, Homs and Hama—an advance of 250 miles when the Armistice was signed.

" The Battalion proceeded to India in July, 1919, and was stationed at Delhi and Jhansi; it left India in 1923 for Khartoum, where it took part in the suppression of the mutiny of Sudanese troops in 1924, returning to England in March, 1925.

" You have a record of which you may be proud, and I trust that these Colours which I am now presenting, will be an incentive to all ranks to carry out their duties to their King, their Country and the Regiment with that keenness and efficiency which they have always shown in the past."

Major-General Sir Edward Woodward, K.C.M.G., C.B., the Colonel of the Regiment, tendered " whole-hearted thanks to Sir Claud Jacob for the honour he had conferred upon the Battalion, one highly appreciated, not only by the 2nd Battalion, but also by the whole Regiment. Lieutenant-Colonel Bromfield had told him of the great kindness Sir Claud had shown to the 2nd Battalion on several occasions during their late service in India. The presentation of the Colours that day recalled vividly to the speaker's mind a ceremony which took place in 1885, when the Colours they were seeing for the last time on parade that day were presented at Lucknow by the Countess of Dufferin. He was present on that occasion, and it was not often that anyone could be privileged to be present on two occasions when Colours were presented to the same Battalion of a Regiment."

The Guard then marched past the Field-Marshal as the old and new Colours were marched away to the Officers' Mess.

At the luncheon party which followed some 120 were present, including past and present officers of the Regiment and their wives, while among those who attended the ceremony were two Chelsea Pensioners, ex-Corporal Aisthorpe and ex-Private Bryce of the Regiment.

In a letter which the Commanding Officer received later from Sir Claud Jacob, the Field-Marshal wrote :—" It was very disappointing that the weather prevented the whole Battalion parading, but if what I saw in the Gymnasium for the ceremony is a sample of the rest, it is evident that you have a splendid Battalion."

Those in possession of Colonel Webb's History of the Regiment will not need to be reminded that on page 266 he states that the Colours now retired from the 2nd Battalion were found, when issued in 1885, to have depicted on the Regimental Colour a Royal Tiger "*proper,*" instead of " green " as heretofore, while the Regimental Colour issued to the 1st Battalion in 1906 was similarly emblazoned. The matter was thereupon represented to the Army Council, but it was not until February 12th, 1908, that approval was given to the " Royal Tiger on the Colours of The Leicestershire Regiment being green with gold stripes."

In April, 1926, the 2nd Battalion was in the Final of the Army Association Football Cup, but was defeated at Aldershot by the South Staffordshire Regiment by two goals to one. In the following year, however, the Battalion team was more successful, winning the Army Cup on the Command Central Ground at Aldershot, in the presence of Their Majesties the King and Queen, on April 18th, 1927, defeating the Royal Army Ordnance Corps, Southern Command, by two goals to one.

The Battalion team was composed as follows : Sergeant W. Booth, goal; Private T. Wardle and Bandsman J. Almey, backs; Bandsman C. M. Mills, Lance-Corporal S. Smith and Private A. Bentham, half-backs; Lance-Corporals J. Bates, G. Fosse and S. Brown, Privates G. Stockton and F. W. Moston, forwards.

The Cup and Medals were handed to the victors by Her Majesty the Queen.

At Colchester the Battalion remained until November of this year, when it was sent to the Rhine to serve in Germany as part of the Army of Occupation.

INDEX

Adie, Capt. W. J., R.A.M.C., 26, 30.
Aisne, the crossing of the, 10 ; battle of the, 47.
Aisthorpe, ex-Corporal, 207.
Allenby, Major-Gen. E., 6, 44, 52 ; Lieut.-Gen. Sir, 187, 190, 194, 197.
Almey, Bandsman J., 207.
America declares war, 46.
Ames, Lieut. R. H., 108 ; Capt., 142, 143 ; killed, 157.
Anderson, Lieut.-Gen., 107, 126 ; assumes command of Indian Corps, 137.
Ansell, 2/Lieut. A. C., missing, 67.
Apton, 2/Lieut. E. R. B., 186.
Armistice, with Germany, 88 ; with Turkey, 196.
Army Association Football Cup, won by 2nd Bn., 1926, 207.
Arnold, 2/Lieut. L. G., 89.
Arras, battle of, 46.
Ath, 95.
Atkinson, 2/Lieut. T. J., 50.
Atter, 2/Lieut. C. F., 50, 54 ; Lieut., 60 ; killed, 67.
Aylmer, Major-Gen. Sir F., to command Tigris Corps, 147, 149, 155, 156, 159.

Bacchus, Capt. J., 8 ; wounded, 13 ; Major, 96.
Baghdad, occupation of, 173 ; Bell captured, 173.
Bagshaw, 2/Lieut. A. N., 50, 54, 59, 62, 63 ; missing, 67.
Bailey, 2/Lieut. C. C., wounded, 140.
Bailey, 2/Lieut. W. M., 26.
Balad, action at, 175, 176.
Bale, C.S.M. W., commands Bn., 161, 165.
Bamford, Capt. C. A., 14, 16, 159 ; wounded, 161, 166.
Barron, 2/Lieut. H. K., 185, 186.
Barron, 2/Lieut. M. R., 159.
Bates, L./Cpl. J., 207.
Batten, 2/Lieut. W., 190, 197.
Batten, Sergt., 182.
Battersby, C.S.M. E., 72.
Bayfield, Lieut. H. L., 8, 10 ; wounded, 13 ; died of wounds, 125.
Beale, 2/Lieut. W. B., 184-186, 188.
Beard, L./Cpl., 182.
Beirut, occupation of, 194, 195.
Belle, 2/Lieut. A., 142, 143, 146 ; wounded, 151.
Bennett, C.S.M., 89.
Bennett, Lieut. P. W., 80 ; Capt., 94.
Bentham, Pte. A., 207.
Bentley, Sergt., 136.
Bexon, Sergt. J., 63.
Billingham, C.S.M., 89.
Billings, 2/Lieut. H., 142, 143, 146 ; wounded, 151 ; killed, 161.
Birch, Sergt. W., 92.
Blackader, Major C. G., 1 ; Lieut.-Colonel, 3, 108, 110, 113 ; General, 117, 120, 127 ; death of, 144, 145, 205.

Blacklock, 2/Lieut. W., 31, 36 ; wounded, 38.
Bogg, Pte. G. H., wounded, 203.
Bohain, 85, 86.
Bois Grenier, 11.
Bolland, R.Q.M.S., 89 ; Lieut. and Quartermaster, 95.
Bonas, 2/Lieut. W. B., 40.
Boote, L./Cpl. T. W., 62.
Booth, Pte. A., missing, 189.
Booth, Sergt. W., 207.
Boulter, Lieut. A. J., 142.
Boulton, Capt. N. P., R.A.M.C., 46.
Bradbury, Pte., died of wounds, 19.
Bradley, Pte., wounded, 100.
Braithwaite, Lieut.-Gen. Sir W., 80.
Brake, L./Cpl., 115.
Brake, 2/Lieut. B., wounded, 161, 163.
Brigade, Infantry, 16th, 2, 7, 10, 12, 21, 52, 53 ; 17th, 7, 21 ; 18th, 7, 10, 11, 17, 52, 53 ; 28th, 147 ; 71st, 21, 27, 52, 53 ; 138th, 86 ; Indian, 19th,; 147 35th, 147.
Brock, Capt. A. W. S., wounded, 132, 134 ; Major, 166 ; Lieut.-Colonel, 185, 186, 197, 198, 204.
Brodie, Lieut. and Quartermaster H. C., 108, 146, 153.
Bromfield, Lieut.-Colonel, assumes command 2nd Bn., 199, 204.
Brooker, 2/Lieut. H. W., 31, 36, 40 ; Capt., 50, 54, 59, 66, 67 ; wounded, 77, 85.
Brounsworth, 2/Lieut. G. A., 26 ; killed, 29, 30.
Brown, 2/Lieut. A. E., killed, 88.
Brown, Brig.-Gen. P. W., 49, 94.
Brown, L./Cpl. S., 207.
Brown, Pte. L., wounded, 203.
Brown, Lieut. H. B., 2, 8 ; Capt., 16 ; Lieut.-Colonel, 50, 54.
Brown, Lieut. M., 14, 16.
Browne, 2/Lieut. H. A., killed, 134.
Browne, 2/Lieut. M. W., killed, 139.
Bruhl, 94.
Bryce, Major W., 8.
Buchanan-Dunlop, Major A. H., 16, 21 ; Lieut.-Colonel, 26.
Buckingham, 2/Lieut. O. H., 142, 143, 146 ; wounded, 151.
Buckingham, Pte. W., 115, 125.
Buckler, L./Cpl. G. B., 62, 63.
Bulfin, Lieut.-Gen. Sir E., XXI. Army Corps, 188, 190.
Bulfin, 2/Lieut. E. F. J., 190, 197.
Bullecourt, battle of, 47.
Bullimore, Cpl. 19.
Buncher, Cpl., 182.
Burn, Lieut. C. J., wounded, 18.
Burnett, 2/Lieut. J., 30, 31, 36 ; died of wounds, 38.
Burns, 2/Lieut. R. V., 89, 95, 96.
Burrell, 2/Lieut. C. H. O. D., 14, 16, 26, 31, 40.

Burrows, 2/Lieut. G. W. C., 182, 185, 188.
Burton, 2/Lieut. W., 89.
Butler, 2/Lieut. E. H., 50, 59.
Buxton, Lieut. V., 121, 166.
Byers, 2/Lieut. H. D., 142, 143, 146.
Bygott, 2/Lieut. H. M., 190, 197.
Byng, Gen. the Hon. Sir J., 52, 61, 71.

CADRE, 1st Bn. sails for England, 96.
Cambrai, battle, results of, 43, 58.
Cantrill, L./Cpl. H. R., 100.
Card, 2/Lieut. R. W. G., 154 ; wounded, 155.
Casualties, 6th Division, March, 1918, 67 ;
    Neuve Chapelle, 128, 129.
Cavan, Lieut.-Gen. Earl of, 28.
Challenor, Lieut.-Colonel E. L., 98, 101 ; Mrs.
    Challenor, wounded by rebels, 100.
Chamberlin, 2/Lieut. R., 184-6, 197.
Charlesworth, 2/Lieut. W. A., 40 ; killed, 44.
Cherry, Pte., 19.
Chesterfield, Acting Quartermaster-Sergeant, 94.
Christmas truce, 1914, 15.
Chudleigh, Lieut. C., 108, 112.
Chudleigh, 2/Lieut. H. E. L., 142, 143, 146.
Clancey, 2/Lieut. W., wounded, 77 ; wounded, 85.
Clarence, 2/Lieut. L. J., 21.
Clark, 2/Lieut. G., wounded, 85.
Clarke, Capt. B. F., 4.
Clarke, 2/Lieut. T. C. A., 60 ; missing, 67.
Clover, 2/Lieut. C. C., 187, 197.
Cobbe, Major-Gen., 166, 168, 169, 173, 183.
Coburn, 2/Lieut. D. F., 204.
Colbourne-Smith, 2/Lieut. G. C., 50 ; wounded, 88
Coleman, Lieut. G. C., wounded, 85.
Cologne, 92.
Collis, Lieut. W. J., wounded, 88.
Colquhoun, Major A. E. R., 159 ; wounded, 161.
Colours, presentation of new, 2nd Bn., 204-6.
Company re-organization, 2.
Congreve, Brig.-Gen. W. N., 7 ; Major-Gen., 20 ;
    to III. Corps, 22.
Connaught, H.R.H. Field-Marshal Duke of,
    presents decorations, 187.
Connell, 2/Lieut. J. H., 50, 54.
Cook, 2/Lieut. E. R., 185, 186 ; Lieut., 197.
Cooke, 2/Lieut. A. E., wounded, 77.
Cooper, 2/Lieut. W., 89.
Copeland, 2/Lieut. M. M. F. C., 197.
Copeman, Capt. M. G. B., 8, 16 ; wounded, 17.
Copeman, 2/Lieut. C. N. C., 176, 185, 186.
Copeman, 2/Lieut. J. Y., 166, 176, 185, 186, 200.
Corbridge, Pte. F., missing, 189.
Corps, Army, I. 6, 10, 11, 39, 118, 131, 137 ; II.
    10, 11, 78, 118, 137 ; III. 6, 10, 11, 34, 55, 70,
    118, 137 ; IV. 61, 64, 118, 127, 131, 137 ; V.
    61, 70, 118, 137 ; VI. 17 ; VII. 62 ; VIII. 35 ;
    IX. 75, 80, 85, 87 ; XIV. 27, 34, 39 ; XV. 34 ;
    XVIII. 61, 62 ; XIX. 62, 78, 79 ; XXI. 187-
    191, 195.
Cox, Capt. C. H. V., 45.
Cox, Cpl. A., 72.
Cox, Lieut. and Quartermaster H., 185, 187, 197,
    198.
Cox, 2/Lieut. D. S., 95.

Creagh, Capt. P. H., 166, 178, 179 ; wounded,
    181 ; Major, 185, 186, 197.
Crisp, Pte. 115.
Croker, Lieut.-Colonel H. L., 2, 8 ; wounded,
    13, 16.
Croker, 2/Lieut. R. J., 59 ; wounded, 85.
Cross, Sergt., 94.
Crosse, Lieut. G. W. M., killed, 134.
Crouch, 2/Lieut. P. A., 50.
Crowe, 2/Lieut. S. L., 29, 31, 36.
Cummins, Sergt.-Major A., promoted 2/Lieut.,
    30, 31, 36.
Curfew order introduced in Ireland, 100.
Curtis, L./Cpl., 41.

DAKIN, Lieut. A. E., 154 ; wounded, 155.
Daur, attack on, 183.
Davies, Capt. C. S., 2 ; Lieut.-Colonel, 102, 203.
Davis, Pte., 136 ; wounded, 189.
Davis, 2/Lieut. R. N., 27, 31, 36, 47 ; Lieut., 50,
    54 ; Capt., 59, 67, 89, 95.
Deane, Capt. E. C., R.A.M.C., 136 ; killed, 139,
    141.
Delmer, Lieut. G., 46, 50 ; Capt., 89.
Demobilization, 92, 93, 197.
Dennis, 2/Lieut. F. S., wounded, 88.
Dent, Major B. C., 2, 8, 16 ; Lieut.-Colonel,
    198, 199.
Dickinson, Capt. G. C., 28, 108 ; wounded, 125.
Diggins, Capt. F. J., 178, 179, 183 ; wounded, 185,
    186, 198.
Divisions, 3rd, 17 ; 6th, 7-9, 14, 17, 20, 34, 35,
    45, 52, 53, 85 ; 12th, 52, 55 ; 14th, 34 ; 15th,
    34 ; 20th, 53, 55 ; 21st, 45 ; 29th, 53, 55 ; 36th,
    52 ; 37th, 45 ; 46th, 86 ; 47th, 34, 87 ; 50th,
    34 ; 51st, 52 ; 55th, 34 ; 56th, 34 ; 62nd, 52 ;
    Meerut Division, composition of, 107, 113.
Dixon, Capt. W. C., 2.
Dodd, C.Q.M.S., 89.
Dods, 2/Lieut., 1, 2 ; Lieut., 8 ; killed, 13.
Dodson, Capt. C. A., 89.
Dolby, 2/Lieut. H. A., 22, 26 ; killed, 46.
Dooley, 2/Lieut. H. T., killed 134.
Douglas, 2/Lieut. A. G., 31 ; killed, 32.
Dowding, Lieut. L., 16 ; wounded, 17, 142, 143,
    146 ; killed, 151.
Dujaila Redoubt, 156, 157, 165.
Dunkirk, 95.
Duvall, Capt. H. H., 82 ; wounded, 85.
Dwyer, Major B. C., 2.
Dyer-Bennet, Lieut. R. S., 2 ; Capt., 27 ; Major,
    31, 35, 40.
Dykes, 2/Lieut. G. N., 8.

EDWARDS, Brig.-Gen. Fitz J. M., to command
    71st Brigade, 30.
Edwards, Lieut.-Colonel F. H., to command 1st
    Bn., 101, 102.
Egypt, 1st Bn. move to, 101 ; 2nd Bn. lands in,
    146 ; 2nd Bn. sails for, 185.
Ellingham, 2/Lieut. V. E., 136 ; wounded, 140.
Ellis, 2/Lieut. H. S., 159 ; wounded, 161.
Elsenborn Camp, 92.
Elsmie, Colonel, 157.

INDEX

England, Cpl. J., 30.
England, 2nd Bn. returns to, 204.
English, 2/Lieut. S. S., 27.
Entwistle, 2/Lieut. A. B., 50, 54.
Escudier, 2/Lieut. A. G., wounded, 67.
Etherington, 2/Lieut. D., 50, 54 ; wounded, 55.
Everitt, Capt. S. O., 2.
Extension of British front, 60.
Eyre, L./Cpl., 189.

Fane, General V. B., 166, 169.
Faulkner, Sergt., wounded, 31 ; C.S.M., 89.
Faulks, 2/Lieut. L., 60 ; killed, 77.
Featherstone, Lieut. J., 89.
Feetham, Brig.-Gen. F., to command 71st Brigade, 39, 49.
Ferguson, Capt. J. F., 185, 186 ; missing, 188.
Fergusson, 2/Lieut. H. G. B., 182, 185, 186.
Fidoe, 2/Lieut. N. G., 59 ; killed, 67, 68.
Foch, General, assumes command in chief, 75 ; Marshal, 88.
Foister, Sergt. P., 112 ; C.S.M., 163.
Folwell, Pte. 24.
Ford, Capt. F. I., 16.
Forbes, 2/Lieut. T., 19.
Fosse, L./Cpl. G., 207.
Foster, Sergt. G., 72.
Fowke, 2/Lieut. L. A., 167.
Fraser, 2/Lieut. C. G., wounded, 151.
Freakley, Cpl., wounded, 100.
French, Field-Marshal Sir J., 6 ; resigns command, 25, 116, 118, 131.
Frost, Pte., 62.

Gamble, R.S.M., 89.
Gandy, 2/Lieut. G. J., killed, 134.
Garbutt, Lieut. J. E., 16, 40.
Gardner, 2/Lieut. W. J., 27, 31 ; died of wounds, 38.
Garner, Pte., 161.
Garton, Pte., 108, 109.
Gas, poison, first mention of, 23.
Geddes, Lieut. S. M., 82 ; killed, 85.
German, Capt. H. B., R.A.M.C., 30, 31 ; wounded 38, 40, 46.
Germany, move into, 91 ; 2nd Bn. to, as part of Army of Occupation, 207.
Gibaud, Lieut. A. B., 190.
Gill, C.S.M., 304.
Gillespie, Capt. R. H., gassed, 24, 26 ; Lieut.-Colonel, 31, 36, 37.
Gilmore, Capt. E. R., R.A.M.C., 197.
Goddard, 2/Lieut. F. S., 185, 186, 197.
Godfrey, 2/Lieut. C. B., 143, 146 ; wounded, 151.
Gordon, Major H., 108, 111 ; Lieut.-Colonel, 117, 132, 136 ; wounded, 139, 140, 142.
Gorringe, Lieut.-Gen., 159, 162, 166.
Gough, General Sir H., 44, 61, 62, 64.
Gould, Lieut. A. B., 95.
Granger, Capt. E. H., R.A.M.C., 89.
Grant, Capt. H. A., 108 ; killed, 111, 112.
Grant-Anderson, 2/Lieut, H. T., wounded, 177, 181, 185, 186 ; Lieut. 197.
Gravers, 2/Lieut. H. A., 31 ; wounded, 38, 46.

Gray, 2/Lieut. A. L., 40.
Gray, L./Cpl. G., 112, 188.
Greasley, Lieut. and Quartermaster J. H., 2 ; Capt., 8, 16, 26, 31 ; Major, 50, 59, 89, 95, 96.
Greenhalgh, 2/Lieut. C. H., 184, 185, 197.
Grimble, 2/Lieut. A. N. H., 8 ; Lieut. 146 ; wounded, 161.
Grimsley, 2/Lieut. F. G. H., 22, 26, 29.
Gristwood, 2/Lieut. G. H., 30, 31, 36 ; died of wounds, 38.
Grossmith, Lieut. G. W., 27, 31 ; Capt., 89 ; wounded, 140.
Gruchy, Capt. F. le M., 2, 8 ; killed, 13.
Grylls, 2/Lieut. T. R., 108 ; wounded, 125.
Gwyther, 2/Lieut. G. L., 142, 143, 146 ; killed, 151.

Hackett, 2/Lieut. D. F. M., 40, 50, 59 ; wounded, 77.
Haig, Lieut.-Gen. Sir D., 6 ; assumes command of the B.E.F., 25, 43, 70, 72, 120, 131.
Haig, Lieut.-Colonel C. H., assumes command of 2nd Bn., 199, 202.
Haigh, Lieut. B., R.A.M.C., 182 ; Capt., 185, 187.
Hall, 2/Lieut. E. L., killed, 181.
Halls, 2/Lieut. W. H., wounded, 77.
Hanna, position at, 155.
Harbottle, Capt. J., 50, 60, 64 ; killed, 67.
Harbottle, 2/Lieut. J., 159 ; wounded, 161.
Hardyman, 2/Lieut. M. L., 186, 197.
Hare, Capt. C. T. M., 2, 8, 16.
Harper, 2/Lieut. O. T., missing, 67.
Harrison, Lieut. E., killed, 17.
Hartshorne, Lieut. S. T., 36, 40 ; Capt., 50, 54, 59 ; wounded, 67, 68, 72.
Hassall, Lieut. A. H., killed, 151.
Hassall, 2/Lieut. C. H., 40.
Hassall, 2/Lieut. T. C. D., 142, 143, 146 ; wounded, 155.
Hasted, Capt. J. O. C., 178, 179, 182.
Hawes, Capt. R. F., 8 ; died of wounds, 10.
Hayball, Sergt. E. B., 14.
Haywood, Pte. B. W., missing, 189.
Heath, 2/Lieut. S. T., wounded, 88.
Hebden, 2/Lieut. G. S., 167 ; killed, 181.
Hemphill, 2/Lieut. H. H., wounded, 140.
Henderson, Capt. E. F. S., 2 ; Major, 142, 143, 146, 150 ; killed, 151.
Herbison, Lieut. C. W., 16 ; Capt. 26, 31, 36 ; died of wounds, 38.
Herring-Cooper, 2/Lieut. J. C., 2 ; Lieut. 8, 16 ; Capt., 82, 83.
Hervey, Lieut. G. C. I., 2.
Hill, 2/Lieut. J. H., 27 ; Adjt., 31 ; killed, 77.
Hill, Pte. J., 125.
Hilton, 2/Lieut. W., 186.
Hindenburg Line 52 et seq. ; capture of, 54, 55, 81.
Hine, 2/Lieut. C. A., 17.
Hodgson, 2/Lieut. G. C., 190.
Hodson, Lieut. St. J., wounded, 100.
Holland, Lieut.-Gen. A. E. A., 39.
Hollingsworth, L./Cpl., wounded, 189.
Homs, 197.

INDEX

Hooge, battle of, 16 *et seq.*, 18.
Horne, General, 39, 44.
Hostilities cease, 89.
Houston, 2/Lieut. J., 59.
Howell, Lieut. A. H., 142, 143, 146.
Huddleston, Major-Gen. H. J., 201, 203.
Humberston, 2/Lieut. H., 28.
Huntley, Lieut. R. J., 50, 54, 59.
Hurley, Bandsman G., 302.

INDIA, 1st Bn. moves to, 101 ; situation in August, 1914, 105 ; 2nd Bn. proceeds to, 198.
Ireland, 1st Bn. moves to, 98 ; troubles in, 99 *et seq.*
Irwin, Rev. R., 140, 141.
Istabulat, action at, 176-8.

JACOB, Lieut.-Gen. Sir C., 78, 137, 139 ; Field-Marshal, 204, 205.
Jacques, Cpl., 182.
Jaggar, Cpl., wounded, 100.
Jeeps, 2/Lieut. F. H., 54 ; wounded, 55 ; Capt., wounded, 88.
Jeudwine, Major-Gen. Sir H., 99.
Joffre, General, 43, 137.
John, 2/Lieut. J. H., 30, 31 ; Lieut., 36 ; wounded 38 ; Capt., 50, 59, 62 ; wounded, 67.
Jones, 2/Lieut. T. B., 182, 185, 186, 188.
Jones, 2/Lieut. V. J., 185, 186.
Jones, 2/Lieut. W., wounded, 67.
Jones, Pte. J. J., 202.
Judd, O.R. Sergt., 36.
Judge, 2/Lieut. H. L., 197.

KEARY, Major-Gen. H. D'U., 107, 116, 157.
Keely, 2/Lieut. T. C. S., 176, 185, 186 ; wounded, 190, 197.
Keir, Major-Gen. J. L., 7, 17, 27.
Keitley, Cpl. R., 125.
Kemball, Major-Gen., 149, 150, 151, 157.
Kennedy, 2/Lieut. J. G., 24, 26, 31, 36 ; killed, 38.
Keymer, Rev. B. W., 30, 31.
Khartoum, 2nd Bn. moves to, 199 ; trouble in, 199-201.
Kidd, 2/Lieut. B., 30, 31, 36, 40.
King's message to the Army, 9 ; inspection of 2nd Bn. by, 112, 113.
Kitchener, Field-Marshal Lord, 6 ; message to the Army, 9 ; inspects 2nd Bn., 136, 137.
Knatchbull, Major R. N., 108 ; wounded, 114, 115, 159, 161 ; wounded, Lieut.-Colonel, 178 ; death of, 182.
Kulbir Thapa, Rifleman, 2/3rd Gurkhas, rescues wounded man of 2nd Bn., 141, 142.
Kut, advance for relief of, 148 ; surrender of, 162 ; re-occupation of, 171.

LADDER of Tyre, 195, 196.
Lancaster, 2/Lieut. C. E., 40, 50, 54, 59 ; killed, 67.
Lancaster, 2/Lieut. H. V., 50, 54 ; wounded, 55.
Lambert, Brig.-Gen. T. S., 99, 100.
Lang, Lieut. E. C., R.A.M.C., 8, 16.
Langdon-Thomas, Capt. J., 30, 31.
Langton, C.S.M., 204.

Latham, Capt. F., 4 ; Lieut.-Colonel, 59, 64, 67, 72 ; wounded, 77, 95-98, 108, 135.
Lawrence, 2/Lieut. S. C., wounded, 24, 28, 59, 62 ; Lieut., missing, 67.
Le Couture, 109.
Le Fanu, Lieut. R., 108 ; wounded, 109 ; Capt., 135.
Lewis, Major F., wounded, 139, 140, 143, 146, 148 ; wounded, 155.
Lingham, Lieut. J., 186, 188.
Littlewood, 2/Lieut. H. S., 184-186, 188 ; Lieut., 197.
Lodge, 2/Lieut. R. E. S., killed, 139.
Lowther, Lieut. R. A. N., 108, 112 ; Capt., 178, 179, 185, 186, 197, 200, 202, 203.
Ludendorff, General, 40.
Lyons, 2/Lieut. J., 185, 187.

McALLISTER, Pte., 80.
MacBean, Major-Gen. F., 3, 107.
McConchie, 2/Lieut. C. A., 21.
McInerney, Lieut. F. E., 178, 185, 186, 188.
McIntyre, 2/Lieut. A. S., 124 ; Capt., wounded, 151, 159, 185, 186.
McIntyre, Capt. R. J., 124, 158 ; wounded, 159, 166.
Mackay, 2/Lieut. S. F., 27, 31 ; wounded, 88.
Mackinstry, Lieut. L. G., 204.
Mansfield, 2/Lieut. G., 60, 65 ; wounded, 67.
Mansfield, 2/Lieut. O. M., 167 ; killed, 174.
Maqil, 184, 185.
Marden, Major-Gen. T. O., commands 6th Division, 49, 55, 64, 71 ; farewell order, 95.
Markillie, L./Cpl., wounded, 99.
Marks, Pte., wounded, 100.
Marner, Lieut. G. L. S., killed, 175.
Marseilles, 2nd Bn. embarks from, 143.
Marshall, Lieut.-Gen. W. R., 166, 167 ; succeeds General Maude, 184.
Marshall, 2/Lieut. W., wounded, 88.
Martin, 2/Lieut. H. E., 142, 143, 146 ; wounded, 158.
Martin, Lieut.-Colonel J. H. (Lancaster Regt.) assumes command 1st Bn., 88, 89.
Mason, 2/Lieut. F. C., 182, 185, 186 ; wounded, 193.
Matthews, 2/Lieut. C., 185, 186, 197.
Matthews, 2/Lieut. V. G., 95.
Maude, General Sir S., 159, 166, 167, 169, 183 ; death of, 184.
Measures, Sergt.-Major A., 2, 8, 36.
Mesopotamia, 2nd Bn. arrives in, 146.
Mills, 2/Lieut. M., 54, 59 ; missing, 67.
Mills, Bandsman C. M., 207.
Milner, 2/Lieut. P. R., wounded, 18, 26, 31, 36, 40 ; Lieut., 46 ; Capt., 82, 83 ; wounded, 84, 85.
Mitchell, Pte., killed, 136.
Mobilization of B.E.F., 6, 106.
Monaghan, 2/Lieut. T., wounded, 161.
Montcerf, 9, 10.
Mont Kemmel, 76.
Morgan, Capt N. A., 121 ; wounded, 125, 129.
Morgan, 2/Lieut. S. B., killed, 17.
Morrison, Lieut. C. E., 16, 26, 31.

Morton, 2/Lieut. L. C., wounded, 46.
Mosse, 2/Lieut. J. W. E., 2, 8 ; Lieut., 16 ; Capt., 26, 31, 36, 40, 47 ; Major, 50.
Moston, Pte. F. W., 207.
Muggeridge, 2/Lieut. A. H., 59 ; wounded, 77.
Muggeridge, 2/Lieut. H. D., 40 ; wounded, 45, 142.
Murphy, 2/Lieut. W., killed, 125.
Mushaidie, action at, 173, 174.

Neuve Chapelle, battle of, 118 *et seq.*
Nicholls, Pte., killed, 31.
Nivelle, General, 43.
Nixon, 2/Lieut. R. H., wounded, 88.
Norman, 2/Lieut. O. M., wounded, 85.
North, 2/Lieut. W., 22.
Nunn, Bandsman, S. J., 203.

Oakes, Pte. C., 125.
Otter, 2/Lieut. R. D., 167 ; wounded, 175.

Page, Pte. 135.
Pakenham, 2/Lieut. E. H., 108.
Palestine, advance into, 192-4.
Palfreyman, 2/Lieut. G. W., 167 ; wounded, 193.
Paling, L/Cpl., 19.
Palmer, Colonel C. H. D., 98.
Panton, Lieut. W. F., 2.
Parry, Pte., 37.
Passmore, Lieut. F. F. S., 166, 185, 186, 197.
Passmore, 2/Lieut. D. G., 89.
Passmore, 2/Lieut. F., 17 ; wounded, 18.
Paterson, 2/Lieut. A. E. W., 59 ; wounded, 88.
Patrick, C.S.M. H., 163.
Paul, Major J. R. A. H., 3, 108.
Pegg, Lieut. K. H., killed, 156.
Penfold, 2/Lieut. E. N., 184-6 ; killed, 189.
Pentelow, 2/Lieut. F. L., 190.
Percival, L/Cpl. T. B., 202.
Phillips, Lieut. H. H., 136 ; wounded, 140.
Pickbourne, Lieut. H., 16, 26 ; wounded, 27 ; Capt., 31, 36 ; wounded, 38, 186, 197.
Pickersgill, 2/Lieut. R., 36 ; wounded, 38.
Pickin, 2/Lieut. W. T., 136 ; killed, 139.
Pinder, 2/Lieut. A. H., 22, 26 ; Lieut. 31 ; killed, 38.
Pinder, Lieut. H. S., 2 ; Capt., 204.
Plant, 2/Lieut. J. C. G., 176.
Plumer, General Sir H., 22, 28, 29, 44, 91.
Pollard, 2/Lieut. T., wounded, 78, 88.
Ponthein, Lieut. L. de V., 197.
Port Said, 197, 198.
Potter, Pte. 31.
Powell, Capt. A. C. L., 159.
Prain, Lieut. T., 8 ; killed, 13.
Priestley, 2/Lieut. W., 89.
Privett, 2/Lieut. A. B., killed, 151.
Puckle, Capt. T. N., 2.
Pulteney, Major-Gen. W. P., 2, 6.
Purdy, 2/Lieut. A. K., 54 ; killed, 55.

Quadrilateral, The, 35, 37.
Quayle, Lieut. G. A., 28, 108 ; Capt., 184-6.
Queenan, L./Cpl., 150.

Rackham, 2/Lieut. A. R., 197.
Raids, 45, 62, 63.
Raine, 2/Lieut. J. H., 166.
Raleigh, 2/Lieut. H. M., 108 ; wounded, 125.
Ranikhet, 2nd Bn. at, 1, 3.
Rawlinson, General Sir H., 34, 38, 44, 80, 91.
Raynes, 2/Lieut. J. H., 89.
Reception of 1st Bn. Cadre at Leicester, 96-8.
Redding, Pte., wounded, 100.
Redwood, 2/Lieut. J., 142, 143, 146 ; wounded, 151 ; Lieut., 167 ; wounded, 190.
Reeves, 2/Lieut. A. J., 182, 185, 186.
Re-formation of 1st Bn., 98.
Regiments, British : Bedford, 60 ; Black Watch, 107 ; Border, 66 ; Buffs, 7, 29 ; Durham L.I., 7, 22, 60, 84 ; E. York, 7 ; Essex, 53 ; Highland L.I., 75, 124, 158 ; King's Royal Rifles, 18 ; Leinster, 7 ; London, 131, 133 ; Loyal N. Lanc., 17 ; Manchester, 87 ; Norfolk, 21, 29, 35, 39, 53, 55, 63, 64, 85, 86 ; North Stafford, 7 ; Rifle Brigade, 7 ; Royal Fusiliers, 7 ; Seaforth Highlanders, 107, 113, 123 ; Sherwood Foresters, 7, 21, 22, 24, 35, 53, 55, 65, 66, 85, 86 ; Shropshire L.I., 7, 12, 19 ; South Lanc., 66 ; Suffolk, 21, 35, 53, 60 ; West York, 7, 11, 84 ; Wilts, 57 ; York and Lancs., 7, 19.
Indian : 28th, 188 ; 39th, 107, 119, 121, 123, 130, 131, 132, 138 ; 41st, 107, 149 ; 51st, 147, 149, 150, 155, 170, 172, 177, 178, 180, 183, 190, 193 ; 53rd, 147, 149, 150, 151, 155, 157, 169-174, 177, 178, 183, 189, 190, 193 ; 56th, 147, 149, 151, 154, 157, 159, 169, 172, 174, 177, 178, 183, 190 ; 58th, 107 ; 92nd, 152 ; 125th, 172, 176 ; 128th, 149 ; 2nd Gurkhas, 107, 123 ; 3rd, 107, 114, 118, 121-124, 131, 133, 138 ; 8th, 107, 131, 132, 138 ; 9th, 107, 158.
Reorganization of Divisions, 60 ; of Brigades, 131.
Richards, 2/Lieut. R. E. F., 89.
Risden, Lieut. T. O., wounded, 85.
Roberts, 2/Lieut. G. A., 60 ; killed, 67.
Roberts, 2/Lieut. H. S., 21.
Robertson, 2/Lieut. F. B., 24, 26, 29, 31.
Rodger, Lieut. G. S., 166 ; missing, 168.
Rolph, Lieut. C. C., 2, 8 ; Capt., wounded, 13, 135.
Romilly, Capt. F. H., 108, 114, 115, 121, 123, 130, 135 ; killed, 139, 140.
Ross, Major-Gen., commands 6th Division, 22, 38, 49.
Royce, 2/Lieut. D. C., 146 ; killed, 151.
Ruckledge, Sergt. H. E., 125.
Rumours of German offensive in March, 1918, 60, 61.
Russian Regiment, message from, 30, 31.

Sadler, 2/Lieut. B. W., 89.
St. Nazaire, 1st Bn. arrives at, 8.
Salmon, Lieut. G. H., 27, 31 ; Capt., 36 ; wounded 38.
Sambre Canal, 87, 88.
Sanders, 2/Lieut. W. N., wounded, 135 ; Lieut., 166, 185, 186.
Sannaiyat, action at, 161, 167, 169.

INDEX

Savage, 2/Lieut. W. A., 40, 44.

Seal, 2/Lieut. J. R., 142.

Seton-Browne, 2/Lieut. C. L., 27, 31.

Seton-Browne, 2/Lieut. M. W., 108 ; killed, 111.

Shaikh Saad, action at, 149-153.

Sharp, Capt. H. W., 184, 186, 197.

Shaw, 2/Lieut. P. J., 186, 197.

Shaw, 2/Lieut. R., wounded, 85.

Shelton, 2/Lieut. F. E., 30, 31 ; Lieut., 40 ; Capt., 54 ; killed, 67.

Sherer, Lieut.-Colonel L. C., 2, 8.

Shewen, Brig.-Gen. M., 21, 30.

Simmons, 2/Lieut. F. A., 197.

Sims, 2/Lieut. D. H., 50, 54, 60, 75 ; wounded, 88.

Sisson, 2/Lieut. F. W., wounded, 85.

Smeathman, Lieut. C., 8, 13.

Smith, C.Q.M.S., 89.

Smith, 2/Lieut. C. A., missing, 85.

Smith, L./Cpl. S., 207.

Smith-Dorrien, General Sir H., 6.

Sneath, Pte., 189.

Somme, description of enemy position on the, 33, 34 ; battle of, 35 *et seq.* ; results of, 39, 40.

Sowter, Lieut. U. H. E., 176 ; died of wounds, 181.

Spencer, 2/Lieut. F. N., 50, 60.

Steele, 2/Lieut. C. J., 95.

Steeples, Pte. J., 125.

Stevens, Lieut. A. L., 44 ; missing, 45.

Stevenson, 2/Lieut. F. B., 30, 31, 36 ; wounded, 38.

Stevenson, 2/Lieut. G., wounded, 85.

Stewart, 2/Lieut. A., 89, 95, 96.

Stimson, 2/Lieut. W. E., 75 ; wounded, 78.

Stockley, Lieut. H., wounded, 161, 166 ; Capt., 167, 185, 186, 197.

Stockton, Pte. G., 207.

Stoney-Smith, Major H., 8 ; wounded, 16, 21 ; Lieut.-Colonel, death of, 20.

Sturdy, 2/Lieut. A. E., 142, 143, 146 ; Lieut., wounded, 158.

Sutherland, 2/Lieut. D. W., 136, 143 ; Capt., wounded, 151.

Sutherland, Sergt., 115.

Swaine, 2/Lieut. J. P., 143, 146 ; Capt., wounded, 158.

Swindells, 2/Lieut. C. G. R., 142, 143, 146 ; wounded, 151 ; missing, 168.

Sykes, Lieut. C., 202, 204.

Symington, 2/Lieut. H. S., wounded, 166, 186.

Tailby, Lieut. J. V., 95.

Tanks, employment of, 51.

Tanner, 2/Lieut. G. W., 31, 50, 136 ; wounded, 140.

Tayler, 2/Lieut. J. G., killed, 134.

Taylor, Lieut. F., United States Medical Service, 50, 54 ; Capt., 59 ; wounded, 67.

Thomas, Lieut. J. A., wounded, 88.

Thomas, 2/Lieut. W. H., 40.

Thompson, Rev. E. J., 180.

Thorpe, Lieut. F. J., wounded, 18, 167, 178.

Tidswell, Lieut E. S. W., 2 ; Capt. and Adjt., 8 ; wounded, 10, 16 ; Brigade Major, 81st Brigade, 17.

Tigris Corps, strength of, 164.

Tipton, Pte., 72.

Tollemache, Capt. L. S. D., 8, 16.

Tompson, Major-Gen. W. D., appointed Colonel Leicestershire Regiment, 1 ; death of, 41.

Tooley, Lieut. H. A. R., missing, 114, 115.

Transports : *Bandra*, 185 ; *Braemar Castle*, 8 ; *Clan MacGillivray*, 143, 146 ; *Devanha*, 107 ; *Elephanta*, 108 ; *Heroic*, 7 ; *Hyperia*, 185 ; *Janus*, 146 ; *Julnar*, 152, 162 ; *Kilkenny*, 7 ; *Londonderry*, 7 ; *Margilief*, 96 ; *Medjidieh*, 147 ; *Mutlah*, 186 ; *Minnetonka*, 186 ; *Moora*, 198, 199 ; *Oranda*, 143 ; *Rossetti*, 185, 186 ; *Urlana*, 143.

Trench warfare begins, 13.

Tripoli, occupation of, 195, 196.

Tristram, Capt. L. B. C., 108 ; killed, 109.

Tunks, Lieut. G. P. de A. G., 108 ; killed, 202, 203.

Tyers, Cpl., 37.

Upton, Lieut. E. R. B., 197.

Utterson, Major-Gen. A. H., death of, 1.

Utterson, Capt. A. T. le M., 8 ; wounded, 13 ; temporary Lieut.-Colonel, 95, 204.

Vessey, 2/Lieut. J. O., 47, 50 ; Lieut., missing, 67.

Victoria Cross awarded to Pte. Buckingham, 126.

Vincent, 2/Lieut. N., wounded, 170.

Viney, Capt. P. E., died of wounds, 13.

Wacks, 2/Lieut. J., 50

Wadi, the position at, 153 ; action at, 155.

Waine, Lieut. J. G., R.A.M.C., 143, 146.

Walker, Lieut. G. M., killed, 77.

Walker, Brig.-Gen. W. G., 136.

Wallace, 2nd Lieut. D. J. W. T., 182, 185, 186, 188.

Waller, Lieut. J. T., 2, 8, 10 ; wounded, 13 ; Capt., wounded, 17.

Wardle, Capt. M. K., 26 ; wounded, 28, 108, 109 ; wounded, 132, 134.

Wardle, Pte., 207.

Waring, Lieut. S., 16 ; wounded, 18.

Warren, 2/Lieut. T. J. R., 166 ; wounded, 181, 185, 186.

Wateridge, 2/Lieut. E. L., 108 ; wounded, 109.

Watson, 2/Lieut. C. H., 45, 50 ; Lieut., 60, 64 ; wounded, 67.

Watson, Lieut. P. C., wounded, 44.

Watts, 2/Lieut. A. W. J., 89.

Webb, 2/Lieut. A. H., 159.

Webb, Lieut. D. V., gassed, 24, 26 ; wounded, 27, 31, 36, 40, 45 ; wounded, 85 ; Capt., killed, 88.

Webb, 2/Lieut. J. C., 30, 31, 36 ; killed, 38.

Weir, Capt. D. L., 108, 121, 136 ; wounded, 139, 143, 146 ; Major, wounded, 158, 159, 161

Wells, C.S.M. W., 163.

Weldon, L./Cpl., killed, 101.

Wesseling, 92-94.

INDEX

West, 2/Lieut. G. S. V., 89.
Westlake, 2/Lieut. H. W. G., wounded, 181.
Weyman, 2/Lieut. A., 2 ; Lieut., 8, 16 ; Adjt., 17 ; Capt., 26, 49.
Whatsize, Sergt.-Major, killed, 181.
Wherry, 2/Lieut. A., wounded, 45.
Whitcher, Sergt. H. T., 89.
Wilkins, Rev. B. D., 40.
Wilkinson, 2/Lieut. W. J., 135.
Wilkinson, Cpl., 178.
Willcocks, Lieut.-Gen. Sir J., 107, 108, 111, 112, 115, 116, 127, 132, 137.
Williams, 2/Lieut. A. W. F., wounded, 77.
Williams, Lieut. W. C., wounded, 20.
Wilson, Capt. D. McD., R.A.M.C., 182.
Wilson, Capt. W. C., 8, 16, 135, 136 ; wounded, 139, 140.
Wilson, Lieut. W., 50 ; Capt., 84, 136.
Witt, Bandmaster C. S., 2.
Wood, Lieut. and Quartermaster A., 3.

Woodburn, 2/Lieut. C. G., wounded, 135, 140.
Woodfield, 2/Lieut. E. W., wounded and missing, 158.
Woods, 2/Lieut. D., 197.
Woodward, Major-Gen. Sir E. M., 6 ; appointed Colonel The Leicestershire Regiment, 41, 42, 206.
Wounded, sufferings of, 152, 153.
Wragg, Sergt., 44.
Wratislaw, Lieut. J. C., 50, 54 ; wounded, 55.
Wright, 2/Lieut. J., 16.
Wright, L./Cpl., died of wounds, 203.
Wrixon, 2/Lieut. P. A. B., 50, 54.
Wykes, Lieut. G. N., 16 ; Capt., 46, 89, 91.

Yardley, L./Cpl. W., 63.
York, Pte. G., 189.
Younghusband, Major-Gen., 150, 156, 166.
Ypres Salient, 17 *et seq.*

www.ingramcontent.com/pod-product-compliance
Lightning Source LLC
Chambersburg PA
CBHW050403110426
42812CB00006BA/1786